GW00497550

THE PLAYS OF CARYL CHURCHILL

The Plays of Caryl Churchill

Theatre of Empowerment

AMELIA HOWE KRITZER

Lecturer, English and Women's Studies
University of Wisconsin-Madison

MACMILLAN

First published 1991 by
THE MACMILLAN PRESS LTD
Houndmills, Basingstoke, Hampshire RG21 2XS
and London
Companies and representatives
throughout the world

ISBN 0-333-52248-6

A catalogue record for this book is available
from the British Library.

Printed in Great Britain by
Antony Rowe Ltd
Chippenham, Wiltshire

11   10   9   8   7   6   5
03   02   01   00   99   98

To all teachers who nurture and demand the best
in their students,
but especially to Louise Leonard
and to the memory of Lucy D. Allen

Contents

Acknowledgements

I have been enabled to research and write this study by different types of help from many individuals and groups. An American Fellowship granted by the American Association of University Women (AAUW) supported me while I wrote the first draft. A Charlene Wackman Travel Grant provided by the Department of Theatre and Drama, University of Wisconsin-Madison, helped fund the research. Robert Skloot offered valuable insight and indispensable guidance. Susan Freidman introduced me to feminist theory and has encouraged me to extend its application to the field of theatre and drama. Meredith Alexander gave freely of her time to discusssions that enhanced my knowledge of theatricality. Caryl Churchill's willingness to meet and correspond with me has helped me understand her work. Churchill and her agent, Margaret Ramsay, assisted me by providing copies of unpublished plays. Linda Fitzsimmons has shared information and insights. Librarians at the British Broadcasting Association, the British Library National Sound Archive, and the British Theatre Association, especially Margeret Cox at the BBC and Enid Foster at the BTA, were extremely helpful in locating needed play scripts and reviews. Finally, Bert Kritzer generously advised me (often at odd hours of the day or night) on the technical aspects of word processing and gave me the constant support and encouragement without which this project would not have been completed. To all these people and organizations, it is with warm affection and deepest thanks that I acknowledge your help.

AHK

1

Questioning and Empowerment

'Playwrights don't give answers, they ask questions', stated Caryl Churchill in an essay published in 1960, as she embarked on her career as a dramatist.[1] In the thirty or so plays she has written for stage, radio, and television since 1960, Churchill deals with some of the most difficult questions of contemporary life – and typically concludes with these questions resolutely left unanswered. Her manner of approaching even the most intractable issues, however, tends to be playful, startling, and subversively comic rather than authoritative and confrontational. Churchill's plays are, above all, theatrical. Their theatricality energizes the process of open-ended questioning that empowers audiences to ask further questions and seek satisfactory answers in the world outside the theatre.

Churchill's continual, imaginative challenges to the conventions of the theatre she inherited distinguishes her work as much as does her overt, thematically based questioning of societal conventions. A dual fascination with ideas and theatrical forms is evident throughout her plays. Churchill began with a vision of social justice and a desire for theatre that would be 'not ordinary, not safe'.[2] In the mid-1970s, she developed an integrated socialist-feminist political analysis which has become increasingly explicit and consistent. Throughout her career, Churchill has continually experimented with form, both in terms of play structure and in terms of the process through which plays are created. Frequently involved in collaborative projects, Churchill also participates actively in the first, and sometimes subsequent, production of her plays. Conscious interplay among the elements of image, structure, and theme is a major characteristic of Churchill's work. The ways in which she uses the materiality of theatre and the often collaborative process of creation in which she engages express

her activist philosophy as surely as do the textual messages of
her plays.

Churchill's work, in common with that of other feminist artists,
stands at a point of intersection between the practice of her chosen art
and theory concerned both with art and with society.[3] An analysis
of Churchill's plays must, therefore, recognize the co-dependent
nature of their political and aesthetic dimensions. Existing theoretical frameworks – Marxism, feminism, or theatre criticism – do
not adequately address or integrate the aesthetic and the political.
Neither do they deal with what can be seen as the production
of socialist-feminist theory by the plays: Churchill's originality
as a dramatist is matched by an unusual ability to perceive and
analyse the basic patterns that maintain an oppressive social order.
Nevertheless, in their very challenges to dramatic convention and
interaction with explicit ideologies, Churchill's plays inevitably
refer the audience or reader to theoretical frameworks outside
the works themselves. The plays relate both to theories of theatre
and drama and to socialist-feminist analyses of social systems.
Some familiarity with major contributions to these two fields, as
preface to discussion of the ways they have been included within
or reacted against in Churchill's work, enriches understanding of
the plays.

Theories of theatre and drama generally acknowledge the primacy
of Aristotle. The Aristotelian ideal is one of structural and stylistic
unity based on a narrative plot that builds progressively to a climax
and resolution, presenting an instructive example of character development. It is one which has pervaded drama throughout its history.
Challenges to it – e.g., romanticism or expressionism – have invariably carried the implication of protest against authoritarian power
and assertion of a need for social change. Contemporary feminist
drama, in its protest against patriarchal authority and struggle to
create forms of expression that affirm the subjectivity of women,
tends to challenge the standards and conventions of Aristotelian
drama. From a socialist-feminist standpoint, the Aristotelian ideal
can be seen as confirming patriarchal ideology and the power
of traditional elites, as well as validating a phallic paradigm of
creativity. Churchill rejects both the forms and the underlying
assumptions of Aristotelian dramaturgy, having recognized the
'"maleness" of the traditional structure of plays, with conflict
and building in a certain way to a climax'.[4] Her plays offer
fragmentation instead of wholeness, many voices instead of one,

demands for social change instead of character development, and continuing contradiction instead of resolution.

The epic theatre theories and practice of Bertolt Brecht have constituted one of the major twentieth-century challenges to Aristotelian drama. Brecht's ideas, which have exerted a marked influence on British theatre since the late 1950s, have been incorporated into much of Churchill's work. Churchill, like Brecht, eschews the Aristotelian evocation of pity and fear in favour of stimulating new understandings of specific social situations through 'astonishment and wonder'.[5] Churchill's plays make effective use of such Brechtian techniques as distancing the audience from the characters and action to encourage a critical attitude, encapsulating the power relations of a particular situation in the simple action of the social gest, or disrupting the flow of narrative through episodic structure and songs. Most important is a commonality of artistic intent: like Brecht, Churchill seeks to empower audiences against oppression rather than encourage serene acceptance of an apparently inevitable fate.

However, as will be seen in the subsequent discussion, Churchill stays within the confines of the epic theatre defined by Brecht in only two of her plays – *Vinegar Tom* and *Light Shining in Buckinghamshire*, both written in 1976. Since then, she has continued experimenting with subject, form, and style. While Brecht has remained a clear reference point for most of Churchill's plays, she alters epic techniques, integrates epic with other forms, and constantly seeks new modes of expression. The most recent of Churchill's plays depart from Brechtian dramaturgy in their demand for a collective reformulation of the *process* through which issues or problems are identified and solutions developed. In this demand, which questions accepted meanings as well as the fundamental cultural and political structures through which meaning is produced, Churchill allies her work with the cultural disruption of such feminist experimentalists as Gertrude Stein, Megan Terry, Ntozake Shange, and Susan Griffin.

Socialist feminism, to address the declared ideological content of Churchill's work,[6] links the elimination of gender oppression to replacement of the capitalist system with one in which all workers, as feminist historian/social theorist Sheila Rowbotham writes, 'no longer have their lives stolen from them, and in which the conditions of their production and reproduction will no longer be distorted . . . by the subordination of sex, race, and class'.[7] The writings of Simone de Beauvoir show a convergence of socialism and feminism at the origins of the contemporary women's movement. In her autobiography, De Beauvoir stated that change in the status of women 'depends on the future of labour in the world; it will change significantly only at the price of a revolution in production'.[8]

Michele Barrett, in *Women's Oppression Today: Problems in Marxist Feminist Analysis* (1980), expands understanding of the 'relations of production' in capitalist-patriarchal society to include division of labour on the basis of race or gender, and identification of work as mental or manual. Barrett's analysis of women's oppression posits an 'integral connection between ideology and the relations of production'.[9] She identifies as crucial to women's oppression an 'ideology of gender division' which has 'been embedded in the capitalist division of labour from its beginnings'.[10] The ideology of gender division operates independently of biology to establish 'the relationship between sexuality and procreation' as 'much closer for women than for men'.[11] By breaking down the components of the ideology of gender division, Barrett argues that it can be changed, despite its pervasive acceptance as simple fact rather than ideology. The means of change proposed by Barrett involve constructing new meanings in the areas of sexuality, gender definition, and relations between the sexes.

Other Marxist-feminist theorists, such as Anna Foreman, Juliet Mitchell, and Gayatri Chakravorty Spivak, though their particular emphases differ widely, share with Barrett a recognition of the primacy of consciously held but largely unexamined gender- and class-related assumptions in structuring the conditions that oppress women and the working class. Challenges to these assumptions will only be mounted by individuals and groups who have gained some power outside traditional patterns of socio-economic interaction. Rowbotham describes the role of art in this empowerment as that of oppressed people creating 'their own ways of seeing' and beginning to integrate a new reality.[12]

The idea of a feminist-socialist aesthetic presents great problems of definition. The debate about socialist standards for literature has been conducted largely in the context of East European communism, and has generally excluded feminist considerations. Socialist drama in Britain has been dominated by the working-class naturalism of the 'angry young men' who emerged in the late 1950s. While feminism has undeniably provided the spark for an outpouring of creative work in all areas of artistic endeavour, feminist critics have barely begun the work of tracing the parameters of feminist aesthetic practice. Feminist theories of theatre have not yet progressed beyond the very early and tentative stages of development. Studies of plays by women – even of contemporary playwrights who identify themselves as feminists – have identified only the most general non-thematic patterns. In *Feminist Theatre*, the best known of such studies, Helene Keyssar points to a 'strategy of transformation'[13] as a primary dynamic among the plays she surveyed. While Keyssar's observation is valuable, it serves best to stimulate and direct more specific and detailed analysis.

The most recent trend in feminist theatre criticism derives its approach from the work of feminist film critics, such as Teresa de Lauretis, author of *Alice Doesn't: Feminism, Semiotics, Cinema* (1984). These analyses tend to situate themselves within a general critique of representation. While this critique is indispensable in pointing out the mechanisms by which systems of representation have excluded women, its view from the outside has sometimes failed to acknowledge the aesthetic possibility and political necessity of working within and changing these systems. Socialist-feminist theorists, while acknowledging that representation has been dominated by men's 'point of view, which they confuse with absolute truth,'[14] argue against wholesale abandonment of representation. Rowbotham, in *Woman's Consciousness, Man's World*, recognizes that 'the immediate response' upon understanding how an oppressive society 'communicates to the individual' may be to 'deny all culture'; but, she cautions, this denial actually perpetuates 'the distortions of oppression'.[15] Michele Barrett states that patriarchal-capitalist ideology 'should be understood as part of a social totality rather than as an autonomous practice'.[16] De Lauretis herself, in the essay that concludes her recent book, *Technologies of Gender*, acknowledges that 'women's cinema has been engaged in a transformation of vision' that has the potential to stimulate 'the redefinition of aesthetic and formal knowledges'.[17]

The dual recognition that women artists in any medium must find ways to combat systematic and systemic exclusion, and that drama may offer both special problems and special potential to feminists who work within it, frames the analyses of Churchill's plays contained in the following chapters. These analyses view theatre practice as a gestic, or actively referential, cultural practice that enacts the text of its governing ideologies. Following Catherine Belsey, the analyses will attempt to deconstruct the scripts and/or

productions of Churchill's plays in order 'to release the possible positions of its intelligibility, including those which reveal the partiality
(in both senses) of the ideology inscribed in the text'.[18] They will
examine what Belsey refers to as 'the process of production'. Of
course, production has a particular meaning for dramatic works,
which achieve full realization only through the set of choices that
culminate in public presentation of a particular interpretation of the
work. This special meaning, however, only heightens the importance of examining production as implied by stage directions and
as carried out in documented stagings or broadcasts of the plays.

Before proceeding to specific discussion of Churchill's plays, I will
lay out a brief and tentative formulation of theatre as a practice
that represents gender relations in and through the 'grammar' of
theatrical production. Patriarchal ideology is, of course, present in
the overt images of powerful men and submissive women that
dominate traditional theatre; less obvious, but equally important,
is the ideological foundation of the rules under which they are
constructed. In theatre, these rules, or modes of production, are
referred to as theatrical conventions. The dominant ideology of
patriarchal-capitalist culture may function most effectively in the
meta-theatrical realm of theatrical convention, structuring basic
expectations and assumptions about dramatic character, action, and
language as well as the use of actors, space, and other theatrical
resources. Its operation in this powerful realm, in fact, has made
representation appear unalterably patriarchal to some feminists.
Feminist ideology, by contrast, must operate at the most conscious
and explicit level, because it constitutes a deliberate challenge to
basic and usually hidden assumptions. Regardless of whether a
feminist play attacks patriarchy on a thematic level, a formal level, or
both, it risks rejection by supposedly neutral arbiters of artistic taste
(and acceptance only by the already converted) on the grounds that it
is stridently ideological, even as the ideological nature of patriarchal
works goes unnoticed.

Theatre's cultural importance derives, at least in part, from its
uniquely analogous relation to individual subjectivity. Theatre
actively represents a dramatic work to an audience in much the
same way that an individual actively represents a self to society.
The operation of patriarchal ideology in structuring theatrical convention mimics its structuring of subjectivity in male-dominated
culture. Individual subjectivity is constructed by means of a self / other
opposition which establishes the self as a mediator between all that

is truly individual (including, but not confined to the unconscious) and the finite choices offered by a given society (including language, appearance, and modes of behaviour).

Patriarchy has organized the self/other opposition primarily around a division of human potential and experience into two opposite and unequal categories, 'masculine' and 'feminine'.[19] Within this division, males' attainment of selfhood, as feminist theorists of psychosocial development agree, depends on inward repression and outward objectification of that which the culture defines as feminine. Nancy Chodorow writes, 'the basic masculine sense of self is separate. . . . Masculine personality, then, comes to be defined more in terms of denial of relation and connection (and denial of femininity)'.[20] Patriarchy compensates for the hidden negativity (the 'denial of relation') in the assertion of masculine subjectivity by claiming priority for the 'masculine' and casting subjectivity in the symbolic mode of psychic separateness and phallic unity. The 'feminine', constructed of the connectedness and relationality rejected as not-man, restricts women to relational roles qualified in terms of objectification. The gendered individual, whether man or not-man, therefore consists of an artificial construct produced, as Barrett emphasizes, by the 'ideology of gender division'.[21]

Because masculine subjectivity depends upon identification of the feminine as other, within the closed structure of the subject/object opposition, the male elite has appropriated the space, apparatus, and products of culture to the on-going project of reifying the repression of femininity and the objectification of women. Theatre, as the cultural institution most reliant upon social/political mediation between the source of the text and the audience, as well as most dependent upon specialized space and equipment, may perhaps be the one most resistant to divestiture of ownership and control by male elites. In any case, when feminists confront traditional theatre, they must deal with more than stages, curtains, scene elements, and lights; they must find ways to reshape a material practice that has been used to legitimize and maintain male hegemony.

Working in theatre as a socialist/feminist means working both in and against the dominant culture to situate oneself in relation both to the dominant culture and to alternate cultures that can only be theorized or imagined. Feminist writers in all genres, as Rachel Blau du Plessis has observed, have found it necessary to 'break the sentence' of a symbolic structure legitimizing masculine authority in order to exist in relation to it or an imagined alternative.[22]

For feminist dramatists, 'the sentence' consists of the conventions structuring the four primary elements of theatrical representation. Theatre, first of all, requires an actual space to accomodate the presentation and the audience. Theatres have taken many forms over time, changing with (and perhaps in response to) alterations in societal organisation. Second, theatre involves the performance of at least one written role by at least one player. A performance consists of the relationship between a given set of players and a given dramatic text. Third, theatre involves, as Roland Barthes points out, 'a density of signs built up on stage starting from the written argument'.[23] This density of signs – created by the gesture, posture, and vocal tones of the actors, and the staging, as well as costume, lighting, set, and the environment in which the performance takes place – comprises theatricality. Such a density allows for complex and even inherently contradictory communication to an audience; in semiotic terms, it permits the simultaneous production of multiple signs. The fourth factor is time: theatre requires a shared experience of both actual and imagined time by performers and audience. Each of these factors has been developed in ways that create and maintain theatre as a patriarchal institution. None, however, can be defined as innately patriarchal: all four contain the potential for feminist empowerment.

The first factor to constitute theatre as such – a public space accomodating performance and audience – has shown the most variability over time. The changes may be viewed as indicative of changing social configurations (though a detailed analysis cannot be attempted here, the historical correspondence, for example, between the domination of theatrical production by vanishing-point perspective scenery and the authority of the absolute monarch, suggests the value of further research into the relationship between political organization and theatrical convention). Since the stage mediates between the individual potentialities of texts and collective receptivity of audiences, the use of such space for productions in which explicit or implicit viewpoints are female, feminine, or feminist[24] constitutes an advance over powerlessness. Of course, as in other struggles for power, tokenism and hierarchization have helped to reinforce the governing elite. All stages are not equal, or equally accessible. Those theatre practitioners who seek ways out of the ghettos of tokenism and marginalization do so with varying strategies and effectiveness.

The most universal commonality among different theatre spaces is the provision of separate areas for performance and audience. This separation allows an acting out of the self/other opposition basic to the structuring of subjectivity in patriarchy.[25] Appropriation of the stage – the self position – for productions that are recognizably female, feminine, or feminist reverses the terms of the patriarchal power equation: women speak and are heard. Many feminist productions go beyond simple appropriation to question the self/other opposition through spatial arrangements and staging choices that deliberately challenge the boundary between performers and audience, though this type of experimentation is certainly not limited to theatre that declares itself feminist. Churchill, while accepting the physical separation of performers and audiences, uses both Brechtian devices (such as seating non-performing actors on stage) and literary techniques (i.e., fragmented narratives and open endings) in her plays to challenge the convention of audience passivity and engage the audience in a relationship of imaginative reciprocity.

The second of the factors to constitute theatre as such, the player/role relationship, gives theatre a unique doubleness. Barthes emphasizes this quality in his description of theatre as 'the site of an ultraincarnation, in which the body is double, at once a living body deriving from a trivial nature, and an emphatic, formal body, frozen by its function as an artificial object'.[26] The doubleness of theatrical representation has traditionally been used to reinforce the masculine/feminine opposition fundamental to patriarchal subjectivity. Theatre's player/role opposition mimics the division and hierarchization of masculine and feminine. The player is real, while the role makes visible the false man – i.e., the feminine – that must be repressed in the attainment of subjectivity. Stage parlance, which places the player 'in' a role, confirms the penetrable, 'feminine' quality of the role, as well as the unitary, 'masculine' quality of the player. (It should also be noted that the player appears 'out of character' for the curtain call at the end of a performance.) The control of theatre's doubleness by the masculine/feminine opposition demonstrates what Gayatri Chakravorty Spivak terms the 'double displacement' of woman in 'the discourse of man'.[27]

Theatre replicates the experience and repression of doubleness that makes possible the discourse of man. Patriarchy, as has been noted, constructs subjectivity as a unity which has as its emblem the phallus. Theatre reifies the substance/shadow or true/false division inherent in the demands of patriarchal subjectivity. This division, with the binary, hierarchized opposition between true man and false man (player and role) has governed traditional theatre. Theatre assures the audience, through enactment of the player/role relationship, that true man – unitary man – exists. The false man of the role reinforces the construction of the subject as phallic unity by offering the concept of the role as an 'other' upon which tendencies or qualities that threaten this wholeness can be projected.[28] This false man does, however, masquerade as the true man on stage. Thus, at the same time that patriarchal subjects are comforted by the role, they are also threatened by it. Theatre's doubleness makes it both a potentially more powerful and a less safe medium for replication of the subject/ object division than other forms of artistic production – a factor which may account for the periodic upsurges of anti-theatricality.[29]

The player/role opposition has excluded women from acting 'at certain moments in time':[30] a woman playing a role would be not-man enacting false man, and the reassuring value of doubleness would be lost. Since the advent of the female player, the stage has idealized and fetishized female physicality, excluding those women who do not construct themselves as ideal feminine objects. It has, despite artistic movements that have challenged many established structures of society, almost invariably offered women players roles that mimic passive acceptance of the subject/object opposition, in which females repress the desire for phallic subjectivity and accept the limiting boundaries of not-man. While generally failing to reflect or address the internal conflict and fragmentation that women experience as a result of societal expectations,[31] these roles equate womanhood and femininity. The patriarchal assumption that the true woman (player) and false woman (role) are essentially the same precludes for women the experience of doubleness and access to subjective power.

The feminist playwright must simultaneously use and disrupt the doubleness of theatrical representation to create the possibility of a non-patriarchal subjectivity. The strategy of equalizing the relationship of body (player) and text (role) highlights the relationship itself, making dissolution of the opposition imaginable. Such an equalization is implied in Cixous' call for an *écriture féminine*, which aims to break the controlling link between phallus and word that marks the discourse of man, and to appropriate *logos* on behalf of the multiplicity and relatedness implied by breasts, clitoris, vulva, and vagina. This project cannot be accomplished by simple or selective reversal or substitution; it must disrupt and delegitimize the artificial unity of the discourse of man. Feminist theatre must attempt to deconstruct the socially constructed wholeness of the gendered subject. To do so, it must break down the masculine/feminine opposition reified in the player/role division, theatricalizing the possibility of a subjectivity based in multiplicity and relationality rather than binary opposition and separateness. In the deconstructed space they themselves create, feminist imaginings of women can then make, in Cixous' evocative phrase, 'the shattering entry into history'.[32]

Modern drama, which developed gradually after the ban on women players was rescinded, subordinates the spoken word of the player to the written word of the playtext. It produces an experience of doubleness at least partly derived from the author/text relationship that characterizes other forms of literature. Authorship, as Gilbert and Gubar have argued, depends on 'fundamental definitions of literary authority' that are 'both overtly and covertly patriarchal'.[33] The authorized text exhibits the author's privileged position in male discourse through the construct of the unified viewpoint governing selection, sequencing, and definition of the material presented. Its claim to transcendental truth, as Gayatri Chakravorty Spivak has pointed out, rests upon penetration of what is seen as separate and 'other'.[34] The 'other' must be metaphorically feminine to play its part in this paradigm of artistic production. The text created in this mode of production, which is itself objectified in the author/text opposition, therefore represents woman in terms of a wholeness that denies the actual experience and theorized subjectivity of women.

The aesthetic standards of modern theatre have generally mandated that theatre's communicative density – its theatricality – be subordinated to a thematic and stylistic unity of production determined by the playwright's point of view. This reining in of complexity particularly characterizes the realistic theatre inherited by Churchill. As Catherine Belsey observes, 'classic realism offers the reader a position of knowingness which is also a position of identification with the narrative voice'.[35] This narrative voice, occupying the apex in the 'hierarchy of discourses'[36] both demands and is legitimized by realistic production. Rather than attempting to reveal something of the full range of inconsistency, contradiction, and ambiguity available in a dramatic situation, or even in a written text, the classically realistic play and its unified production reduce the range of meanings within the boundaries of a single voice. This simplification focuses audience attention on the message of that voice and away from the means by which the voice is produced. The play is performed from the standpoint of what it says, not what it is.

Feminist theatrical production, to extend feminism's conscious challenge of familiar and unexamined patterns to the realm of theatre, must approach the play from the standpoint of what it is as well as what it is about. The process of production, as well as the overt message of the play, is taken as an area of choice and meaning. Feminist production uses the inherent density of theatre to actuate its potential for multiplicity, relationality, and unresolved contradiction. In this use of theatricality Brecht led the way for contemporary feminists by theorizing and using 'alienation effects' to make familiar situations 'appear strange and even surprising to the audience'.[37] For example, Brecht's attempt to develop an acting style to simultaneously portray the character and express an awareness that the character is a fiction being consciously portrayed by a person on stage depends on theatre's capacity for complex communication through multiple signs. Brecht, however, used the authorial voice and often used traditional male authority figures to resolve the dilemmas he had set up. Feminist theatre makes use of alienation effects, but also goes beyond this partial fragmentation to shatter the unitary viewpoint into a range of perspectives. These varied perspectives allow for audience identification with the situations presented at the same time that they challenge customary perceptions of them. Both by highlighting situation as such (both as drama and as dramatization) and by offering multiple character and player messages arising out of a situation, socialist-feminist plays give the audience more than one way of seeing.

The temporal element of theatre has traditionally been dominated by the linear narrative – again, emphatically so in realistic plays. The narrative, which begins with conflict and builds to a climax and *dénouement*, contains imaginative time within its unitary thrust. Its archetypally masculine form parallels a combative courting ritual, conquest, and release of sexual energy. Brecht's plays, which superimpose a didactic theatricality on the linear narrative,[38] and interrupt without disrupting its progress, offer scant alternative to Aristotle in this area. The anarchic disruptiveness of the Artaudian *avant garde* initiated the contemporary movement away from traditional narrative structure. Twentieth-century feminist writing in all genres has disrupted narrative continuity with anti-narrative forms. Some feminist dramatists – notably Megan Terry – have substituted symbolic image and such anti-narrative forms as repetition of phrases for traditional narrative. More analytically-minded dramatists, such as Churchill, create disrupted narratives by using shifts of style and viewpoint as well as interposing anti-narrative devices. The cumulative effect of such a play is less to tell a story than to examine and question a social construct. Janelle Reinelt refers to the focus on situation at the expense of narrative as 'gestic experiment'.[39] Open-endedness characterizes the structure of such plays and allows for continued engagement with the questions it has posed. Rachel Blau du Plessis refers to this technique of feminist empowerment as 'writing beyond the ending' so as to subvert the 'prescribed script' of 'quest and romance'.[40]

Churchill's dramas stand among a growing number of feminist works for theatre that analyse patriarchy at the levels of both content and form. Her plays question the conventions of theatre as sharply as they question societal norms of gender and class, attempting to disrupt the unconscious operation of patriarchal-capitalist ideology in theatrical representation – and ultimately to challenge its place in the all-encompassing fabric of given social relations. Churchill reorients theatre in a number of ways to admit the possibility of a non-patriarchal subjectivity. She uses the doubleness inherent in theatre as a means of analysing and resisting the ideology of gender division. She theatrically deconstructs the hierarchized opposition between player and role by demanding a reciprocity in their doubleness. Churchill exploits the full complexity of theatricality to expose the range of possible meanings in the situations she presents and to reinforce a multiplicity of viewpoints. Finally, she experiments continually with conceptions of time, testing both the materiality of stage time and the linearity of assumptions about historical time through her highly theatrical presentations of the temporally impossible.

Churchill's theatre is remarkable for its channeling of the anarchic energy associated with performance art, as well as with such early drama and ritual as the satyr play and the Feast of Fools, to animate a materialist-feminist analysis of oppression based on race, gender, sexual preference, and socio-economic class. The social and collaborative nature of theatre is a crucial element in Churchill's work. She speaks in a cacophony of voices, mobilizes a multiplicity of forms. Above all, in her determined experimentation with the limiting traditions of the theatre she inherited, she empowers audiences to experiment with and alter the roles and power relations which they have inherited.

2

Questions of Power: The Radio Plays

CHURCHILL'S BACKGROUND AND EARLY WORK

Caryl Churchill first became known as a radio dramatist, but her radio plays had their origin in her interest in the theatre. Born in 1938, Churchill spent her childhood in London and Montreal. In 1957, she entered Lady Margaret Hall College of Oxford University, where she studied English literature.[1] Though Churchill had decided as a child to become a writer, it was at Oxford that she developed a strong interest in drama, influenced by the exciting theatre of the late 1950s, including the work of John Osborne, Samuel Beckett, Bertolt Brecht, T. S. Eliot, and Christopher Fry.[2] Churchill wrote three plays while a university student: *Downstairs*, a one-act which was performed at the NUS drama festival, 1958–59; *You've No Need to be Frightened*, a play for voices; and *Having a Wonderful Time*, which was produced by Oxford students at the Questors Theatre.[3]

Churchill's completion of her university degree, in 1960, was followed by an Oxford Playhouse production of *Easy Death*. This verse play uses the character of a young drifter to expose the absurdity of endless technological innovation, the hollowness of a life spent 'climbing over' other people, and the cynicism of a 'Speak for Peace' contest intended as corporate publicity.[4] With a structure splitting concepts of time to show a single day for one character and the lifetime of another, and in a style fluctuating between absurdist and parodic, the play denounces the callous competitiveness of domestic, business, and political life. It introduces the social concerns that underpin Churchill's later writing.

Radio served as an important training ground for Caryl Churchill, as indeed for many writers active in the 1960s. Under the directorship of eminent theatre critic Martin Esslin from 1963 to 1976, the

15

BBC Radio Drama Department produced approximately 300 new, mostly unsolicited, plays per year,[5] making it the most important venue for non-commercial drama in the years before the small theatres of the London Fringe sprang up. In addition, BBC Radio organized conferences and workshops aimed at the developing playwright. Furthermore, it provided inspiration for new writers by producing the experimental work of established dramatists such as Samuel Beckett and Tom Stoppard.

Churchill's agent first encouraged her to write for radio. Of *The Ants*, broadcast by the BBC in 1962, Churchill has written, 'I thought of it as a TV play, but my agent Margaret Ramsay sensibly sent it to radio.'[6] Churchill continued sending plays to the BBC, but another was not accepted until 1965. Thereafter she became a regular contributor to BBC radio drama until the early 1970s. Radio presented Churchill with important advantages in this stage of her career. Most important, of course, was its openness to new playwrights. In addition, it offered an unusual freedom in that it placed few limits on length; as Churchill has said, 'If your play was seventeen minutes long, they wouldn't ask you to make it thirteen.'[7] Finally, radio had already proved its potential for serious drama: Churchill has said that 'Beckett plays . . . like *All That Fall* made a huge impression on me' and showed 'what radio could be at its best'.[8]

The length of Churchill's ten-year apprentice phase in radio was undoubtedly affected by the fact that its demands proved compatible with caring for the three children born to Churchill and her husband David Harter between 1963 and 1969. While writing for radio, Churchill looked beyond it to the challenges of theatre. During the 1960s, she wrote several plays for the stage, but had none produced.[9] One submission, in fact, elicited a rejection later referred to by Churchill as 'one of those encouraging, friendly letters' from the Royal Court, the theatre with which she was eventually to become most closely associated.[10] Finally, she rewrote two of her most successful radio plays for stage performance.

Between 1962 and 1973, Caryl Churchill had eight plays produced on radio. They include *The Ants* (1962), *Lovesick* (1966), *Identical Twins* (1968), *Abortive* (1971), *Not . . . not . . . not . . . not . . . not enough oxygen* (1971), *Schreber's Nervous Illness* (1972), *Henry's Past* (1972), and *Perfect Happiness* (1973). The radio plays vary in length from approximately fifteen minutes to approximately fifty, with an average length of twenty-five minutes. With the exception of *The Ants*, all were directed by John Tydeman.

It was in writing for radio that Churchill first learned to empower audiences. Since the radio audience is by definition a group of listeners, it was Churchill's task, as for any radio dramatist, to empower the audience to see the action. She had to consider, in her choice of dialogue, music, and sound effects, the likely effect on the imaginations of her listeners. Thus, at this early stage of her writing career, Churchill became accustomed to allying her work with the imagination of the audience.

THE ANTS

The best known of Churchill's radio plays, *The Ants* (1962),[11] asks questions about the human capacity for caring. In the play, a school-age boy passes a lonely summer holiday with his mother and grandfather in a seaside home. Both the boy's personal world, and the greater world in which he lives, are threatened by failures of caring: his parents are engaged in a bitter divorce battle; the grandfather marks off his days in the numbness of neglect; and the papers bring news of war and the dropping of 'a big bomb'. The boy, Tim, withdraws into close observation of a colony of ants. He evidently cares about these tiny creatures, as he treats them gently and talks to one he calls 'Bill'. Tim's mother, on edge as she expects the father for a visit, calls the ants 'disgusting' and demands that they be killed. Tim protests, and his sympathetic grandfather assures him that the ants will not be harmed.

As Tim and his grandfather converse about the war, the old man's personal regrets, and the question of which parent Tim will live with if they divorce, the dual nature of Tim's relationship to the ants becomes evident. As long as he is in control, coaxing one or two into his hand, he views them kindly; however, when the ants swarm up his arm, Tim becomes frightened and reacts with instinctive violence. In the tape of the original production, the ants are identified by an odd, tinkling music which gives them a clearly identifiable non-human presence in the play. At the moments when Tim feels overwhelmed by them, the music gradually becomes a loud and vaguely discordant cacophony.[12]

Interspersed with Tim's reactions are a series of comparisons through which the ants are identified with humans. Tim, watching his parents walk on the beach below the house, remarks that they 'look very small'. The grandfather says of the ants, 'Look at them, they're just like people. Greedy . . . they're very intelligent, ants, as intelligent as people, anyway. They've got everything organised.' He goes on to say, ominously, 'They have terrible ants in foreign countries. They march in great armies, enormous ants eating their way through a jungle. They eat everything in their way.'

When the parents return and break the news of their divorce, his mother demands that Tim live with her and reject his father. A fresh quarrel starts between the parents, and Tim cries at both of them, 'I hate you! Ant! Ant! Ant!' As his father leaves, Tim's grandfather quiets the sobbing boy by showing him how to kill the ants, carefully spreading petrol and referring to the ants as 'the enemy'. When the blast occurs, the strange music of the ants rises to a climax, then dies out entirely. Tim explodes with laughter, then lapses into a silence made more profound by the unceasing background noise of the ocean.

In *The Ants*, through a combination of direct argument and metaphor, Churchill presents a central dilemma of caring: it is impossible to really care about and not feel threatened by abstract and faceless masses. Yet, as the play illustrates, the power struggles that may arise in intimate relationships can also annihilate caring. The adults in the play have all, to a greater or lesser extent, given up caring; they enact unthinking rituals of violence that question the assumption of their superiority to animals. Tim, surrounded by a quarrelsome mother, a mostly absent father, and a bitterly regretful grandfather – each of whom fails him at this crucial time – might well seek in the insect world a model of peaceful co-operation.

In a tenuous world, the uncertainty of which is underscored by the background sounds of the ocean, with its classically dual implications of comfort and threat, the play reveals a hierarchy of power. Farthest away but most powerful are those who decide to drop bombs. Fighting with each other for control on a familial level are Tim's parents. The grandfather, handicapped by his ageing eyes that 'can't see' and his conviction that 'it's all too late,' has little power; Tim, a child, has even less. The ants, mere insects, have the least. Thus, it is only in relation to the ants that Tim, the central character, has any power at all. His impulses toward the ants are nurturing, but he lacks the power to oppose the adults who consider his preoccupation with them foolish. Young and uncertain, Tim appeals to his sympathetic grandfather for answers, at one point asking, 'Does water burn?' The grandfather, however, feels himself poised on the edge of an ordered system threatened by the nameless chaos of 'great armies' of 'enormous ants' that 'eat everything in their way'. Therefore he transmits to Tim the patterns of aggressiveness, self-protection, and isolation which he himself questions but beyond which he cannot see.

The play thus links violence and power, suggesting that betrayal and violence are an inevitable outcome of power disparities. The ants represent an ideal of co-operation, working together for common survival and posing no real threat to the world of the humans. Despite the harmlessness of the ants, the humans destroy them with systematic brutality. Tim and his grandfather light the petrol as a diversion from pain, to feel less helpless as they wield power over creatures weaker than themselves. The destructive behaviour of all the characters derives similarly from a desire to maintain power, or the semblance of power, in relation to others. Churchill's anti-war message, then, is one which questions the fundamental ordering of human social relationships. It is the structuring of human societies on the basis of a power hierarchy, rather than on a model of egalitarian co-operation, which inhibits caring and promotes the tendency toward war and other forms of violence.

In using a child as the main character, *The Ants* offers an example of human potential in its simplest form. Tim, whose imaginative caring contrasts with the rancorously stalemated world of the adults, has not yet exercised his innate capacity for evil. The first intimation of Tim's fall from this original state of grace comes when he feels overwhelmed by the ants and, panicking, hits at them. The actual fall – and entry into the self-centred/violent world of the adults – occurs when he reacts to his parents' withdrawal of love by betraying the ants, participating in his grandfather's military-like preparations to destroy this 'enemy'. Tim's explosion of laughter suggests that his fall is also his destruction, as he has helped to annihilate the only model of community offered by his environment. *The Ants* gives a tangible feeling for the intensity of the relationship between the child and the insect emissaries of the natural world. This intensity sharpens the sense of loss when, in the end, neither the innocence of the child nor the experience of the grandfather has enough power to heal the poisoned relationship between the parents or to redeem either of the two worlds headed for destruction.

The play takes place as night falls. The grandfather, as he makes the final preparations for destroying the ants, repeatedly asks Tim if he is able to see. Tim, of course, is blinded not only by the night but also by the tears brought on by his parents' dispute and his own lack of power. At the end, there is silence except for the sounds of the ocean and the occasional cry of a sea bird. The darkness and roar of the ocean suggest the eternal night threatened by nuclear war. At he same time, they open the play's ending, going beyond the closure of the explosion and appealing to the listener to see what the characters could not.

The Ants offers, in its dramatization of the issue of caring, significant hints of the techniques Churchill would employ in future work. The use of a central metaphor that is both poetically and analytically evocative would prove to be important in her early work. A section of dialogue, near the end, in which Tim's mother and father compete in telling him their separate versions of the decision to divorce, nearly overlaps, and offers a first example of Churchill's technique of presenting conflict through juxtaposition rather than direct confrontation. Finally, the inclusion of unusual sound effects or language, and the use of time as a means of expressing theme indicate an attention to the materiality of the medium that will be found throughout Churchill's plays.

Structurally and stylistically, *The Ants* offers several examples of creative patterns that have become hallmarks of Churchill's work. The plot is based on a before-during-after structure which takes the place of the traditional pattern of conflict, build-up, climax, and resolution. The 'during' movement consists of Tim's father's visit, whose arrival and subsequent departure are indicated by the sound of an automobile motor. During the visit, the parents agree to permanent separation and Tim learns the lessons his grandfather has to offer. Despair marks the aftermath, in which the ants are destroyed. Using the ants as the central focus of the play, Churchill gives the audience the opportunity to 'see' them through multiple perspectives. These different views are not, in the end, resolved into one correct way of viewing the situation: they are presented without overt judgment, leaving the audience to draw its own conclusions. Stylistically, *The Ants* combines realistic dialogue and sound effects and the expressionistic music of the ants. This integration of styles testifies to Churchill's early interest in stretching the conventions she had inherited from a predominantly realistic theatrical tradition, as well as to her boldness in adapting the construction of a play to best express the ideas paramount in its conception.

LOVESICK

Lovesick (broadcast 1967) focuses on the power of desire and the question of expression versus repression. Surrealistic in its mixing of explanation and riddle and its alternation of bizarre action with documentary-like language, *Lovesick* juxtaposes narrative monologues and multi-character episodes. Hodge, a psychiatrist who cures patients of unacceptable desires through aversive conditioning, dictates the case history of his own obsession with Ellen, the niece of one of his patients. Hodge's opening lines establish both the repugnant criminality of some patients' forbidden desires and his own half-realized identification with them:

> When Smith raped he didn't find what he was looking for, so then he dissected with a chopper and was left with a face and meat to stuff in a sack. I cured Smith. But I could dissect Ellen, not so crudely, not even surgically, but in the laboratory applying every known stimulus to that organism and getting all her reactions, by analysis, by hypnosis, by abreactive drugs, by shaving her red hair and laying bare her brain, yes surgery perhaps or a chopper.[13]

The key to Hodge's obsession is Ellen's aura of mystery, although he explains it in more conventional, if necessarily contradictory, terms: 'It wasn't Ellen's dirt and ugliness that attracted me but her beauty which must have been great to outweigh them.' From the beginning he tries to dominate Ellen by relating to her as a patient, but she steadfastly maintains that mysterious otherness which so fascinates him.

In pursuit of Ellen, Hodge enters a world of unsanctioned desire. Two adult sons turn a water hose on their mother's lover to drive him away. The mother has an incestuous relationship with one of her sons. The mother's lover eventually returns to his wife and finds happiness by trading clothing and roles with her. Ellen herself is in love with Kevin, a homosexual.

Trapped in his own narrowly prescriptive realm, where he efficiently cures a young nymphomaniac and sends her off to marry a curate, Hodge diagnoses Ellen's attraction to Kevin as a fear of sex. Hodge then conceives a plan to redirect Ellen's desire away from Kevin and toward himself, through conditioning. On the pretext of curing Kevin's homosexuality, Hodge hospitalizes both Ellen and

Kevin, then leaves their treatment in the hands of an assistant. However, when Hodge returns to inspect the results, he discovers that, because of interference from Kevin's brother, the program has gone awry. Kevin, still a homosexual, now desires Hodge, and Ellen is now a lesbian and in love with her nurse.

As the play ends, Hodge is heard dictating his own case history. He now sees himself as one of his own patients. Depressed and suicidal at the loss of Ellen, he prepares to take a drug that will cure him of his desire for her, yet hesitates: 'It can't be fear of nausea that makes me hesitate. By next week, if I don't turn back, I could be free to concentrate on my work, with no thought of Ellen, whose beauty is great.'

Lovesick explores the way in which society maintains existing power relations through repression of certain types of sexual desire. Hodge, who represents the power of the social status quo, is the first of a number of Churchill characters to embody overtly patriarchal attitudes. A behaviouristic psychiatrist, he oppresses women and homosexuals through paternalistic imposition of behavioural norms based upon male dominance. At the same time, he identifies with the most horrific expressions of misogyny, although he also gains satisfaction from curing the rapist/murderer and returning him to a productive place in society with 'only a slight distaste for sex and butchers in an otherwise well balanced personality'. Fusing the concepts of doctor and patient, abnormal and normal, healing and destruction, Churchill questions both the accepted norms of behaviour and the institutions which attempt to enforce them.

While the narrative segments focus on society's marginalization and stigmatization of individuals who express deviant desires, the multi-character episodes indicate that such desires are too strong to be suppressed by a mere social power structure. Those on the margins of the social order continually threaten and undermine that order with their anarchic power. *Lovesick*'s scenes of playful deviance – in which, for example, one character replies to Hodge's suggestion that he be cured of his Oedipal fantasies with the information that he has not found it necessary to resort to fantasy since he began having sexual relations with his mother – celebrate marginality in the serio-comic mode identified with the plays of Joe Orton. Hodge finds himself distracted and his work disrupted by Ellen because she refuses to behave in a socially approved – or, to Hodge, rational – manner.

His obsession with Ellen presents Hodge with two choices: either join her in the marginalized world of deviant behaviour, or bring her into the conventional one. Long conditioned to play a God-like role in relation to his patients, Hodge does not even consider the first option, but easily constructs a clinical justification for modifying Ellen's desire and producing conventional behaviour. The conventional social construct that he wants to produce, of course, coincides with Hodge's own desire. Thus, the re-made Ellen he wishes for is the type of 'man's creation' that Churchill would later explore in the stage play *Cloud Nine*.

To the extent that he limits his own options, Hodge is himself a victim of the system he upholds. His double-edged relation to power illustrates the dual nature of subjectivity in patriarchal society: men, while subjects within, are also subject to the conventional order. His obsession can be seen as Hodge's intense desire for knowledge and experience outside this conventional order. Hodge cannot gain knowledge, however, without giving up his secure position of dominance and centrality as a guardian of social authority. He does not even acknowledge the obsession as part of himself until the end, instead externalizing it as Ellen's problem. While he can manipulate it in powerful ways, Hodge does not understand desire. Without understanding, he is condemned to repeat endlessly the patterns in which he has been conditioned, as is evident at the end when, although he has now become a patient, he prepares only to submit to his own regimen of repression. Hodge's attempt to control his own or Ellen's sexual obsessions, though fueled by desperation, is futile. He is constantly drawn to the borders of marginality by the anarchic force of desire, which can be controlled only through extinction – and with it a partial destruction of the person.

The structure of the play gives form to the power struggle between the representative of societal authority and the sexual anarchists. Repeatedly, the barely contained *jouissance* – replete with sound effects – of the multi-character episodes spills out over the rationalized structure of the expressionless, scientifically worded monologues confusing the time sequence and replacing the single voice with multiple voices. Even Hodge's precise language and careful reasoning undergo strange distortions when he takes part in the dramatized episodes, as when he advises Ellen, who has confessed that she smacks her child when he wets his pants, 'You should smack him before he does it, it's a better deterrent.' Though the single voice prevails at the end, it is a voice that has been stripped of its authority and reduced to the level of one hopeless, obsessive desire.

Lovesick points to several areas that will prove to be continuing concerns for Churchill in future plays. In this play she allies herself with the repressed, the taboo, the socially unacceptable, as she will in the stage plays *Vinegar Tom*, *Cloud Nine*, and *Softcops*. She questions the relationship between violence, sexuality, and resistance to authority, as she will later in *Objections to Sex and Violence*. Finally, in the subplot of the character who swaps roles with his wife, she hints at an analysis of societal role-playing that will later be central to several of her plays.

IDENTICAL TWINS

Identical Twins: A Duologue for Radio (1968) is a dramatic poem which uses one voice, both on its own and recorded over itself, to create the effect of two voices speaking in unison. Using rhythmic lines, softly chanted for a dream-like effect, the play explores questions of identity through the fragmented memories of Clive and Teddy, identical twins. The story is their struggle for separate identities. They reveal that they fought as children and always felt different from each other, but that they enjoyed the confusion caused by their sameness and took advantage of it for their own purposes, such as trading girl friends. At the age of seventeen, they got on separate trains going in opposite directions. Together the voices exult: 'We slid apart. That was my happiest time.'[14] Since then, they have pursued very different lives: Clive is a 'stick in the mud' farmer, Teddy a busy urban real estate agent.

Beneath the external distinctiveness, however, the two men have developed exactly parallel lives. Both are successful men with a wife, a mistress, and two children. Each displays a pervasive sense of guilt: Teddy gives money to a repellent beggar, while Clive finds he cannot shoot a dying dog he hits with his car one dark night. Significantly, both are dissatisfied with their current personal situation. Clive wants to leave his wife Janet for Nicola, the children's nanny who has become his mistress, but Janet keeps him tied to her through continual suicide threats. Teddy is bored with his mistress, Dawn, and would like to turn both her and her abusive husband out of the shabby upstairs apartment they rent from him.

When one of Janet's suicide attempts succeeds, her death disrupts the parallel pattern of the brothers' lives. With Nicola, Clive arrives on Teddy's doorstep for an unannounced visit. The resemblance between the twins amazes their families; at the same time, each brother thinks of the other, 'How ugly he is.' Clive hopes the visit will somehow allay his guilt over letting Janet die, evidently expecting consolation from comparison with his brother. Teddy, however, feels superior to Clive, reminding himself of an occasion when he saved the life of his mistress's husband and concluding that he 'couldn't let someone die because he was in my way'.

As the visit progresses, Teddy proves more interested in Nicola than in Clive, but he has still not persuaded Dawn and her husband to leave. Clive, depressed and unable to sleep, swallows some sleeping pills. Teddy, who has seen his brother take the overdose, does not summon help but instead takes a bus ride to the end of the line, feeling 'great joy' that he has caught the last bus. Returning in the morning to news of what has appeared to be his own death, Teddy assures everyone that it is he who is still alive.

Speaking alone, Teddy tells of inheriting the farm, Clive's children, and Nicola. At the end, although his identical twin is dead and he has assumed both their identities (when he visits the farm, the neighbors call him Clive), he is no closer to a firm sense of who he actually is. When he asks Nicola if she loves him, she says, 'What's the difference?' His wife divorces him, saying it was Teddy she loved. His sense of guilt has grown yet more pervasive and difficult to define. He reflects, 'Probably Clive meant me to save him,' and then states, 'What keeps me awake is that I haven't the relief of feeling guilty.' The one facet of identity left to him is the tenuous one of relation to his 'own' children, as he affirms in the final line: 'Clive's children are very sweet and I'm fond of them, but my own are the ones I love.'

Identical Twins questions the meaning and power ascribed to individual identity by fusing the concepts of self and other. Each brother speaks individually but can make his identity clear only by referring to the other. Both define themselves as morally superior to the other, but when Teddy allows Clive to die he proves himself no better (or worse) than his brother. Teddy and Clive have moved apart but have established the same patterns in different locations. When Clive dies, Teddy expects finally to make undisputed claim to his own identity, but instead finds that his twin's identity is now inseparable from his own. In the end, it is only by referring to his relationship with other family members – his own children

– that Teddy clings to any sense of himself as an individual. Since Teddy's voice is indistinguishable from that of Clive, the listener has no external referent by which to verify which twin is speaking at any given time or which one 'really' survives at the end.

As recorded using the then-new technique of stereophonic sound, the play questions individualism not only in a way which uniquely uses the medium of radio, but also in a way that addresses the dominant issue in postwar British drama. The fact that Kenneth Haigh, who played the role of Jimmy Porter in the original production of John Osborne's *Look Back in Anger* (1956), provides the voice(s) in *Identical Twins* gives it a resonance with the stage play that is probably not accidental. If Jimmy Porter's famed anger is the result of his inability to establish a satisfactory individual identity, Churchill is suggesting, in this play, that such an identity may simply be an illusion.

While analysis of capitalism and patriarchy does not constitute an explicit element of *Identical Twins*, there are, of course, political dimensions to the questioning of individual identity. Capitalism and patriarchy intersect in their construction of the individual subject as separate, non-relational, and competitive. Teddy's failure to save his brother can be seen as a metaphor for the way in which the individualistic construct of identity encourages people to compete with, rather than identify with, one another. Thus, as she did in *The Ants*, Churchill calls attention to the negative effect of individualism on community. However, Teddy's occupation as a real estate dealer and the assumption of both Clive and Teddy that wives, mistresses, and children serve as accessories to their own identities, go further in implicating capitalism and patriarchy in the denial of relatedness and community.

The styles and techniques used in *Identical Twins* are ones that have begun to establish themselves as distinctive of Churchill's writing, even in the few plays written by this time. The heightened language and rhythmic currents of the narrative monologues show Churchill's interest in developing a poetic diction for the contemporary theatre. The plot is constructed on a before–during–after pattern, evident in the background of the relationship, the visit Clive pays to Teddy, and the aftermath of Clive's death. Throughout the play, fragments of memory intrude upon the narration of events as they are occurring, disrupting the sequential flow of time and forcing the listener to question information and to work at integrating what is being said with what has already been stated. This play again mixes styles, alternating traditionally sequential and descriptive storytelling with poetic expression of psychological states.

ABORTIVE

Abortive (broadcast February, 1971) deals with the way in which intimate contact between the powerful and the marginalized might unsettle power relations. It takes shape from the voices and the silences of a man and woman, Colin and Roz, who talk intermittently as they lie in bed in their weekend home near London. A realistic sense of spontaneity animates the protracted two-sided conversation revolving around Roz's recent abortion. Opening with the sound of a fretful whimper, which might be the sound of a baby waking, but turns out to be Roz refusing Colin's sexual advance, the play centres on the couple's attempt to come to terms with their recent trauma. Roz reminds Colin that it has been 'only three weeks since the abortion,' and says, 'I won't be permanently frigid,' but he inquires uncertainly, 'Do you love me?'[15]

In their troubled, frequently interrupted and redirected conversation, Roz and Colin reveal the intense feelings they have about the recent events in their lives. Roz's pregnancy was the result of a rape – which she, in the end, did not resist – by Billy, a drifter taken into the household on the husband's generous impulse. In the wake of it, both husband and wife are experiencing doubts about the other: Colin says he 'can't help feeling jealous' of Billy, and Roz accuses Colin of interest in the *au pair* girl. They discuss 'the child', giving a suggestion of agonized deliberations preceding the decision to abort.

When it begins to rain, Roz rushes outside, followed by Colin. They embrace and frolic in the downpour, momentarily happy. When they return to bed, Roz tries to initiate sex, but now Colin refuses, prompting her to remark bitterly, 'We might as well have had the baby.' He replies, 'See, you do want it,' to which she rejoins forcefully, 'I want something.' Crying, she recalls the abortion: 'It was such a load off my mind . . . the best part is getting the anaesthetic and knowing you'll miss all the unpleasantness.' Now, however, there is nothing to alleviate the residual unpleasantness.

The two return again and again to their inescapable contradiction: they cannot live as if the rape and abortion had never happened, yet they cannot find a way to integrate these events into their lives.

Attempting to fit their separate and partial perspectives together to form a more complete view, they go over the whole history of their involvement with the enigmatic and personally magnetic Billy. Taking him into their household, they first treated him as a sort of foster child and introduced him to the wonders of affluence. Finding that he 'told lies' and 'took advantage,' they tried unsuccessfully to fit him into the role of a domestic servant, coping with the various problems he created, but finally threw him out – only to have him constantly return, crying and begging.

The play ends with its issues unresolved, as Roz sees the sun coming up and says: 'I do find I'm afraid to go to sleep. Just as I'm going off I get that feeling like in a nightmare, but with no content. I'm frightened something's about to happen.' The hard questions are left implicit as the two gropingly attempt to regain a hold on the confidence and ease they enjoyed before the rape and abortion.

This play offers an ironic contrast between the extreme affluence and comfort in which the couple live and the very painful way in which they are spending the night. Roz and Colin are part of the powerful establishment, but the intrusion of the once-powerless drifter has shattered their status quo. Their economic power holds no sway over the personal kind of pain he has inflicted on them. That this disruption may result in a new state of consciousness for Roz and Colin is a possibility held out, but only dimly. It is notable that their happiest moment occurs when they leave the shelter of their house and go out into the pouring rain; however, their transient elation as past regrets seem washed away by the rain leaves them with no lasting indication of how to reconstruct their life together.

Roz, for whom the sexual and gender-related experiences of the rape and abortion have had a direct, physical effect, as well as a psychological one, is clearly the most devastated of the two partners. The double trauma has pushed her across the line separating the powerless from the powerful, thus confronting her with the ephemeral nature of the power she has previously taken for granted. Her marriage, the basis of her social power, is threatened. Her sense of control over her own destiny – the psychological power that allowed her to choose the option of abortion – has been undermined. She can neither respond to nor elicit response from her husband in attempts at reestablishing sexual relations. The dawn of a new day brings no change, as she continues to feel at the mercy of forces beyond her control, 'frightened', as she tells Colin, that 'something's is about to happen'.

Although Colin raises the question of why Roz did not, after being attacked, clearly resist, the two never discuss what Colin's unacknowledged motives may have been for bringing Billy into the household. Both acknowledge an inexplicable attraction to this 37-year-old man of mixed race 'from another walk of life'. Neither can quite fathom why their 'moment of feeling close to him' has, in its wake, so shaken their confidence. Again, as in *Lovesick*, Churchill directs attention to the power of marginalized individuals to disrupt the orderly world of entrenched power.

Churchill has used a highly naturalistic style in this play to heighten the material sense of the discomfort and frustration which have intruded into the ordinarily comfortable and well-ordered personal domain of the upper-class couple. In combination with a sequential time frame – here, the progression from night to day – the naturalistic dialogue and sound effects (i.e., of shifting positions in bed) give immediacy and an almost tactile substance to the issue being addressed. Bits of dialogue alternate with Pinteresque silences, which provide a contrasting sense of formlessness. The silences are infused with Roz and Colin's uncertainties about, as well as their continued fascination with, Billy. The contrast leaves the listener with a curiosity about this stranger who, during his brief period of close contact with Roz and Colin, left indelible marks on their lives but who has left behind no tangible evidence of his existence. The key to their dilemma may be to gain a sure sense of Billy's identity and motives, but such knowledge remains elusive.

NOT. . . NOT. . . NOT. . . NOT. . . NOT ENOUGH OXYGEN

With *Not . . . not . . . not . . . not . . . not enough oxygen* (broadcast March, 1971), Churchill moves from naturalism to science fiction, presenting a future world where everything necessary for life is running out and, within that world, two different responses to the failure of resources. As the title implies, the play deals with panic in the face of environmental collapse; yet the panic is muted, having become part of everyday life. Those caught up in the disaster, Mick and Vivian, are quite ordinary people who occupy a tiny room in a huge high-rise building. Shut up in their small world, they shut out

the larger one. Their concerns are purely personal – enough food,
water, and oxygen, as well as television and jigsaw puzzles to 'keep
the mind active'.[16] They worry about sharing space, even with each
other: Vivian has been staying with Mick and wants to move in
with him, but he hesitates to make their arrangement permanent,
because he has so little space in his allotted room. Vivian, who
speaks in broken phrases as though brain damaged, nevertheless
cares for Mick in practical ways, buying the things they need and
dealing with the building manager.

Nick and Vivian place their hopes for personal survival on an
expected visit from Claude, Mick's son, from whom he has been
separated for many years. They assure each other that Claude, a
wealthy pop singer, is 'a sweet, kind boy' who will help them move
out of 'the Londons' to the country. As they nervously wait by the
window, two things draw their attention: black smoke, which they
attribute to 'the fanatics' they have seen on the television news; and
a live bird, the sight of which they greet with amazement.

Claude arrives nearly unconscious, having walked to their building from his. When he revives, he reports the news of the rest of the
family. His mother has given up her property and joined the 'fanatics'. 'It's a madness they say sweeping the country,' Vivian remarks.
A half-brother and his wife, both doctors, had an unlicensed child,
attempted to hide it, then finally killed it and turned themselves in.
Mick says he would rather not have known about these things, then
brings up his desire to live in the country. Claude says people in the
country are starving. Mick begs Claude not to let him starve, but
Claude reveals that he no longer owns anything.

The news that Claude has given away his entire fortune brings an
outburst of anger from Mick:

> You didn't think of me . . . . I think of you all the time. You were
> one of the last children born in the Londons . . . . What do you
> think a license cost to have a second child? Can't you even pay
> that money back? How dare you give five million pounds away
> to strangers?

Vivian, however, understands immediately that Claude has joined
the fanatics, and fears that he has come to kill them. Claude assures
them that he simply wanted to see his father once more and hints
at a climactic event 'not happening til this evening'. Mick then
urges Claude to reconsider, retracting his angry words and arguing

that life is still worth living: 'Even without children, even with everything the way it is and getting worse you could be happy at times. There are always moments.'

Claude departs, and Mick and Vivian watch as he seems to merge with the flames of a burning building nearby. Then, in the face of a hellish existence where fire is consuming what little oxygen remains and where Claude's heroic but futile act of self-sacrifice provides the only alternative, Vivian and Mick go back to discussing, as before, the minutiae of domestic life.

Despite its grim situation, this play emphasizes the power inherent in positive collective action. In a strongly affirmative tone, it asks whether a movement composed of people with Claude's courage could have turned things around before the world reached such a hopeless state. By combining barely imaginable horrors with mundane characters who might have been borrowed from a television soap opera, the play warns against the tendency to concentrate on personal relationships and individual concerns, while ignoring global dangers and the fate of others besides oneself. Mick and Vivian are not, of course, powerful enough to be responsible in a major way for the horrors of the environment around them. Their relatively low place in the power hierarchy is indicated by the building manager's reply to Vivian's request for more oxygen: he says that such decisions are not 'up to . . . down to' him. Mick and Vivian's failure, however, lies in their lack of attention to anything beyond their immediate relationships and personal needs. They have adapted and attempted to cope in isolation, rather than joining with others to present an effective opposition while there was still a possibility of reversing the destruction. In the world allowed by, if not created by, Mick and Vivian, personal relationships and plans are not just called into question, but finally rendered absurd by the nearness of total annihilation.

The isolation of Mick and Vivian in their personal realm is reinforced by references to the small room in which they live and to the very limited contact they have with anyone outside the room. Such minimal contact with the outside world has contributed to their passivity and dependence on others. Mick and Vivian cannot improve their own situation and therefore hope that Claude will save them. They live by proxy, depending on television for experience. The only way in which they can relate to Claude's death is to discuss the fact that it will probably merit a mention on the evening news. Their ignorance of direct experience and blindness to the implications of what they do see allows them to assume that television will continue to bring news into their encapsulated world even as the buildings surrounding theirs are consumed by apocalyptic flames.

This play marks Churchill's first use of science fiction and first attempt to place a concept of collective action in contrast to a vision of social and environmental dystopia. Here she uses both the representative and descriptive capacities of dialogue – evident in Vivian's halting, repetitive speech and Nick's awe at the sight of a sparrow – to evoke a setting and an act of personal sacrifice that can be imagined more effectively in the absence of visual representation. The before-during-after plot structure is again used, with an open ending that invites the audience to formulate an alternative to Nick and Vivian's absurd response to annihilation.

SCHREBER'S NERVOUS ILLNESS

Schreber's Nervous Illness (broadcast July, 1972) initiates an exploration by Churchill of the interplay between gender division and power relations. It is the first of many works in which Churchill would address questions of gender. With a length of fifty minutes, *Schreber's Nervous Illness* also marks the beginning of a transition period during which Churchill wrote longer works for radio. Based on a turn-of-the-century document, *Memoirs of My Nervous Illness* by Daniel Paul Schreber, translated and republished by Ida Macalpine and Richard A. Hunter in 1955, *Schreber's Nervous Illness* dramatizes the story of a man who rose to be President of the Court of Appeals in Dresden by the age of fifty, then suffered a mental breakdown, became schizophrenic, and spent ten years in an asylum. Uniquely in Churchill's work, it focuses intensely on a single character. The most textually rich and intellectually provocative of the radio plays, it draws much of its force from the original, which Churchill came across while browsing in a library.[17] It deals with what can be seen as the ultimate power relation – that between God and the individual human being. At the same time, in the selection and focus applied to the original material, Churchill directs our attention to issues of sexual and gender identity. On the surface merely an interesting and rather bizarre case history presented through the voices of the patient and his doctors, *Schreber's Nervous Illness* asks fundamental questions about the definitions of masculine and feminine in western culture.

Schreber is presented sympathetically throughout the play; yet there is no doubt that by any conventional standards he is mad. The central question is not whether to judge Schreber insane, but instead whether traditional definitions of masculine and feminine constitute womanhood as a 'nervous illness' – a question suggested in other forms by such theorists as Elaine Showalter.[18] Conflict is generated in two ways – first through Schreber's courageous and strangely moving struggle to survive the alien forces he feels are attacking him. Second, and more subtly, it results from the tension between two extremes of experience within the same personality: the model of power and exemplary rationality Schreber took on in his role as high court judge, and that of irrationality and powerlessness embodied in the 'woman submitting to intercourse' which he believed himself to be at times after his breakdown. The issues of power *versus* powerlessness and rationality *versus* irrationality gain complexity in the original production through the use of one actor – Kenneth Haigh – to play both Schreber and his doctors.

Schreber, even while under siege by what he perceives as overwhelming forces, attempts to use logic to bridge the gap between the extremes of his experience, working out a religio-scientific explanation that reveals his view of the deity as an irresistible but totally anarchic force. In his opening monologue, Schreber states:

God was always in a precarious position. The human soul is contained in the nerves of the body. God is all nerve, and his nerves turn into whatever he wishes to create. But, although he enjoys what he has created, he has to leave it to its own devices and only rarely make contact with human nerves, because they have such an attraction for God's nerves that he might not be able to get free and would endanger his own existence.[19]

Schreber goes on to say that God made 'nerve contact' with him, 'regardless of the danger,' after which he began to attract more of 'God's nerves,' as well as the 'nerves of . . . dead souls . . . they dripped on my head, like thousands of little men'. Periodic intrusions of the distorted voices and obscene or unintelligible words of the 'little men' he comes to refer to as 'rays' convey the sense of Schreber's mental chaos.

Sure that he is witnessing the destruction of the world, Schreber feels himself to be 'the last human being left' and speaks of 'miracles' in which he is 'demasculinized' and impregnated 'so as to bear children and repopulate the world'. 'Twice,' Schreber observes, 'the male genitals have withdrawn into my body, and I have felt a quickening.' Even though he believes himself the potential savior of humankind, Schreber feels his continued existence is an 'embarrassment' to God. He reports 'remaining immobile for several months' in the hope that such stillness would lessen his attraction for 'rays', allow them to return to God, and end the embarrassing predicament.

Schreber's diary entries and letters alternate with brief clinical reports and court testimony presented by his doctors. Thus the play offers inside and outside views of Schreber as he goes through treatment in the asylum. The doctors note gradual improvement, from complete incoherence, through a period of passive withdrawal, to a state of lucidity only occasionally interrupted by fits of rage. As he progresses, Schreber is allowed a piano in his room and encouraged to read and play chess.

Though he acknowledges improvement in his situation, Schreber becomes increasingly convinced that he is simply being transformed into a woman: 'The signs that I was turning into a woman became so marked that I could not ignore them.' He resists at first, seeing feminization as an attempt to 'degrade' him. Then, with renewed faith in a 'divine plan', he embraces what he sees as his fate, giving himself up to 'voluptuousness': 'God demands constant enjoyment . . . since he cannot escape from my nerves, it is my duty to provide it.' A new skepticism toward God, however, is evident in his reference to 'a thoroughly mismanaged affair', and conclusion that 'God can no longer claim infallibility'.

Wanting to return home, Schreber petitions for release from the asylum, but his requests are repeatedly turned down. Finally, after many appeals, Schreber appears before the high court over which he had once presided. This court, though it recognizes the abnormality of Schreber's persistent attempts to publicize his unusual religious views, his episodes of cross-dressing, and his bouts of uncontrolled shouting, decides that his behaviour is not sufficiently disruptive to warrant continued confinement. Schreber leaves the asylum confident that divine justice will reward his suffering with 'something magnificent'. He finds some compensation in the extreme 'voluptuousness' he enjoys at times. Strange voices still assail him, though the 'miracles' grow more harmless. He continues to dress up in women's clothes and jewelry periodically, and the urge to 'bellow' still comes upon him. Though he usually controls this urge, his final speech describes occasional release:

> While going for walks along country lanes or in the fields, I make things easy for myself and simply let the bellowing happen. Sometimes it continues for five or ten minutes, during which time I feel perfectly well. Anyone who saw me, however, would hardly understand what I was doing, and might really think he was seeing a madman.

Schreber's Nervous Illness focuses on the opposition between the rational and the irrational. Gender analysis is an important, though implicit, part of this focus. As a judge, Schreber is expected to uphold the ideal of the blindfolded goddess with the scales of justice – an image that implies a fusion of the rational and irrational in its demand for both blindness and precise measurement. The ideal, of course, is a God-like one, and Schreber's illness can be seen as a metaphor for the conflict between God-like ideal and human social norms. Patriarchal societies – of which turn-of-the-century Germany provides a good example – do not allow the fusion of such oppositions in normal social relations. Patriarchy separates rationality and irrationality according to gender expectations, linking the former to masculine identity and the latter to the feminine. Thus, Schreber must maintain his position as judge on the basis of rationality alone. When God, as he says, makes 'nerve contact' with him, the irrationality he has suppressed in order to be a proper masculine authority figure surfaces. Fusion of the rational/irrational opposition can only be seen by society as confusion – a 'nervous illness'.

Gender division provides the basis not only for behavioural norms, but also for power disparities. Power is accorded the masculine and the rational. When Schreber begins to feel overwhelmed by the chaotic voices of the 'rays', he identifies his new state as feminine and gradually comes to believe that he is turning into a woman. The more 'feminine' he becomes, the more dangerous he is perceived to be. The belief that he is being 'demasculinized' therefore coincides with his actual removal from power and confinement in conditions of absolute powerlessness. Schreber's nervous illness reverses his position in the power structure, turning him into one of the judged.

Interestingly, Churchill uses as her main character a man afflicted with the 'female malady'[20] of madness, rather than a woman reacting madly to the world of male-imposed structures. In taking an approach that defies habitual divisions and avoids reinforcing such division, Churchill emphasizes that any individual – male or female – may be both a perpetrator and a victim of patriarchal oppression. At the same time, Schreber's story, as presented in this radio play, gives a compelling capsulization of the relation of women to patriarchal power. Schreber's interactions with authority may be seen as emblematic of the strategies by which women attempt to cope with the patriarchal establishment. First, he tries to invest his new role with a distinctive power, viewing himself as the regenerator of the human race, or the mother of a new race of beings. Second, he gives up any claim to power and lapses into complete passivity, remaining largely immobile and eschewing all responsibility for his own welfare. Finally, he trivializes his femininity, reducing it to harmless pursuits such as dressing up in jewelry and crying aloud on lonely roads. This final strategy is the most successful, winning him a measure of freedom.

The implications of the traditional division of the world into 'masculine' spheres of law, philosophy, and science, and 'feminine' spheres of imagination and intuition, with most power allocated to the former, are clear. Those who seek to transcend the division risk actual madness or, at the least, being seen as mad and disqualified from any position of power. The success of Schreber's final strategy has equally strong implications: women or those viewed by male-dominated society as feminized (i.e., mysterious, irrational, and thus dangerous) can gain a measure of power over their own lives only if they channel their feminine qualities into inconsequential acts, such as dressing up or venting rage in solitude. It is important, finally, to note that Schreber expresses himself in two forms traditionally identified with women: writing in a diary and crying out in a wordless, inarticulate release of emotion.

Two major aspects of *Schreber's Nervous Illness*, one technical and one thematic, indicate directions of Churchill's work in the future. First, she shows a talent for translating a non-dramatic work into a dramatic genre, effectively selecting, condensing, and reshaping the material. Non-dramatic sources – essays, documentary works, histories – would significantly extend Churchill's range of subjects in future plays. Second, this play shows a preoccupation with androgyny, evident in a God both identified as 'all nerve' and referred to by the pronoun 'He', as well as in the ambivalent identity of Schreber, that would be further developed in later plays focusing on questions of gender.

HENRY'S PAST

Henry's Past (December, 1972), written and broadcast the same year as *Schreber's Nervous Illness*, makes a more explicit, though less dramatically effective, analysis of gender relations – again through the perspective of a central male character. A sprawling, hour-long play originally intended for the stage,[21] it explores Henry's fixation on past events and highlights the issue of masculine control. Henry, who wants to dominate the women in his life, can be seen as an exemplar of patriarchal attitudes. He has, however, lost the private kingdom he once ruled, and throughout the play tries to regain the power he lost, or perhaps never had.

Henry, as the title implies, is obsessed with the past – particularly with the time when he, his wife Alice, and his daughter Lydia lived together as a family. This time ended when Henry, suspecting Alice of having an affair with his friend Geoffrey, attacked Geoffrey with a hammer. That incident put Henry in prison for five years and Geoffrey 'in a wheelchair for life'.[22] Alice, Lydia, and Geoffrey have since established a new and satisfying life together in Canada. Henry, on the other hand, does little but think and talk about the past.

The play begins when Paulina, the friend with whom Henry has lived since he 'came out of prison', interrupts a discussion between Henry and a young, unmarried woman. This woman, Silvy, has just given her newborn baby up for adoption. Although Henry has not fathered the baby, he professes concern for it and tries to persuade Silvy to reclaim it. To Paulina, Henry casually offers the news that Alice, Geoffrey, and Lydia will arrive at any moment for one of their infrequent visits.

The visit brings Alice into the debate over Sylvy's decision. While others had suggested tossing a coin or making a list of pros and cons, Alice recommends that Sylvy wait two days and then ask herself, 'would it be fun to get the baby?' Discussion of the baby provokes a verbal free-for-all of accusations and personal revelations. Lydia asks Sylvy to join their household, volunteering to help care for the baby. Paulina regrets the 'ten years of nothing' with Henry, but asks him to remain a while longer. Sylvy remains in a quandary. Henry, perhaps arriving at a new understanding of his life, murmurs, 'What happened then is the present moment.'

Although *Henry's Past* lacks the purposeful construction and clear line of inquiry of the best of Churchill's radio plays, it juxtaposes characters with intriguing differences and does manage to raise significant questions about the future of patriarchy. Henry, who attempts to command total loyalty from Alice, contrasts with Geoffrey, who quietly tolerates her liaison with another man, describing this lover as 'only an episode' and saying, 'Alice and I will be together till we're ninety-five.' Alice, who has 'weak hands' and has not held to any person or interest for long, contrasts with Paulina, who has taken care of Henry for ten years despite the lack of commitment from him. Henry's possessiveness and lack of interest in the quality of his relationships contrasts directly with the attitudes of Geoffrey. Sylvy and Lydia show contrasting attitudes toward the baby. While these contrapositions do not necessarily point to good or bad attitudes in relationships, it is notable that the non-controlling and adaptable Geoffrey seems happiest – even though confined to a wheelchair – and least hurtful toward others.

Henry, the patriarch, has failed to adapt to new conditions. He cannot accept the change in his relationship to Alice and Lydia, complaining, at one point, that a recent newspaper article featuring Alice made no mention of him. Changes in society have left him behind, as he acknowledges in the statement that he is, 'in effect, already dead'. He has no watch or clock, and spends his days trying to 'destroy time' – a compulsive and impotent effort to exert control. Meanwhile, the people Henry wants to dominate continue their lives beyond his reach. His compulsion to control others, a product of patriarchal attitudes which have lost force in the present, has become a weakness. Instead of dominating others, Henry is himself dominated by the past to which he obsessively clings.

The play, then, suggests that changes in society have made rigid and extreme patriarchal attitudes obsolete. Henry, because he violently asserted possession of Alice, is shown to have lost Alice, Lydia, and years of freedom. He has become a pathetic figure playing the role of victim, while his ex-wife and the real victim of his attack have gone on to build a new and successful life. Alice has proved that she does not need him. Geoffrey and Paulina testify to the fact that love has nothing to do with possession or dominance. Lydia envisions an alternative nurturing group to replace the patriarchal family in caring for the baby. Her attitude towards close relationships reveals that she is more Geoffrey's child than Henry's. The crippled but powerful Geoffrey presents a new model of masculinity.

The primary question asked by the play is whether or not Henry, the exemplar of patriarchy, can adapt to this new order. Churchill attempts to answer this question in the affirmative: she has referred to *Henry's Past* as a play 'about accepting the way things are without necessarily being able to encapsulate them or make versions of them'.[23] Henry's continual withdrawal into the past (or future), a 'way of doing time' he learned in prison, shows his determined effort to control time and force it to express quantitative, rather than qualitative, meanings that would, of course, deny the possibility of personal or social change. His ambiguous comment at the end may indicate his capacity to 'change a little for the better',[24] as the characters of *Cloud Nine* would later do. This positive ending, however, achieves insufficient realization to carry the impact implied in Churchill's description of the play.

Henry's Past contains two thematic concerns, in addition to gender, that play a major part in later works. The first consists of a focus on the nature and function of time. A structure in which narrative flow is frequently disrupted by Henry's recollections of his past reinforces this focus. Henry's desire to make time stand still shows an interplay between theme and character. Second, an emphasis on possessiveness in relationships emerges here as a major concern which Churchill was to explore further in subsequent work. Rather than condemning Henry's possessiveness, Churchill merely contrasts it with other ways of relating, such as Paulina's friendship, Sylvy's disinterest, and Geoffrey's tolerance. As she would in subsequent work, Churchill here shows more interest in empowering audiences to find a way out of the central dilemma than in pointing out one particular route.

PERFECT HAPPINESS

Perfect Happiness (1973), continues the critique of gender relations in a fast-moving comedy pitting an anxious housewife against a pair of disdainful young office workers. Their encounter exposes the insecurity of the traditional wife and, of course, satirically dismantles the romantic ideal of 'perfect happiness' in marriage.

Felicity, whose name underlines the irony of her position, has initiated the encounter. 'I completely fail to understand why girls today are so unhappy,' Felicity announces at the outset of a brisk lecture on why marriage should bring women 'perfect happiness'.[25] While she talks to Leanne and Margo, two young women from her husband's office, Felicity demonstrates her control of the situation by mixing up a cake. The resulting clatter conveys a sense of Felicity's well-equipped kitchen as a power base. Nevertheless, one of the young women immediately challenges Felicity's viewpoint, scorning household skills and rejecting the label of typist, saying 'typing is what I do, not what I am'.

Felicity gradually reveals that her real worry centres on her husband's overnight absence. At first she intersperses careful and casual-sounding questions about lunch dates with claims that she and her husband have never had a 'real row', and assurances that she has 'never wanted a *single* thing that [he] has not given me'. Forced to admit her strongest fear, however, Felicity grows more aggressive, 'I just need a little filling in on the details. How *often* did you meet? Has he ever kissed you? Where? When he kissed you on the mouth, did he put his tongue in? How often?' Finally, she attempts to justify her husband's infidelity: 'Forty is such an age, isn't it?'

Margo and Leanne, the two office workers, counteract Felicity's power play with sly humor. When Felicity urges them to 'find boys [their] own age', they soberly agree that many supposed men are really women masquerading as men to gain higher salaries. The two thoroughly turn the tables on Felicity, however, when Leanne ventures, 'I think we should tell her . . . how we got rid of the body,' and Margo replies, 'We'd better tell her what happened first, then.' An uncomprehending Felicity inquires, 'Body . . . do you mean yoga?'

The two young women alternate in narrating the story of 'what happened', reeling off ever more outrageous details without hesitating or losing control. They report that Felicity's husband, having kept them late at the office, asked them to indulge his fantasy by pointing a loaded gun at him. Detouring briefly into a disagreement about guns and self defense, they further confuse Felicity, who says, 'I seem to have lost the thread. Are you talking about a film?' Returning to their story, the two explain that Margo, on an irresistible impulse, shot her boss. They describe how, with great effort they disposed of his body by throwing it into the river from Westminster Bridge. Felicity finally begins to understand. She stammers then shrieks in horror, while Leanne helpfully takes the cake out of the oven.

The sound of a car roaring into the garage interrupts them, and a glance out the window assures the now-hysterical Felicity that her husband is not dead. The two young women wonder aloud how Felicity's husband spent the night and what he will claim to have done. Aiming a final blow, Leanne asks Felicity, 'Do you want to hear what he said about you?' Felicity begs to know, insisting, 'He can talk to me, but not about me.' As she leaves, Leanne ruefully admits, 'He said he was very happily married and didn't know why he kept seeing me.' Felicity calls after her, 'There's more to us, Leanne, than you might think.'

In Felicity, Churchill presents a view of the traditional wife that is satiric, yet has an edge of pathos. Felicity initially conducts the meeting with the artificial friendliness of a poised hostess, confidently exercising proven skills in her own territory. However, the threat of losing the man upon whom she depends for her identity activates uncertainty and defensiveness. Assailed by confusing and frightening messages, Felicity can no longer maintain the pretence that she is anything but powerless and dependent.

Perfect Happiness points toward the Marxist-feminist idea that gender, rather than apparent economic position, determines a woman's class. At the beginning of the play, Felicity's position seems much more secure and powerful than that of Leanne and Margo. Her actual insecurity, however, becomes obvious as the encounter confronts Felicity with her total lack of control over her husband's actions outside the home – a set of conditions reinforced by the 'his' and 'her' sound effects of the car and the kitchen. Felicity's readiness to believe Margo and Leanne's story heightens the sense of her terrifying vulnerability. That this vulnerability is, at least in part, the result of wilful blindness and passivity does little to mitigate the pathos of Felicity's position.

Leanne and Margo, the tough and self-reliant single women working in an office, offer a contrast to Felicity. With their ability to argue complex issues and concoct on-the-spot fictions, they verbally triumph over Felicity's prim lectures and fatuous invocations of romantic myth. They, however, are not really more powerful than Felicity; after all, they have come at her bidding. The problems alluded to in their hilariously exaggerated stories – lack of opportunities for women and sexual harassment at the office –

are real enough. Furthermore, though they have avoided deluding themselves with romanticized myths of 'perfect happiness', they also do not seem to have found alternative routes to personal satisfaction. What power they do have, as is also true of marginal characters in other radio plays, lies in their ability to expose underlying weaknesses in traditional structures through the force of their imagination.

The crowning irony of *Perfect Happiness* is that the romantic ideal invoked by its title serves to divide women and turn them against one another. The male, physically absent but overwhelmingly present in the consciousness of Felicity, Leanne, and Margo throughout the play, controls their access to happiness. Their competition for the male's attention denies them the strength of unity. Leanne and Margo's blackly comic fantasy of killing Felicity's husband hints at a positive and possible strategy of killing the romantic dream of 'perfect happiness'. There is, however, no indication that they have gone beyond this point, even in imagination. *Perfect Happiness*, then, offers a critical view of the traditional position of women in society, and acknowledges some difficulties faced by women who attempt to step out of traditional roles.

In *Perfect Happiness*, Churchill exults in her newly-discovered comic voice. Written during the same period as the stage play *Owners*, *Perfect Happiness* shows a similar ability to approach familiar character types with fresh humor, pit them against one another with tongue-in-cheek playfulness, and make valid criticisms through mocking and witty dialogue. With this first of her feminist comedies, Churchill signals her intent to avoid the simplistic polarization of masculine and feminine, while focusing on power relations and analysing the ways in which women and men use what power they have. Comedy will assume increasing importance as Churchill's work matures, becoming one of her major strategies of empowerment.

Though Churchill has not written for radio since *Perfect Happiness*, she retains her affection for the medium and may return to it in the future.[26] Exemplifying Churchill's response to a particular set of conventions at an early stage in her work, the radio plays demonstrate both her strong sensitivity to the medium and her boldness in manipulating it. Language, which varies from the realistically conversational, through the poetically rhythmic, to the disturbingly erratic and even the non-human, carries the full weight of Churchill's urge to experiment. At the same time, dialogue in the radio plays efficiently and consistently serves its necessarily multiple functions of telling a story, suggesting setting, and revealing character. Churchill's ability to exploit radio's uniqueness is further apparent in her construction of characters. Deliberately heightening the ambiguity resulting from the absence of a definitive visual image, she makes ambiguity a crucial element of character. The radio characters thus evoke the listeners' sympathy as they grapple with difficult and universal human dilemmas, but at the same time fail to extricate themselves from the chain of exploitation they help to maintain. The importance of character ambiguity in fostering a simultaneously empathic and critical attitude may explain the fate of the two radio plays adapted for lunchtime theatres. Both *Schreber's Nervous Illness* and *Perfect Happiness*, though very effective when presented on the radio, failed as stage plays.[27]

Questions about the nature and extent of individual power animate all the radio plays. Based, as Churchill has stated them to be, in personal experience rather than on movements or theories,[28] the radio plays tend to focus on individual choice and judgment. The sense of one-to-one communication between Churchill and the listener, through stories that share subjective experience and psychological insights, is very strong. The emphasis is on individually experienced moral and philosophical dilemmas beneath the surface of sociopolitical issues. Concern with the equivocal nature of individual power engages Churchill in an ever-widening project of charting power relations in contemporary society. Taking on such diverse issues as war, environmental disaster, repressive social control, economic exploitation, and gender relations, the radio plays concentrate heavily on the ills of the current social order, but are also infused with a vision of change.

The key to Churchill's vision of change lies in those members of society who occupy its margins. A consistent dynamic in the radio plays is the tension between entrenched societal structures and the marginalized person in society. With the relative freedom of their position on the borders of societal expectations, the marginalized pose a continual threat. The plays highlight the power of subversive, deviant, and anti-establishment impulses and attitudes to disrupt the traditional structures which have maintained the status of established elites. The bastion of family, as in *Henry's Past* and *Perfect Happiness*, trembles under the impact of changing times. The traditional small acts of caring, charity, and tolerance made in deference to conscience appear, in *The Ants, Abortive,* and *Identical*

Twins, as futile or actually destructive. Institutions responsible for maintaining order, such as the judiciary and psychiatry, fall victim to the very chaos they attempt to control in *Lovesick* and *Schreber's Nervous Illness*. Repeatedly and in various contexts, then, those who derive their personal power from traditional roles are shown to be losing it to those others who are on the margins of traditional structures and thus free to imagine alternatives.

From the beginning, then, Churchill empowers herself and others by writing from the margin, deliberately positioning herself in the space allotted to women who in any way challenge patriarchal culture. This space, as Toril Moi has observed, is the space of ambiguity, 'the frontier between man and chaos' that is 'neither inside nor outside, neither known nor unknown'.[29] In addition, some of the specific strategies of empowerment that distinguish Churchill's major work begin to emerge and take shape in the radio plays. Accepted meanings and structures of meaning are challenged through convention-breaking fusions of such commonly used oppositions as 'self' *versus* 'other'. The use of such fusions – a general pattern carried through all of Churchill's work – invites formulation of new structures and meanings. The 'gestic' presentation of power relations – particularly in the plays dealing with gender issues – provides the audience with a 'way in' to the analytic process. Finally, the before-during-after pattern of action in the radio plays, coupled with the non-resolution of conflicts at the end, allows the listener to order the play's information and find her or his own 'way out'.

3
Questions of Freedom: The Television Plays

Evidence of Churchill's interest in the potential of television appears in the same germinal essay quoted at the beginning of this study. She wrote: 'There is no reason why the demands of the small screen . . . shouldn't stimulate our drama as the technical requirements of the Greek and Elizabethan theatres stimulated them.'[1] The BBC's regular production of new and classic plays made that medium available for serious work, although costs limited the number of new scripts accepted. In the 1970s, both the Thirty-Minute Theatre and Play for Today series provided outlets for single-episode television plays with sophisticated content. Between 1972 and 1981, Churchill wrote or contributed to six television plays, including *The Judge's Wife* (1972), *Turkish Delight* (1974), *Save It for the Minister* (co-written with Cherry Potter and Mary O'Malley, 1975), *The After-Dinner Joke* (1978), *The Legion Hall Bombing* (1979), and *Crimes* (1982).

While she welcomed the chance to try writing for television, and continued doing television scripts even when she became quite well known as a stage dramatist, Churchill eventually found television work unsatisfying. As early as 1974, while insisting on keeping all options open, Churchill compared television unfavourably to the stage:

> Television . . . attracts me very much less . . . . It has the attraction of large audiences and being the ordinary peoples' medium and not being the sort of effete cultural thing that no one ever pays any attention to anyway. But as an actual medium, as a physical thing that happens, I don't find it anything like as exciting myself [as the stage]. I do like things that actually happen.[2]

She has spoken of feeling like an 'outsider' during the production of

45

a television play.[3] In addition, the rigidly timed format of television programs and the heavy dependence of the medium on realistic conventions may have seemed confining to a playwright who had enjoyed the flexibility of radio and has consistently searched for alternatives to realism.

The television plays, like those for radio, relate individual actions to societal issues, but the context of the television plays is more often public and overtly political. Tension between freedom and constraint raises the question of how much choice – and how much responsibility – a given individual actually has. Ambiguous endings leave audiences with conflicting impressions and no certain answers to the central question. The middle-class setting for many of the plays again emphasizes restrictions placed upon individuals by the demands for propriety, conformity, and support of powerful elites.

Churchill was highly conscious of the particular demands of television, as distinctive from those of radio, to create images for the eyes as well as for the mind. Throughout the television plays, she strives to achieve visual images that match the dialogue in impact. Conscious play with the visual element is the primary form of experiment in the television plays. Churchill loosens realism's hold with such techniques as disrupting the linear time sequence of scenes, breaking up the flow of multi-character scenes with long closeups of one character, and using images for their symbolic rather than purely representational value. Throughout, she attempts to reach television's mass audience with explicitly political questions often linked to current events and issues.

THE JUDGE'S WIFE

The first of Churchill's television plays, *The Judge's Wife*, broadcast on BBC2's Thirty Minute Theatre in October, 1972 – several months after broadcast of *Schreber's Nervous Illness* on the radio – continues the analysis of gender relations begun in that play. It opens with a filmed image of a man, later to be identified as the judge, lying on the ground in a wooded area. Action then jumps backwards twice, as the man is shot, then gets out of a car prior to the shooting. In a voice-over monologue during these sequences, the judge states:

> Every criminal is a revolutionary. And every revolutionary is a criminal . . . . For they both act in defiance of laws that protect

us . . . . In either case he is challenging our society. And he must take the heavy consequences. For our society is upheld by force. (2)[4]

A shift of scene shows the judge concluding this speech by sentencing Vernon Warren to twenty years in prison for political activities. Demonstrators protest the sentence, but the judge ignores them and goes home to his wife Caroline, who bathes him and serves him dinner. Even in his own home, however, the judge finds no peace. Caroline's sister condemns the harsh sentence, the Irish cook quits, and threatening phone calls interrupt their meal. Only Caroline remains supportive of the judge, despite his ill-tempered treatment of her.

Studio-taped scenes in the judge's home alternate with filmed scenes showing, in backward progression, the acts which culminate in murder of the judge by Vernon Warren's brother Michael.[5] Michael makes the threatening phone calls received by the judge. The judge responds to the threats with a challenge to meet, then abruptly goes out for a walk. Michael's car pulls up, and the judge gets in. The sequence of the judge getting out of the car, being shot, and lying dead in the woods then runs again in forward sequence. A newspaper headline reports the judge's death.

In the concluding scene, Caroline and her sister Barbara discuss the judge's death. Caroline explains that the judge had secretly sympathized with revolutionaries like Vernon Warren, but was prevented by his house, money, and career from joining them:

Oppressed people were rising all over the world, and he found himself on the wrong side . . . . And then at a brilliant stroke he saw what he could do for other people. He could be the enemy . . . . He could help them to revolt by making . . . the establishment so despicable that every one would see it had to go . . . . (23–4)

Barbara responds simply, 'I don't believe you, Caroline. I think you're making it up' (24). This final line leaves the audience with no indication of whether Caroline's explanation constitutes bizarre truth, deliberate deception, or complex self-justification.

The Judge's Wife exemplifies Churchill's transition away from psychologically oriented themes and toward explicitly political debate. It merges psychological and political elements as it attempts to bring together themes of gender oppression and political repression. By focusing on the wife Caroline and emphasizing the judge's dependence on her support, the play implicates this peripheral figure in the unjust sentence imposed by the judge. Churchill thus calls to account those who do not exercise power directly, but nevertheless provide vital support to a repressive political system. Caroline's final speech calls attention to her covert rejection of this system, regardless of what it indicates about the judge's actions. Questions then multiply about why she has, for most of a lifetime, carried out a role contrary to her beliefs. The question of her responsibility is, of course, complicated by the issue of gender implied in the title, with its emphasis on the role of wife. As the judge's wife, Caroline forbids herself even the freedom to disagree with her husband.

Societal limitations on freedom of choice appear important, not only for Caroline, but also for the judge and his assassin. The apparently powerful judge is constrained by his position, whether or not he ever acknowledges the fact. Michael, though he kills the judge, cannot free his brother and has no effect on the system that brought his brother into court in the first place. In fact, the intertwined fates of the judge and Michael, shown in the backward-progressing scenes, seem almost predetermined by the wider context that encompasses them both. Although the ending makes no final assessment of Caroline's claim that the judge has actually helped the opposing revolutionary cause, the assertion provokes thought about political oppositions. It raises the question of whether political extremes do depend on, and thus automatically limit each other.

The Judge's Wife, in common with a number of Churchill's works for radio and stage, experiments with time. In this case the time manipulation disjoins the visual and aural elements of the production. Scenes that are propelled aurally – i.e., by dialogue – unfold in a forward progression, while those propelled visually start from their end point and progress backwards. This device undermines the cause-effect assumptions implicit in the realistic dramatic style. A double before-during-after construction permits the 'during' section to be seen as either dinner or the judge's death, depending on whether the viewpoint is that of the judge or Caroline. The filmed sequences, of course, reverse the order to after-during-before. Churchill's play with time in this piece translates to the structural level the sense of ambiguity evident in Caroline's final self-justification. The empowering defiance of sequence is at odds with the sense of constraint communicated by the emphasis on temporality and the hint of fate. Churchill's abrupt ending, however, fails to draw the issues of this play in suggestive directions, resulting in an indecisive rather than ambiguous conclusion.

TURKISH DELIGHT

Turkish Delight, a thirty-minute television play broadcast in 1974, as part of the 'Masquerades' series, deals with the issue of female sexuality in a world controlled by men. Alternating scenes of comic mix-up with serious monologues, the play presents a traditionally feminine space dominated by a mirror, and five female characters psychologically dominated by an important and powerful man named John, who is never seen. The women are identified only by function or role – the Call Girl, the Fiancee, the Ex-Wife, the Attendant, and the Other Girl. The setting is a bedroom suite used as a ladies' room for guests at a masquerade party.

The focus on sexuality is established in the Call Girl's opening monologue:

Sex is the most dreary pastime I know. Yes all right and it's also the most exciting. But there's nothing as boring as something that might be interesting if it isn't . . . . The trouble is now I've lost my amateur status . . . it's like losing all that money if you do it for love. (1–2)[6]

At the party, two women dressed identically as harem girls pass each other without speaking. Subsequent scenes reveal that the Call Girl, the Fiancee, and the Ex-Wife, as well as the Other Girl, have all come to the party wearing identical harem costumes. The first three have all dressed to be seen by John. The Call Girl wants to blackmail him. The Fiancee, whose engagement to John is to be published the next day, wants to call attention to their relationship. The Ex-Wife wants to remind John of when they used to live in 'a semi-detached house in Gerrard's Cross', and pretend 'he was a sultan and I was his concubine' (18).

Each woman's monologue reveals her thoughts and feelings. The Call Girl seeks revenge against John, because 'it's him that's put me right off . . . being alive'. The Fiancee goes over her discarded ambitions – dancer, veterinarian, explorer – then reflects brightly that when married 'I won't need to be anything' (11). The Ex-Wife admits that she ought to have taken 'more interest in things', but claims 'it's hard when you're married to a boring man not to be boring yourself. It seems like treachery to be less boring than him' (20A). The ladies' room Attendant, who otherwise serves as sounding-board for the others, speaks in turn, describing her loneliness as a widow and her hope that two remaining friends 'don't die before me' (26).

Realizing that John has used all of them, the Call Girl, the Ex-Wife, and the Fiancee turn against one another in angry and tearful confrontations. Even the Other Girl, briefly pulled into the melee by mistake, is treated as a rival. The three women barricade themselves in the ladies' room against a mob of reporters. The Ex-Wife stops the fighting by reminding everyone that each made the choice to participate in the sultan-concubine fantasy: 'none of us had to do it' (22). Realizing they must go out and face the photographers eventually, each chooses a new costume. The Call Girl, whose nose is still bleeding, spreads the blood to create a 'horror film' image. The Ex-Wife wraps herself with toilet paper to resemble a mummy. The Fiancee decides to go out naked, as Lady Godiva.

The quiet and dreamy final scene presents the Other Girl's monologue:

> When I get home after a party, the first thing is I look at the baby to see if she's all right. Then . . . make a cup of tea and . . . think back over the party, or about what I'll do at work today, or about the baby . . . or about my friends. And by then it's quite light and I drink the last sweet bit of tea . . . and I go to bed. (23)

In *Turkish Delight*, Churchill's first work with an all-female cast, the harem-girl costumes place a strong visual focus on the issue of female sexuality. These identical disguises do not, of course, express the women's sexual desires. They represent the women as female sexual objects on display for the male gaze – a gaze represented by the ever-present mirror before which the women adjust their appearances to please the unseen John. The role of erotic object, as the costumes indicate, obliterates individuality, just as the lack of names negates identity. In choosing the harem-girl costumes, the women have substituted for their own sexuality a disguise intended to attract the powerful male and, they hope, gain second-hand access to the power of social status or money. The reward for their collusion is at least temporary avoidance of the lowly and solitary status of those, like the Attendant, who are unable to attract men.

Turkish Delight shows Churchill's ability to make provocative feminist analyses of social conditions well in advance of their articulation in theory. Five years after the broadcast of *Turkish Delight*, French feminist theorist Luce Irigaray would state, in her 1977 essay 'This Sex Which Is Not One', that the 'dominant phallic economy' denies female sexuality, treating a woman's genitals only as an 'instrument' with which the male can 'touch himself'.[7] Irigaray would attribute to the phallic economy the definition of women's sexuality not as difference but as 'lack' – the absence of a penis, and therefore of positive sexuality. She would write of 'masquerades' as the devices through which women excite and maintain male desire.[8] Mary Russo, who interprets Irigaray's term *masquerade* to mean 'women experiencing desire only as male desire for them', has developed the concept further, arguing, with Jacques Lacan, that what the masquerade masks is 'nonidentity'.[9]

Turkish Delight views the issue of female sexuality in the context of social realities. The Call Girl's monologue about sex for money refers not only to a theorized 'phallic economy', but also to an actual economy in which women's most valuable resource is their sexual attractiveness. The play highlights three roles – the prostitute, the wife, and the ingenue – in which women present a particular sexual image as a medium of exchange. The prostitute presents a purely physical sexuality and a simple bargain – money for sex. The wife's image is that of sex inseparable from love; she offers both, along with subordination, in return for the financial support and social status of marriage. Youthful beauty and the challenge of conquest constitute the ingenue's appeal, but her terms demand commitment to marriage in exchange for the promise of sex. The assumed differences in these roles, however, merge in the image of the concubine, as the play makes evident through the identical costumes. For all three women, the actual relationship with John turns out to be less one of exchange than of consumption, as is implied in the title *Turkish Delight* – a type of confection.

The Ex-Wife, Call Girl, and Fiancee eventually confront their objectification and emerge from the mirrored enclosure of the ladies' room to vent unladylike anger. Each of the women first strikes out at an imitation that renders her own image absurd. In the end, however, they co-operate in devising new images that make visible the 'lack' governing their sexual and social lives. The Call Girl presents herself as the bleeding victim of unnamed horror. The Ex-Wife is a 'mummy' bound and gagged by the stuff of prosaic domesticity. The Fiancee, taking Lady Godiva as her model, presents her naked body as a protest against an oppressive establishment – despite her expectation that the male reporters will not interpret her nudity as protest. These changes, of course, do not signify positive sexuality; that, like asserting names, still lies ahead. But the women do take a first step in ending their collusion with the male gaze.

The monologues convey a sense that each of the women has maintained some part of herself separate from the phallic economy, despite its pervasive demands. These presentational scenes set against a plain background contrast sharply with the representational ones in the mirrored ladies' room. The monologues – a risky experiment for television drama – thus suggest a theoretical and potential space of subjectivity. The monologue of the Other Girl, which ends the play, asks the question of whether femininity can exist apart from objectification. The Other Girl was costumed like the other three women at the party but showed no interest in or relation to John and only entered the mirrored ladies' room when dragged in by mistake. Her costume, she states, was meant to please 'nobody . . . myself . . . ' and 'anybody,' in that order. Her life seems satisfying. Has she discovered an alternative to the limiting roles of the other three women? Or is she merely at an early stage of development – yet to meet her version of John? The play gives no clear answer. On one hand, the Other Girl seems to embody the best qualities of the other three – independence, maternal caring, and youthful vigor. On the other hand, she, like the others, has no name.

Churchill's next television venture was a collaborative project, quickly assembled with co-writers Mary O'Malley and Cherry Potter in 1975. Written for the Eleventh Hour series, a weekly program providing immediate commentary on major news events, *Save It for the Minister* dealt with Parliament's establishment of a ministerial post to handle race and sex discrimination claims. Episodic in form, *Save It for the Minister* focuses on a black man and white woman who set off to find the new Minister and seek redress for the injustices they have suffered.

En route, the couple encounters symbolic scenes of race and sex oppression. A tethered woman cheerfully maintains, 'If you never go to the end of your rope, you just wouldn't know you were tied up.'[10] A black girl lovingly paints a portrait with yellow hair, blue eyes, and a pink face. A nightclub comedian's fragmented act highlights the racial and sexual stereotypes on which he relies for laughs. A black man hanging upside down by one foot while he reads Dickens' *Great Expectations* explains that this position is most conducive to acquiring an English education. A woman is sawed in half by a magician. A woman seated in front of a mirror applies cosmetics and talks about health risks of such products. White businessmen cannibalize a black man. When they reach the Ministry of Equal Rights, the man and woman register their complaints, but find that the Minister offers only vague sympathy and bureaucratic procedures. Disappointed, the two nevertheless resolve to fight discrimination themselves.

Hastily and collaboratively written, *Save It for the Minister* occupies a minor place in Churchill's body of work but shows several tendencies important in her work as a whole. First, it demonstrates the interest in topical writing that would identify later stage plays such as *Top Girls* and *Serious Money*. It indicates skepticism toward simple solutions to social problems, focusing symbolically on examples of culturally engendered attitudes that may require complex approaches. The wide-ranging episodic structure – here assembled with haste – will be used provocatively in other work. Perhaps most important, this play shows Churchill developing increasing skill in the use of humor as a weapon.

THE AFTER-DINNER JOKE

The After-Dinner Joke, an hour-long exploration of the charity business, aired on BBC-1's Play for Today series in 1978. It moves on double tracks, simultaneously presenting general and specific views of charity's place in the world of capitalism. A montage of scenes demonstrates the links between charity and profit. A disaster aid worker distributes blankets to hurricane victims, then retrieves one from a confused recipient in order to re-enact the handout for news cameras. Meanwhile, a businessman calculates the hurricane's impact on banana prices. A British government minister pledges aid to 'friendly' nations. The head of a corporation lists five charity boards on which he serves. A mother urges her toddler to eat by describing starvation in India. A scene of black women living on a garbage heap in Johannesburg serves to advertise their handicrafts. An upper-class woman threatens to cut off money to charities which imply, in their appeals, that it is 'wrong to be rich' (20).[11] A plump Bengali says, 'I wouldn't like you to think everyone in Bangladesh is starving . . . . Take me, for instance. I own extensive lands . . . . There are some people you could help, like a tenant of mine . . . ' (96).

The panoramic view parallels the story of Selby, an idealistic young woman who quits business to work for a charity. Selby's story unfolds in reverse sequence, starting with her admission to a mental hospital. In her role as charity organizer, Selby appears in many of the montage scenes. She worries about raising ever-increasing amounts of money without being unpleasant. She tries to avoid politics in a world where, as the mayor of one town conclusively demonstrates to her, everything is political. She refuses money obtained illegally. Selby finds, however, that the values of the system in which she works consistently undermine her attempts to help people. The boats she obtains for Bangladeshi fishermen merely replace those smashed by owners in a rent dispute. An American visitor recuperating from a heart attack praises the 'private room, pretty nurses, vases of flowers', he enjoys in an Arab hospital, while acknowledging that the locals for whom the hospital was built receive no medical care (85–6). Finally, after being kidnapped by revolutionaries who educate her about the root causes of poverty, Selby tries to promote genuine social change, but her efforts provoke only disbelief and hostility. When she breaks down and goes into the hospital, Selby receives a visit from her former employer, who offers her a holiday and a good sinecure.

Charity, as Churchill presents it in *The After-Dinner Joke*, makes no real difference in a system built on profit and exploitation. A joke told in one scene demonstrates the futility of generosity. Discussing how to disburse one million pounds, a businessman suggests that they either 'give each poor person in the third world one-thousandth of a penny' or give the entire sum to one man and 'at least make one very happy Indian' (41). *The After-Dinner Joke* may be regarded as Churchill's single venture into agit-prop drama. As such, it lacks subtlety, repeating the same message insistently in each of the many scenes. At the same time, the play does show a sophisticated interrelatedness of medium and subject, using the mass medium of television to question a social institution that relies on mass response to public appeals.

The play indicates the creative habits Churchill was in the process of developing, as the demand for her work increased. One notable aspect of *The After-Dinner Joke* is that the central character, a woman, grapples with the problem of poverty in a public and professional capacity. It shows Churchill's interest in expanding the range of dramatic roles available to women but refusing to dilute the strength of her socialist-feminist vision. In addition, the play exemplifies Churchill's emerging pattern of learning about a particular area of endeavor, but not hesitating to use newly-acquired knowledge critically. Structurally, *The After-Dinner Joke* resembles *The Judge's Wife*, with a simultaneous backward and forward motion suggesting that Selby's unhappy outcome may have been predetermined by a larger context. Finally, the use of colour separation overlay to give the production the look of a moving comic strip[12] testifies to Churchill's continuing urge to experiment with visual images.

THE LEGION HALL BOMBING

While working with Margaret Matheson on *The After-Dinner Joke*, Churchill received a document from one of Northern Ireland's Diplock Courts, which she has described as follows:

> I had the transcript of a trial of a boy who was given sixteen years. A bomb had been planted in a British Legion Hall . . . . The trial was extraordinary because there was no evidence to say the boy who was accused did it, except the police saying he'd confessed, which he denied. There was no signed statement by him. And there was an old man who'd been in the hall who said, 'I don't know what boy it was but it was definitely not *that* boy.'[13]

Churchill persuaded Matheson to produce a play based on the transcript for her Play for Today series, and then set about condensing the nine-and-one-half-hour record. The resulting play, *The Legion Hall Bombing*, was broadcast on BBC in 1979. Its broadcast was attended by considerable controversy, because BBC officials had substituted an introduction they deemed to be less 'political' for the original voice-over introduction written by Churchill to explain the origin and function of the one-judge Diplock Courts in Northern Ireland. In protest, both Churchill and the director, Roland Joffe, removed their names from the credits.[14]

The Legion Hall Bombing presents what begins as a typical courtroom drama but ends with a shocking challenge to the belief that justice triumphs over all obstacles. Justice, instead, appears fragile and embattled by the very system constructed for its preservation. Through the visual close-ups which are the special province of television, the play shows the wide gulf between the world of the judge, who presides in his wig and robes, and that of the frightened defendant who averts his pock-marked face, slouches defensively, and mumbles replies to questions. Two youths are tried for planting a bomb which caused no injuries, but extensive damage to a building; but the second defendant refuses to participate in the proceedings.

The prosecutor brings in both eyewitnesses and law enforcement officials. An anxious elderly woman makes contradictory statements about the identity of the bombers. An elderly man says he had a good view of both bombers, remembers that one of them had 'dirty fair hair',[15] and states his certainty that neither defendant planted the bomb. An expert in explosives identifies the material used in the bomb as one frequently found in home-made devices. A detective sergeant who questioned the second defendant in jail presents an unsigned confession, allegedly written by the defendant, giving such details of the bombing as the type of explosive and get-away car used.

The counsel for the accused, rebuffed in his attempts to get the charges dropped, but successful in exposing irregularities in police records of their interrogation, calls two witnesses – the participating defendant and his father. The youth maintains that he was looking for work in Limerick (in the Republic of Ireland) at the time of the bombing. He disclaims the confession, accuses police of beating him and denying him access to counsel while in custody, and calls attention to the fact that he was not charged until a year after his initial questioning. Cross-examination centres on a defiant remark admittedly made by the youth during interrogation, offered by the prosecutor as evidence that he was not threatened. The defendant's father supports his son's statements and comments bitterly that he should have hired witnesses from Limerick to back up the alibi.

The judge's long summing-up speech emphasizes his lone role in determining the trial's outcome. At first he seems to recognize the weakness of the prosecution case, acknowledging the lack of positive identification and the eyewitness testimony supporting the defence. However, he then returns to the woman eyewitness's testimony, citing the portion that implicated the second defendant as 'the real truth' and denying credence to the contradictory portion.

The judge then rules the confession valid, finds both defendants guilty on all three counts with which they are charged, and sentences each to twelve years.

This play occupies a unique place among Churchill's works. Adhering closely to a single factual source, it could almost be called a documentary – and Churchill has referred to it as such.[16] Although the production reveals dramatically heightened conflict, fictionally represented characters (i.e., the arrogant Crown Prosecutor and the thoughtful, unassuming counsel for the accused), and well-crafted dramatic action, *The Legion Hall Bombing* remains the nearest thing to documentary that Churchill has written. Furthermore, in its original form with the prologue and epilogue written by Churchill, this play stands alone in offering an unequivocal and emphatic answer to its central question. The defendants are judged guilty and given heavy sentences in the face of conflicting and incomplete evidence. The play's original epilogue, with its statement that 'the Diplock Courts were set up to make it easier to get convictions, and they have been successful', gives a clear answer to the question of whether this trial represents the typical result of a deliberate policy or an isolated incident due to chance factors.

Though one must consider general thematic elements as quite secondary in a play written with a narrowly defined goal and in a near-documentary style, a theme centred on freedom of individual action links *The Legion Hall Bombing* with Churchill's other plays for television. While most of the play's action focuses on the defence put forward by one youth, the second defendant provides a continual, usually visible, contrast in the background. The silent and self-possessed defendant who refuses to co-operate differs from the active one not only in behaviour but also in physical appearance; he is good-looking and well-groomed. The play reveals nothing about the silent youth or his reason for not presenting a defence; however, it might not be unreasonable to assume that the two youths, though allegedly accomplices in a bombing, do not know each other and have little in common. While the active defendant admits to previous arrests for minor delinquency, the silent one may have come to the attention of the police because of political activities. In the end, both defendants receive exactly the same verdicts and sentences. Thus, while the contrast between them certainly emphasizes the futility of attempting a defence before a Diplock Court, it can also be seen as a hint at wider limitations on individual action.

CRIMES

Crimes, produced by BBC1 on its Play for Tomorrow series in 1982, is the last of Churchill's plays for television. Set in the future and employing a video-within-a-video technique which distances many of the situations and characters seen on screen, this play questions the concept of crime. It opens with a close-up of Jane, a teenage girl, describing the murder and arson she has committed and concluding, 'I've done a lot of bad things but luckily people are very kind to me and they figure I'm sick. And I'm now just about better' (1).[17] The camera pulls back to show that Jane's speech is a videotape being played by Mel, a 'criminologist', for the benefit of several prison inmates. Mel points with pride to the progress made by Jane since she had an electrode implanted in her brain; now she acts as 'a real partner' in her treatment by activating an electric shock whenever she is tempted to commit a crime (16). He then asks the inmates to discuss their own experiences.

The camera pulls back a second time to reveal the prison session as a videotape watched by Mel and his wife Veronica, in their fallout-shelter home. The dimensions of the social dystopia they inhabit begin to take shape in the stories shared by the prisoners. Ron, a passionate nature-lover, was sent to prison for trespassing on the property of a nuclear power station and an army training area. Elliott tried to defend a 67-year-old grandmother who was arrested for watching while police beat demonstrators, and he now intends to go on a hunger strike to protest the woman's treatment. When Mel turns off the videotape, Veronica switches on a program called 'Select and Survive' that instructs viewers on how to install a machine gun to protect a fallout shelter. Veronica, who has been arguing intermittently with Mel, asks him about his best friend Larry, who has no shelter. Mel firmly rules out sharing their shelter with Larry, and Veronica accepts this decision, reasoning, 'the world's full of people, we can't fit them all in, can we?' (50). Larry arrives for a visit, bringing flowers and scotch, but his actual presence does nothing to change Mel's attitude. The play concludes with the host of 'Select and Survive' urging viewers to 'join me next week at the same time when I'll be talking about the family group and how to bury the dead. Dig! Dig!' (56).

Techniques, characters, and themes in this play connect and overlap with those from several other Churchill plays. As in *Turkish Delight*, Churchill alternates action with monologues by each of the primary characters. Jane, a girl who kills because she wants 'to be frightening' rather than 'frightened' (12), shows similarities to Angie in *Top Girls*. Mel's use of behaviour modification for social control overlaps with themes and characters of the radio play *Lovesick* and the stage play *Softcops*. Veronica exemplifies yet another middle-class woman collaborating in her own oppression as she oppresses others. Finally, the condemnation of ownership which emerges as the major statement of the play is a theme that runs through a number of Churchill's works.

Crimes goes furthest of all the television plays in emphasizing limitations on individual freedom and power of effective action. In the world of this play, the subversive power of marginalized individuals has been neutralized by effective technology and systematic cruelty. Neither the pathological disruptions of Jane nor the political disruptions of Ron and Elliott make any difference. The video-within-a-video technique, which first gives a speaker the power of immediate presence and then removes and reduces him or her to an image within a tiny box, reinforces the sense that advanced technology has robbed people of power. Veronica's passivity, in this context, can be seen less as a personal failing than as the only likely response to her situation.

Having presented this grim view of the future, Churchill wrests the focus away from the unforgettable image of a strangely appealing young girl reciting a bizarre litany of criminal acts, and aims it accusingly at viewers in their proverbial living rooms. *Crimes* presents the actions and attitudes exemplifying different views of crime. Jane poses a danger to others, but lacks the moral awareness associated with responsibility. Ron and Elliott have violated laws in order to uphold a moral system that values the natural world and respects other people. Mel, though he has not broken any laws, announces himself ready to murder his best friend in the name of survival. Veronica's passive acquiescence toward Mel's callous attitude further complicates questions of responsibility. Churchill delegates judgment to the audience.

The video-within-a-video technique visually contains all the described crimes within the exclusive enclosure of Mel and Veronica's fallout shelter. This enclosure, an example of and metaphor for private property, thus shelters all the evil it is meant to exclude. The play subtly points to a parallel between television watchers Mel and Veronica in their fallout-shelter living room and the viewers of *Crimes* watching television in their living rooms. The central issue that finally emerges in the play concerns the moral implications of a private retreat that admits the outside world only in the form of televised images.

The dichotomy between institutions of traditional authority and marginalized people set up by Churchill in the radio plays remains in place throughout the television plays. In the television plays, however, there is less evidence of anarchic disruption and greater acknowledgment of pervasive limitations on those who might challenge traditional authority. Given the remarkable sense of constraint in the television plays, it seems possible that Churchill translated the limitations she encountered in writing for television – inflexibility as to length, realistic conventions, remoteness of the production process, and actual government interference – into the form and content of her works for that medium. Though they deal with compelling issues and make an honest attempt to confront and use, rather than merely adapt to the medium, the television plays are Churchill's weakest area of work. They lack the intangible but vital current of possibility with which her plays for radio and the stage are infused.

The empowering potential of Churchill's television plays lies in the ways they intersect with her life. While she has not made her own experiences an explicit part of her plays, Churchill has spoken to interviewers at various times about important decisions that altered her personal direction. The dilemma of the judge's wife invokes the life she and her husband repudiated when he left private law practice so as 'not to shore up a capitalist system we didn't like'.[18] The idealistic young charity organizer in *The After-Dinner Joke* recalls a youthful Churchill who volunteered with the Samaritans organization until she realized such work was 'like applying Bandaids on a fatal wound'.[19] When she refused to quietly accept the BBC's alteration of *The Legion Hall Bombing*, she provoked a controversy that served to generate much wider publicity for her questions about the Diplock Courts than the original program would have done on its own. Thus, while the television plays highlighted obstacles to challenging oppressive structures, her own actions held out the possibility of change.

4

The Power of Choice

After a dozen years of writing primarily for radio, Churchill finally got her chance to 'see if I could make things happen'[1] on stage when Michael Codron, who had introduced the work of Harold Pinter and Joe Orton, commissioned her to write a play. The resulting work, *Owners*, was produced by the Royal Court Theatre in 1972. Despite an accident that postponed the play's opening, necessitated replacement of the lead actor, and shortened its run, *Owners* earned Churchill considerable recognition. Moreover, it brought her into the sphere of the sometimes conflict-ridden but always politically daring and artistically committed theatre often referred to simply as 'the Court'. Churchill's association with the Royal Court quickly solidified. She became its resident dramatist – the first woman to hold the position – in 1975,[2] and later served as tutor to its Young Writer's Group.[3] During this period *Objections to Sex and Violence* (1975), *Moving Clocks Go Slow* (1975), and *Traps* (1977) were all produced by the Royal Court. The four frankly experimental plays that mark Churchill's transition into theatre all 'make things happen' to, as well as with, theatrical conventions. Churchill's experimentation takes various forms: using farcical humour to rupture realistic style, assaying the potential of science fiction, playing with absurdist techniques, and challenging ordinary perceptions of three crucial but often under-exploited elements of theatre – time, space, and actual objects. While none of these experiments fully succeeds, and some fall far short of their ambitious conceptualization, all have moments in which Churchill's mature potential can be glimpsed. Most important, they show her determination to move boldly into the realm of theatre, testing its limits and marshalling its own vitality against stale and limiting orthodoxies.

OWNERS

Owners, produced in 1972 at the Royal Court Theatre Upstairs,

directed by Nicholas Wright, challenges the norm of property ownership, suggesting that private property produces exploitation and
violence. A philosophical contrast between the Western ideal of
individual achievement and the Eastern one of passive acceptance
addresses the interrelatedness of the institution of private property
and underlying cultural attitudes. Churchill has acknowledged such
diverse influences as Zen Buddhism and Joe Orton in the writing of
Owners,[4] and has said it contains 'things that had been building up
in me over a long time, political attitudes as well as personal ones'.[5]
Heavily loaded with ideas and images, the play nevertheless moves
with manic energy.

Written in two acts (of which the first has six scenes, the second,
eight), *Owners* begins when Marion, a steely and successful property
developer, buys the house in which Lisa and Alec, along with
their two children and Alec's senile mother, rent the third-floor
apartment. Marion, who intends to 'develop' and sell her new
purchase, assigns her employee Worsely the task of gaining 'vacant
possession' of the house. Worsely uses threats and monetary induce-
ments, but finds Lisa and Alec surprisingly resistant to moving.
A past affair with Alec, and the attraction he still holds for her,
complicates Marion's relations with these top-floor tenants.

The situation gets even more complex when Lisa finds Marion
and Alec together just as she goes into labor with her third child, and
impulsively offers the child to Marion. The barren and supremely
acquisitive Marion snaps up the offer. Her husband Clegg, a loutish
butcher with an unexpected nurturing streak, takes care of the
baby and visualizes a chain of Clegg & Son butcher shops. Clegg
dreams of murdering Marion, then switches the focus of his anger
to Alec. He enlists the help of Worsely in his absurd plots, which
parallel Worsely's own farcical suicide attempts. Lisa, meanwhile,
has changed her mind and desperately wants the baby back. She
is ignored by Marion, tricked by Worsely into signing adoption
papers, and sexually exploited by Clegg.

Marion's obsession with conquest gradually shifts from the house
to Alec. As Churchill's exemplar of the tranquil acceptance associated with Far Eastern philosophies, Alec is Marion's antithesis.
Without actively opposing her, he continually eludes her attempts
at control. Alec accepts without complaint the new, well-to-do
owners, who remodel the house and use the upstairs couple as
babysitters for their child. With casual detachment, he disconnects
the life-support tube of his hospitalized mother, to save 'a lot of

bother' (48).[6] He avoids taking sides in the tug-of-war between Lisa and Marion over the baby. Alec's passive resistance finally so infuriates Marion that she decides to kill him, and sends the ever-useful Worsely, always 'wonderful at anything unpleasant' (20), to set fire to the house.

In the final scene, a bandage-swathed Worsely reports to Marion. First he took the baby, who had been left, forgotten, in its infant carrier, and returned it to Lisa. Then he started the fire, but wanted to save Lisa and the baby, of whom he had grown fond, and shouted a warning upstairs. The entire family escaped, but Alec re-entered the burning house to save the child downstairs. He and that child died. Worsely's own resolve to throw himself into the fire failed. Seeing both Clegg and Marion rejoicing over Alec's death, and hearing Marion exult that she is 'just beginning to find out what's possible' (67), Worsely places a gun against his temple, pulls the trigger, and misses.

The uniqueness of *Owners* arises out of a basically realistic style and traditional structure presented through a distorting lens that bends and disjoins the play's elements from their anticipated pattern. Action splits into multiple channels, diverges as some lines of action become progressively more farcical while others become more serious, and never fully converges in the climax. The inconsistencies of action, rather than intensifying conflict and directing it toward resolution, continually deflect and redirect it. Self-parodying dialogue creates comic – and critical – distance between a character and his or her speech, as when Marion ironically confirms Clegg's sexist dismissal of her as 'a talking dog' by boasting, 'Most women are fleas but I'm the dog' (11, 30). Every character, moreover, displays a quirky inconsistency that defeats attempts to integrate her or his actions into a conceptual unity: the demented Worsely, for example, takes a rational view of what would be 'better for the baby' (61). Even Alec briefly sheds his passivity when he disconnects his mother's life-support system. Plot verisimilitude is stretched by Worsely's increasingly ludicrous acts of violence against himself, then mocked outright in his final action of shooting himself point blank, and finding he has 'missed'.

The lens through which Churchill projects the action of this, her first professionally produced stage play, indicates that, even at this point, she writes as a feminist, seeking representational space not governed by the male gaze.[7] The splittings and divergences in character and plot preclude stereotyping and reinforce multiple viewpoints, thus dislocating the play from its framework of traditional theatrical convention. Churchill's rejection of the male viewpoint becomes explicit in the scene at the nightclub where Marion, Clegg, and Worsely celebrate Marion's purchase. While Clegg watches the performance of a female stripper, he, not the offstage stripper, forms the object of the audience's gaze. This objectification exposes his sexual desire to derision: he pants and gasps helplessly while Marion and Worsely coolly take advantage of his distraction.

Churchill uses the construct of a house unequally divided between 'haves' and 'have-nots' to show how private property destroys caring and community. Only the top-floor portion is represented on stage. When first seen, it has been ransacked by burglars. Worsely immediately violates what sanctuary it still offers by walking in late at night and threatening to remove the roof if Lisa and Alec do not vacate. Thus, the portion of the house that nominally shelters Alec, the pregnant Lisa, their two children, and the near-helpless grandmother fails to provide the protection, comfort, and autonomy associated with the concept of home. The new owners underscore the system of exploitation with luxurious surroundings and demands for unpaid service that constantly remind Alec and Lisa of the unbridgeable gap separating them from the well-to-do. Vulnerable as they are in this flat, the family has few alternatives, since the world outside it offers even greater threats. As propertyless individuals, they have no real power of choice.

Although the larger portion of the house remains unseen, a number of striking visual images reinforce the sense of threat attached to those who wield the power of ownership. Clegg's meat cleaver and blood-spattered apron provide a visual reference point for their aggressive ruthlessness toward the weak. Marion signals her insatiability through constant eating; she even grabs a piece of fruit from a bowl in Alec and Lisa's impoverished flat. The owners have a monopoly on choice. Their power, however, only feeds the desire for more power, as they apply the principle of ownership to human relationships, in what the play's original director referred to as a system of 'emotional capitalism'.[8] Worsely articulates this system's incontrovertible principle: 'A man can do what he likes with his own' (36). The owners refuse to accept the sense of powerlessness that those without property cannot escape. When Alec and Lisa suddenly decide to move, Marion protests unbelievingly, 'But you can't just go like that. I haven't paid you to go' (62).

Ownership not only confers control, but also justifies taking life – the ultimate form of control. Marion declares, 'Empires only come by killing' (63). She, of course, decrees death for Alec after her attempts to control him through ownership of the house and possession of the baby have failed. Clegg deals mercilessly with betrayal. He has his dog 'put down' for biting him, because 'I couldn't feel the same to him again. He made himself into just another animal' (58–9). He would like to murder Marion because he regards not only her liaison with Alec, but also her independence and business success as an injury to him. Both Clegg and Worsely, nevertheless, ultimately fail to establish control over the bodies they view as their own. Clegg says of Marion, 'She is my flesh' (56), but can only fantasize about punishing her insubordination with death. Similarly, Worsely's suicide attempts show the futility of his efforts to gain control over 'my flesh and blood. The contraption I am in. The contraption I am' (35). The Samaritan 'befriender' who interferes with all of Worsely's attempts (until he slips on a fire escape and falls to his own death) affirms the privileges of property but attributes ownership of this 'contraption' to God: 'Life is leasehold. It belongs to God the almighty landlord. You mustn't take your life because it's God's property not yours' (35).

The perversely comic emphasis on death testifies to Churchill's stated aim to wrench unremarkable actions 'out of context', because 'an awful lot of the horrible things people do are made to seem perfectly all right by their context'.[9] Context-switching begins in the first scene in Clegg's butcher shop, when Clegg offers Worsely some 'nice rabbit'. Worsely says, 'Rabbit's one of those things I think of you know as a rabbit . . . a nice lamb chop though is definitely a dish,' then continues, 'I like lambs in a field mind you in the spring time. I had quite a pet lamb one holiday when I was a kiddy. Hard for a child till it gets the knack. If the lamb's a pet don't hurt it. If the lamb's a chop it's not got a name' (7). More pointed questioning of context-justified behaviour occurs in Act Two, when Clegg, again conversing with Worsely, boasts of killing a man. Informed that the incident occurred during military service, Worsely scoffs, 'It doesn't count if you were in uniform. Everybody knows it's not the same thing . . . bombing's not what I call killing' (37–8).

Churchill cross-cuts the issue of property ownership with that of gender, confounding a simplistic equation of capitalistic and patriarchal exploitation by reversing conventional sex roles. Marion, who includes herself in the phrase 'we men of destiny' (31), pursues her desires with an aggressive singlemindedness that precludes preserving, nurturing, or caring. She buys the house only for the profit she can make in selling it, and cannot be bothered to care for the baby after she has taken possession of it. She callously uses the devoted Worsely and betrays her former friend Lisa. Alec, on the other hand, has lost the capacity for desire; therefore, he avoids the claims of possession, either as owner or as owned. His detached compliance gives him an aura of mysterious otherness which, of course, intensifies Marion's desire to possess him. Alec is a caretaker, repairing the windows of buildings and nurturing the downstairs family's baby. While Marion's focus on desire places her entirely in the present, Alec's non-possessive caring connects him to the future. This link draws Alec into the burning house, where he turns 'into fire quite silently' (66), joining with a force beyond anyone's control.

With the characters of Clegg and Lisa, Churchill extends and clarifies her questioning of 'natural' gender roles. These two simply want their respective spouses to fulfill traditional roles. At the same time, both appear better suited to those roles than the spouses are. Lisa, when not under exceptional stress, appears capable and practical, supporting the family by working as a hairdresser. Clegg shows considerably more maternal behaviour and sensitivity toward others than Marion does, not only taking care of the baby but also offering sympathy to the hapless Worsely and attempting to soften Marion's attitude toward Lisa. While the role reversal for Alec and Marion functions primarily to 'make their attitudes show up clearly as what they believed rather than conventional male and female behaviour',[10] her use of this pattern for Clegg and Lisa indicates a concern about how the entrenched system of gender relations functions with property ownership to limit the power of choice.

Marion, the first of several rapacious women to be created by Churchill, signals Churchill's conviction that empowerment means more than simply making a grab for the power of men or owners. Marion, of course, has made that grab successfully. In the terms of Virgia Woolf's famous metaphor, she is certainly no 'angel in the house'.[11] Her independence and power – not to mention her triumphs over a chauvinist husband and her own mental illness – defy the idealized and dependent images of women in traditional drama. Within the farcical element of action, Marion infects the play with a delight that is not entirely perverse. In becoming master of the house, however, Marion has become a death-dealing monster.

On the serious level of theme, the play condemns the ruthless acquisitiveness by which Marion has made herself a 'talking dog' (11), or freakish exception, within the patriarchal system. *Owners*, of course, does not resolve the conflict between the 'angel' who tends the house and the 'man of destiny' who owns it. Instead, it suggests that the house itself, as a metaphor for society, must be changed in a manner more fundamental than Marion's partial remodeling.

At the end of the play the house burns, metaphorically hinting at revolution and rendering moot the issue of its ownership; however, the future of that supremely vulnerable emblem of the future in the infant carrier remains unresolved. The outcome of this question, and the play's potential for empowerment, centre on the equivocal figure of Worsely. An agent of the owners, but not yet an owner himself, Worsely mediates between the 'haves' and the 'have-nots'. He lacks Marion's urge toward conquest but is not hampered, like Alec, by an inability to take positive action. His growing fondness for Lisa and the baby shows an impulse toward community which he wryly resists, remarking, 'I'm getting fond of too many people' (59). He nevertheless honours the claim of this nascent community in the end, when he shouts the warning that enables Lisa and her family to escape. Though driven to self-destructiveness by the inherent contradictions of his position, he never achieves this resolution. In the final moment of the play, Worsely transmits to the audience Churchill's newfound sense of power: when his point-blank gunshot defies its mark, Churchill proclaims that in the theatre, she can make anything happen.

MOVING CLOCKS GO SLOW

Churchill's next stage play, *Moving Clocks Go Slow*, gives an indication of the unpredictability for which she has become known. Leaving the familiar territory of North London real estate addressed in *Owners*, she uses a futuristic outer space fantasy to explore questions about the nature of time and action. Of course, the science fiction genre was not new to Churchill, who had previously written the radio play *Not . . . not . . . not . . . not . . . not enough oxygen*. Written soon after *Owners*, *Moving Clocks Go Slow* was not produced until June, 1975, when it was done as a one-night Sunday program at the Royal Court Theatre Upstairs, directed by John Ashford.[12]

In two acts combining six scenes, the play focuses on an earth depleted of natural resources and relegated to the bottom rung of a hierarchical universe. 'Outward' lures earth residents with its power and wealth, but only robots and 'specials' – people with superhuman powers such as telepathy – are permitted to go there. Kay, a human proud of her ability to 'serve space', and her outward-born lover Apollo, work in an emigration station. Their job necessitates moving carefully between earth's governor, the impossibly old and fantastically large Agent Fox, and his rival Q, king of earth's underworld. As the play begins, earth is under attack by aliens. Fox decrees defence measures because he understands earth's value: 'it's invaluable, like death. It makes life worth living outward. Demotion to earth is a real fear' (7). Apollo and a robot named Luna become inhabited by the invisible aliens. They take Kay with them to earth, where they find people living in ruins, scavenging on dumps, and subsisting on food pills. Mrs. Provis, an old vagabond they meet, who remembers earth before 'plastic in the rivers' and 'bad air' made it unlivable, turns out to be Kay's mother (31). As they wander, they are joined by Rocket, a rotund and telepathic young man obsessed with the desire to go outward, and Stella, Kay's daughter who had been in prison for killing her children, but has won release through a 'lottery amnesty' (17).

As Kay readjusts to earth and renews human ties, earth approaches destruction. Kay shields Stella from the police and tries to reestablish a caring relationship with this daughter she had deserted to go outward. Loudspeakers warn of invasion, as lifeless bodies resurrect themselves. Torn between her training to 'serve space' and her earth ties, Kay laments, 'I should have a job. If I knew what my duty was, I'm sure I'd do it' (29). Quarreling over food gives way to sharing. The mothers and daughters exchange recriminations, then reconcile. Fox broadcasts the news that earth is now outward.

Apollo, meanwhile, finds earth fascinating, explaining that 'where I come from . . . there's not what you'd call matter at all' (30). Asked what happens there, he says:

> Nothing happens because time isn't one thing after another for us. It's all available at once like space is with you. And . . . space is one way like time is here. You can never go back. (30)

Stella replies that 'even in this universe time depends on how fast you move' (30), assuring him one can 'trip round the singularity and back to earth before you ever left it' (30). Apollo describes one-way space:

> I go right through the hole. Look, I come out in a different universe, here. I go back through the same hole, and that's not home, that's into a third universe. And back again through the same hole isn't back to here. (30)

Time on earth bends and skips, with Kay and Rocket twice having an identical conversation and Stella and Kay regressing to childhood.

Loudspeakers suddenly proclaim a 'force 9 emergency' and evacuation of 'specials' (44). Kay informs the others that a 'force 10 emergency' automatically detonates earth. Meanwhile, in his outer-space office, a battered-looking Agent Fox shows Q an electronic map charting the spread of aliens. Fox admits defeat, but maintains, 'It's my little globe and . . . I'm not leaving till saturation (47). Q disputes him: 'I'm in love with earth . . . I'm going to have it all for myself just while it dies' (47). He shoots Fox, whose huge body is slowly reanimated by the invisible aliens. Rocket bursts in, warning Fox of assassins and begging to be transported outward. Q laughs and, in a whimsical exercise of power, sends him outward. Kay, Apollo, Stella, Mrs. Provis, and Luna surge into the office. Stella shoots Fox, but there is no effect. Q shoots Stella and Mrs. Provis, who die and then slowly get up. As they stand, the map shows complete saturation. The loudspeaker broadcasts 'force 10 emergency' and starts a countdown. Q shoots himself. The stage goes black. The map remains illuminated for a moment; then it, too, goes black.

In the darkness, the silence is first broken by music. Then Kay's voice is heard asking, 'Where am I? When am I?' (49). Apollo's voice answers 'We've all come away' (49). Kay protests, 'I don't want to. I want to go back . . . back to earth before I ever left it' (49–50). Apollo and Luna remind her, 'You can't go back in space, only in time' (49). Kay calls, 'Earth? People?' Just before he slips 'into the black hole', Apollo reports that Kay has gone back, by reversing time and reassembling earth: 'She opens her eyes. On a rubbishy plain. Old tin cans and weeds. Up on her feet. Walking. Something – what. Losing her now. She's crying' (49–50). With the stage still dark, Luna asks the final, unanswered, question, 'Happy or sad?' (50).

While recognizing that *Moving Clocks Go Slow* only partly succeeds in its attempt to 'make things happen' within an abstract and cosmic framework, one must regard it as a further exploration of the dramatic terrain Churchill had determined to map. The grotesque characters, 'telepathic' dialogue (using tapes), action repetitions and reversals, and fantastic settings defy realistic conventions and test the limits of stage representation.

Churchill, furthermore, plays with the materiality of time and space in the basic construction of the play. She divides the action between earth and outer space, but opposes conventional perceptions of both by placing the outer space scenes in small, enclosed spaces and the scenes which take place on earth in large, open spaces. She attempts to create contrasting experiences of time by alternating short, rapid-fire scenes in outer space with long, slow-moving earth scenes. In the earth scenes, continual walking – that most linear of human activities – reinforces a sense of relationship between linear experience of time and patterns of life. The structure of the scenes, while straining audience attention,[13] proves integral to the play's central question of whether time and space constitute immutable limitations on choice. The alternating pace of the action suggests different realities of time and thus a broader scope of choice than that commonly perceived.

It is, however, in the remarkable final scene of *Moving Clocks Go Slow* that Churchill demonstrates just how daring an innovator she can be. This brief scene takes place in total darkness. Knowing her background in radio, one could speculate that she was trying to bring to the stage radio's potential for stimulating audience imagination. Perhaps this scene does indicate a temporary nostalgia for radio, but the important point is the attempt in this scene to place special demands on the imagination of the audience. Its action can be seen only in the mind. The audience must join their imaginations with Churchill's to answer Luna's final question. Churchill empowers the audience to imagine a reconstructed earth by deconstructing, in as literal sense as stage representation can manage, the existing one. Into the deconstructed space of the black stage, the audience member projects her own theoretical construct – one that may be either 'happy or sad'.

For all its strange and spectacular images, *Moving Clocks Go Slow* presents, in the end, a simple dilemma for its central character, Kay. She may choose either to go with the aliens 'outward' or return to earth. In the space-bound alien universe, places follow one another in sequence, but all time is available at once. On the time-bound earth, events follow one another in sequence, but space is available all at once. Kay returns to earth, accepting time-boundedness as the price of things happening. Her choice is free – not dictated by external conditions. Instead it constitutes the conditions in which it can exist; for when she goes back to earth, Kay re-creates earth within the world of the play. Though she returns alone, Kay seeks not only earth itself, but also people – and the pleasure in human relatedness she had re-learned from her mother and daughter. Finally, Kay's choice is ambiguous: at the end, the questions of how she feels about her decision or whether she will ever find the people she seeks, remain unanswered.

Against Kay's choice is set that of Rocket, who twice attempts to betray his comrades and finally manages to make the coveted journey outward just before earth explodes. His choice throws into relief the part played by the human ideal of community that Kay rediscovers during her experiences on earth. Rocket, who shows the self-serving talents for lying, theft, disloyalty, and blackmail that could make him a rival of Agent Fox and Q, may have found a place where he can, in Q's words, 'hang onto' himself while earth's system comes apart (22). Although Rocket's choice carries the risk that he himself will 'come to bits' outward, it does indicate continuation of the selfish attitudes that have brought about the devastation of earth.

As in *Owners*, empowerment follows cataclysm. When the air grows 'thick with aliens' (34), change becomes a possibility. Here and there fuse, as Fox announces: 'Earth is outward. I repeat, earth is outward' (27). Stella sees the aliens as 'our best hope' (42), but earth's male rulers have set in motion a process of destruction that cannot be stopped. Detonation of earth enables Kay to make a powerful and positive choice. Out of the 'cloud of hot gas' (50), Kay emerges as an authentic feminist hero unique in Churchill's work. Through her power of choice, she reverses and heals her earlier abandonment of the earth and her daughter. Kay's heroic action is not, however, represented directly or visually on stage. It takes place in a space that cannot be seen. Its acceptance as action depends on the ability of the audience to theorize Kay's fusion of power and caring. That this single moment of powerful, positive, and regenerative choice takes place in one of Churchill's most openly experimental (and most marginalized) plays, and still defies representation, indicates how difficult it is for this most rigorously honest of writers to give substance to a theorization of genuine (and traditionally masculine) power for women that does not negate the (traditionally feminine) element of nurturing.

OBJECTIONS TO SEX AND VIOLENCE

Objections to Sex and Violence, written after *Moving Clocks Go Slow* but staged a few months prior to it, was produced on the main stage of the Royal Court Theatre in 1975, the year Churchill was the Court's resident dramatist. Directed by John Tydeman, who had been the director for most of Churchill's radio plays, *Objections to Sex and Violence* opened on January 2 and ran for twenty-seven performances.[14] It was Churchill's first play to receive main-stage production at the Royal Court, *Owners* having been presented in the small Theatre Upstairs. It received generally unfavourable critical notices and played to less than thirty percent capacity.[15] While the management of the Royal Court is known to be relatively sanguine about such losses – Max Stafford Clark recently describing low attendance at plays by new dramatists as 'a risk we want to take'[16] – it was not until four years (and three plays) later that Churchill saw another of her plays, *Cloud Nine*, on the Royal Court's main stage.

Objections to Sex and Violence presents, in two acts set on a quiet beach, an unlikely assortment of characters with often surprising connections to sex and violence. Jule, a young woman committed to violent revolution, is camping near the beach with her friend Eric; both have gone underground since police jailed some members of their group. Jule's sister Annie, worried about newspaper hints of Jule's involvement with 'explosions' (15),[17] has traced Jule and come to try to dissuade her from endangering herself or others. Annie's friend Phil, who is disabled from an industrial accident, echoes Annie's condemnation of violence. Arthur and Madge, a middle-aged couple, go through the motions of vacationing while Madge complains that a 'sinister character' has been following her, and Arthur attempts to conceal and read a pornographic magazine (15). The elderly Miss Forbes has come to revisit the scene of a romantic meeting years ago, the memory of which has obsessed her ever since.

Through an afternoon of rain showers that frequently send them running for cover, these oddly assorted people confront one another with their conflicting viewpoints. When Annie describes her wealthy employer and his wife, and tells of a sexual affair through which she attempted, but failed, to hurt them, Jule urges her to 'put a brick through their window' (26). Phil later reveals to Jule the guilt-ridden sexual fantasies he has long had about her; when she rejects this overture, he reacts violently, attempting to throw gasoline on a fire as she bends over it. Eric, who surpasses Jule in verbal aggressiveness during early discussions, eventually tells her that he plans to quit the group. Jule turns on him with accusations of disloyalty and cowardice, begins half-deliberately throwing sand at him, and ends by attacking him with stones. Immediately afterward, while burying Jule in the sand, Annie asks her about the sexual incident Phil has revealed. When Jule treats the episode with casual superiority, Annie's suppressed anger erupts: she screams at her sister and nearly chokes her with sand. Arthur offers kind words to the distraught Miss Forbes, but then exposes himself to her.

The final scene on the deserted beach brings together Jule and Terry, her former husband. After attending his father's funeral, Terry has, like Annie, sought Jule out in her hiding place. Terry tries to convince Jule to return to the communist ideals they once shared, arguing that violent acts 'drive people the other way' (46). She, in turn, challenges him to name a time 'when the communist party hasn't stood in the way of revolution' (46). Jule accuses Terry of limiting her during their marriage, and he counters that the child who has remained with him is 'much better off' without her (47). Despite their sharp differences, the two end on a note of partial reconciliation. Terry accepts Jule's invitation to stay the night. Jule, however, refuses Terry's suggestion that she come back and live with him.

The title of *Objections to Sex and Violence* implies a link between sex and violence, but Churchill has stated, in an afterword to the play in Volume Four of the series *Plays by Women* that she did not write it with such a link in mind. Rather, she started from the idea that 'Jule's sexuality and violence (not violent sexuality) are subversive, and the other characters have different objections to them both'.[18] Patterns of action in the play, however, inescapably point to relationships between violence and sexuality. Jule and Terry, again reversing traditional gender stereotypes, illustrate opposite extremes in both sexual expression and violence. Annie and Arthur have both attempted to use their sexuality as a form of violence, but have only succeeded in increasing their own confusion and feelings of worthlessness. In any case, questions about violence dominate the play's exchanges, with sexuality providing complications but remaining a secondary issue. Jule's choice to use violence in the service of her political ideas, much more than her sexual choices, defies the precepts of her anxious sister and friends, as they emerge in the play.

Though Jule argues fiercely for the necessity of violence in bringing about political change, her personality and actions question the extent to which the choice to pursue violence is a deliberate one. While Jule advocates a conscious commitment to violence, her own violent acts seem more a reflexive expression of personal displeasure. This dichotomy between Jule's ideas and actions poses the question of whether the origin of such a choice can truly be ascribed to political belief or instead lies in the realm of basic personal tendencies. Jule's self-centredness, her tendency to dismiss the opinions of others, and her quick resort to ridicule in the face of disagreement point to a basic insensitivity to others. When her argument with Eric gradually escalates into physical attack without an apparent decision on Jule's part, it appears that violence may be her ingrained response to opposition rather than a consciously chosen strategy.

The play extends its exploration of whether violence is or can be a conscious choice and positive means to political change by demonstrating the near-universality of the violent impulse, regardless of intellectual position. Phil, who begins by saying, 'I think I'd always resort to non-violence' (24), vents his rage at Jule for rejecting him sexually by attempting to ignite an explosion in her face. Annie, in whom the continual efforts to take care of Jule can be seen as a manifestation of suppressed anger, finally unleashes the full force of her desire to limit the freedom with which Jule continually taunts her, by burying and choking Jule with sand. Madge bullies the less assertive Arthur, and he, in turn, assaults the weak and already distressed Miss Forbes with the display of his genitals. Miss Forbes voices self-destructive thoughts. The moment of violence shows each character at his or her least powerful, raising an additional doubt about the use of violence as a political tactic.

As the would-be revolutionary who has turned her back on middle-class background, husband, child, and conventional politics, Jule testifies to Churchill's continuing effort to expand the range of female dramatic roles available to actors and images of women available to audiences. After nearly two decades of 'angry young men', from Jimmy Porter in *Look Back in Anger* (1956) to Jed in Howard Brenton's *Magnificence* (1973), this play introduces an angry young woman. Of course, Jule's response to the injustices of society is no more constructive than that of her male counterparts: as she admits to Terry, 'we haven't done anything yet. They're onto us too soon' (45). While not a model of positive action, any more than is Marion in *Owners*, Jule does exemplify a woman who has 'more to do than loving another person' (50) and attempts to make active, first-hand choice.

In *Objections to Sex and Violence*, Churchill focuses on the materiality and imaginative possibilities of space. The large, neutral, outside setting of the beach offers no apparent restrictions and thus no evidence of the external conditions that have generated the characters' internal states of anger, frustration, and desire. In this wide open, public space the play unfolds through a series of duologues. The two-way verbal exchanges usually associated with more intimate, enclosed spaces, are at odds with the environment in which they occur. Churchill may have intended, through this combination of personal issues and public space, to synthesize the personal and political aspects of the issue of violence, but if so, the synthesis largely fails. Instead, the expanse that surrounds these duologues merely imparts a strangely impersonal flavor to the very personal conversations.

On the nearly deserted beach, family relationships, friendship, and the need to shelter from rain bring together characters whose personal choices represent sharply opposing views about sex and violence. Pairing off in various combinations, they engage in what almost amounts to debate of the issues brought into the foreground by their actions. Compression of the action into a single day, with heavy reliance on exposition to inform the audience of previous events, means that the characters do a great deal of talking – much of it in long speeches. The non-conversational rhythms imposed by these long speeches give the play an abstract and static quality. Speech, rather than action, propels the play: even such violent acts as stone-throwing, covering with sand, or genital exposure serve mainly to extend the verbal debate.

A call for active choice that overturns previous personal boundaries is implied in an analogy between the characters and the setting. Just as the ocean tides ebb and flow in an undeviating pattern, the characters show movement but no change from the basic positions they occupy at the beginning of the play. Although multiple points of view are maintained throughout the play, each character moves within a similar pattern of his or her own personal choices – a pattern which has, for one reason or another, encompassed the space of this particular beach at this time. While they inhabit the same space, they clash with one another momentarily, but the day of debate and challenge finally leaves each one with his or her original boundaries intact. The lack of restriction implied by the open space surrounding them seems to invite the characters to expand their power of choice into a tidal wave of change, but its weak theatricality prevents it from imaginatively connecting with either characters or audience. Thus, while the play intellectually engages with an issue of great concern in the early 1970s, when a wave of political violence struck Britain, it does not offer a sense of experiential expansion.

TRAPS

Churchill's next play, *Traps*, displays another of the abrupt jumps in style for which she has become known. In it she again experiments with making things happen – this time making everything happen at once. Churchill has explained the action thus:

> It is like an impossible object, or a painting by Escher, where the objects can exist like that on paper, but would be impossible in life. . . . The time, the place, the characters' motives and relationships cannot all be reconciled – they can happen on stage, but there is no other reality for them. . . . The characters can be thought of as living many of their possibilities at once.[19]

Churchill wrote *Traps* early in 1976, then turned her attention to projects she had agreed to do with the Joint Stock and Monstrous Regiment theatre companies. Its production, therefore, did not take place until a year later. *Traps* opened in the Theatre Upstairs at the Royal Court, in January, 1977, directed by John Ashford.[20]

Traps presents a continuous flow of brief, realistically presented snatches of life in the living room of a city apartment/country house where a group of young people live communally. The multi-dimensional structuring of time makes this play unique: for the characters in *Traps*, like the aliens of the earlier *Moving Clocks Go Slow*, time is 'all available at once'. Ordinary activities like walking a fussy baby, ironing, mending a broken bowl, shelling peas, and practicing a card trick mesh with conversations about personal anxieties and interpersonal conflict. Syl complains about the demands of her infant. Albert worries that he is being followed and nags at Jack to get a job, reminding Jack that it was for him he left his wife and children. Roles and relationships change constantly. Syl later says she is torn between continuing her career as a dancer and interrupting it to have a baby. Syl and Jack kiss behind Albert's back and talk about running away. In a later scene, Jack announces his marriage to Syl and her pregnancy. She tells Christie that she lives alone. A few lines later, Albert refers to Syl as his wife and accuses her of deceiving him with Jack.

Sudden arrivals punctuate the action. First is Reg, looking for his wife Christie. Jack, Christie's brother, says he has not seen her for a year, but adds that he expects her soon because he has been 'willing' her to come (80).[21] Then Del bursts in, slamming objects to the floor, angrily shouting names, and cursing the city. He constructs a mobius strip to illustrate his inability to separate from the group. The others soothe and calm him. Christie does come, seeking sanctuary from an abusive Reg. When Reg finds her there and pressures her to return to him, the others support Christie's decision to stay. Act One ends with the reappearance of Del, who repeats the accusations and gestures of his earlier scene, but is met with hostility and driven away after he destroys a potted plant and breaks a bowl.

The protean materiality of the objects that give the texture of realism to the stage environment becomes an integral part of the shifting reality of this play. A door is locked at one moment, not locked a few seconds later. A bowl is mended in one scene, broken in a following scene, and visibly unharmed in the scene after that. Objects associated with daily routines seem to regenerate themselves and demand repetition of the routine. Albert irons the basket of damp, wrinkled clothes Syl has just finished ironing. Del peels and slices some vegetables, cutting his finger slightly. Jack carries out the same task and experiences the same minor accident immediately afterward.

In Act Two the six characters drift in and out of the room as the sun sets successively. Christie and Del cuddle in an armchair and eat chocolates, while Del describes a rape/murder he once committed. Christie shows him the deep bruises on her back inflicted by Reg. Jack builds something out of planks and chicken wire, chatting about life in the country. He and Del, in turn, figure the dimensions for a chicken coop, then prepare vegetables for a meal.

Christie watches a sunset with Reg, then casually converses with
Del about her past incestuous relationship with Jack. Syl announces
that she will name her expected baby in memory of Albert, who
killed himself. The others speculate about the sex of the baby and
reasons for Albert's suicide. When Syl says she does not want a
baby, Jack volunteers to take care of it. Jack and Del make plans to
go away together, asking Syl if she wants to come. Christie clears
the table for dinner, and Del places a metal bathtub in one corner
of the room. Alone, Reg and Christie embrace and speak lovingly.
Then, turning violent, Reg curses, hits, and kicks Christie, while she
repeats, 'Sorry . . . Sorry' (119). In the final scene, all six gather in
the room to bathe and eat.

The temporal fluidity of *Traps* creates an aura of freedom that,
like the expansive space in *Objections to Sex and Violence*, surrounds
but does not liberate the characters. While they 'live many of their
possibilities at once', all seem trapped on a mobius strip that spins
them around the same points of reference again and again. Since the
space of the room remains constant, whether defined as an upstairs
flat in the city or a country cottage, the boundary between inside
and outside provides the primary reference point for choice. It
corresponds to the pattern of binary choice available to all the
characters: to stay within the communal group or leave it. Gender
imposes restrictive patterns as well. Syl and Christie define their
choices almost exclusively in terms of sexual and reproductive
issues, lose at games, denigrate their own abilities, take upon
themselves the blame for behaviour of others, and spend the most
time within the confines of the room. Thus, conventional and social
patterns limit choice and, from the standpoint of realistic dramatic
action, trap the six characters of this play.

The removal of temporal limitation, however, intensifies the
complexity of the play's exploration of possibility and limitation
by rendering choice literally impossible. Action in the realistically
conventional sense of choice and consequence does not occur in
Traps, because the world of the play does not acknowledge the
chain of material limitation linking actions and outcomes. By thus
disengaging from the linear action of realistic narrative, the play
calls attention to the basic pattern on which such fictions are based.
This fixed pattern corresponds to the mobius strip that appears
to offer forward motion but actually allows only circularity. The
possibility of authentic choice depends on breaking this structure
that represents choice but actually denies it.

In its negation of conventional choice, *Traps* potentiates meta-conventional choice. Its unconventional action arises out of a dynamic of displacement: one image, speech, or scene substitutes for another in a continuously reproduced present.[22] This continuous flow of present moments, each of which stands by itself, without relation to the other moments in the play, produces a theatricality not governed by the framework of narrative. This pure theatricality questions representation, which depends on a relationship between the representative work and something prior to it – 'a present outside time, a non-present'.[23] It is this basic relationship that *Traps* problematizes by avoiding reference to anything prior (and therefore definitive of what is being presented). In an ironic contrast to the plays of Pinter (whom Churchill cites as an influence on this play), which minimize reference to the prior by minimizing words, gestures, and objects, *Traps* negates reference through an excess of words, gestures, and objects. It presents more information than can logically be integrated, contradictory actions, and a room filled with 'plenty of clutter' (73). Churchill refuses to inscribe this excess with order and sequence, instead mocking the concepts of order and sequence through the onstage jigsaw puzzle and clock showing real time.

Interviewed about the play, Churchill has stated that it is not only about 'traps that people get into with each other', but also about 'traps that the audience is led into by being given certain information'.[24] In *Traps*, scenes of equal verisimilitude offer conflicting information. Words do not point to a truth that lies beyond them. They cancel one another, and therefore, in the parlance of Artaud's theatre of cruelty, 'cease to govern'[25] the meaning of the presentation. This negation of meaning points to a challenge of the basic linkage of signifier and signified that gives language its symbolic function. Churchill, in common with other feminist writers, thus signals a 'complicated and charged relationship' with language and other structures of meaning, which necessitates strategies of escaping the trap – or 'breaking the sentence' – of patriarchal discourse.[26] Her description of the play as 'an impossible object' suggests the impossible possibility of non-patriarchal subjectivity.

Churchill's questioning of representation in *Traps*, therefore, is more than a passing flirtation with absurdism. It is another step in her process of empowerment. A key factor in the play's potential for empowerment, as with other plays Churchill wrote during this period, is its placement of violent images in a playful context. The card tricks and games with which the characters amuse themselves reinforce the sense of playfulness. Sly and unexplained textual borrowings from other plays, such as *Comedians* (1976) by Trevor Griffiths (from which the opening line of *Traps* is taken) and

Christie in Love (1970) by Howard Brenton (which has as its central character the famed mass murderer Reg Christie) tease the audience. Churchill's refusal to treat serious issues seriously deflects debate and discourse while drawing the audience into a process of immediate experience. Churchill thus asserts for *Traps* the function of play, rather than metaphor.

As the play nears the conclusion of the second act, it appears that it might remain wholly within the non-referential, non-metaphorical realm of convention breaking for its own sake. As such, it would shun connection with the audience and fail to transmit anything more than a denial of discourse and concomitant admission of political impotence. However, in the final scene Churchill suddenly changes tactics. The possible impossible emerges through the rupture of discourse, as Albert, whose death has been mourned, walks through the door apologizing for being late because he got caught up in his work of preparing the vegetable patch and 'went on digging in the dark' (119). His entrance initiates a strategy that combines a forceful connectedness with the prior and a strong sense of metaphor to assert a new discourse of political change. In communally created rituals suggestive of Christian baptism and communion, the members of the group signal trust by removing their clothes, shed the soil of their past actions in the bath, and eat the food they have prepared.

The space where political change is finally enacted as a possibility is that of a nurturant community, not an arena of confrontation. All the members of the group co-operate in preparing the meal and bath. Warmth envelops the room as hot bath water and steaming food are brought in. Individuals share and exchange towels and clothing as they take turns bathing and eating. The bathing order, in which the relatively clean go first and then add hot water for those who, like Albert, have gotten dirty doing outside chores, ensures a rough equality: 'Clean and shallow or deep and dirty' (120). Food is apportioned according to 'how hungry' a person is (125). Conversation around the table reveals that 'the baby' is cared for communally and has not ended Syl's work as a dancer. Comfort, food, and companionship contribute to a general sense of well-being.

Only Reg, finally, remains separated from this general enjoyment, inhibited from joining by his possessiveness toward Christie and his lack of trust in the others. Embarrassed to undress, he wants to skip the bath and just eat dinner, but is informed by Jack that the group's rule is 'no bath, no dinner' (124). Reg then 'undresses slowly and gets into the bath' (124). The others immediately include him in the group's warmth. Albert inquires whether the water is 'warm enough still' (124). Jack washes Reg's back and brings him his dinner while he reclines in the warm water. As pleasure suffuses the group, they 'gradually, each separately . . . start to smile' (125). Even Reg, drawn out of a painful memory of abandonment and into the collective pleasure, begins to smile.

This moment, of course, is not definitive, despite its occurrence at the end of the play; it is just one possibility. Yet it, alone, has a power that transcends its artificial boundaries. This power arises from its embodiment of collective choice and its assertion of a new paradigm of political change. The pleasure of inclusion, not the pain of confrontation, has wrought change. In a reversal of phallic logic, the communal group has changed Reg, not by penetrating his being, but by being penetrated by him. Perhaps the realization of this irony is what prompts Reg, in the final instant of the play, to laugh.

The four plays that mark Churchill's entry into professional theatre demonstrate her determination not to choose a permanent or consistent area of concern, style, set of conventions, or line of argument. In them she initiates a pattern of experiment, innovation, and unpredictability that extends to her most recent stage plays. As she moves out from the one-to-one intimacy of the radio plays, she widens the focus of the presentation to include multiple situations and viewpoints, refusing consistently to subordinate this variety to a single, predominant perspective. As a result of the increasing multiplicity of perspective, the balance between individual and ensemble shifts radically in favour of emphasizing the latter. All four plays call for six or more players, and each one places special demands on scene designers. Churchill thus indicates her willingness to risk rejection – not only at the level of audience approval, but also at the level of access to production – rather than settle for the ordinary and safe.

The political perspectives for which Churchill's later plays are known emerge in these plays. Three of the four have a female central character, indicating Churchill's interest in highlighting and exploring women's experience. Her developing socialist-feminism can be seen in the emerging plurality of viewpoint. The refusal to reduce or unify the diversity of voices signals a sharp questioning both of power disparities and of existing power structures. Coinciding with Churchill's emergence as a playwright, the emerging feminist movement created a demand for new plays written by women. Churchill had begun her exploration of gender relations in radio and television plays written concurrently with the stage plays discussed in this chapter. By the time *Traps* was produced, she had already gained recognition as a feminist playwright on the basis of *Vinegar Tom,* which was written after *Traps* but produced before it was. Although they touch upon feminist issues, the project of these four plays is less that of issues than of feminist empowerment. In them, she works to prove that she, a female writer, can make things happen on her own terms in the male-dominated sphere of theatre.

Though Churchill does not often display, in these early plays, the brilliant synthesis of idea and image which would distinguish her later plays, she does illuminate the hidden structures that perpetuate the status quo, dislocate elements of those structures, and fill the gaps with dense outpourings of imagination. Isolated strategies gradually join and take shape as a mode of production empowering her to make choices where other playwrights would assume none existed. In this mode of production, she chooses theatre over drama, experience over argument, polyphonal complexity over simple narrative. She reworks conventional frameworks of time and materiality. Churchill's increasing power to make choices and changes suffuses these plays with hopeful idealism. Unlike her works for radio and television, they focus less on defining problems than on imagining mechanisms of change. Crucial to these mechanisms is her assertion of the possible through the impossible – her rupturing of patriarchal unity to create space in which her own experience and imagination can exist.

5

Reclaiming History

Moving on from the individual experimentation of her early plays, Churchill entered a new phase in the mid-1970s, when she began to ally her talents with two of the artistically ambitious and ideologically committed groups operating in the burgeoning London Fringe. Contact with the two groups, Monstrous Regiment and Joint Stock, multiplied Churchill's ideas, intensified her energy, expanded the range of viewpoints she was able to encompass, presented fresh avenues for theatrical experiment, and helped her develop an integrated feminist-socialist critique of society.

A common factor in the two groups with which Churchill became associated was their interest in the political orientation and theatrical techniques of Bertolt Brecht. Theirs was a second generation of Brecht-influenced British theatre practitioners. Twenty years after the visit of the Berliner Ensemble to London in 1956, Brechtian theatre had become an established tradition. This new generation of writers and directors combined ideas absorbed from such productions as Theatre Workshop's *Oh What a Lovely War* (1963) and William Gaskill's 1965 staging of *Mother Courage* with a diverse range of newer influences, including the work of the Living Theatre and the Cafe La Mama Troupe from the United States and Dario Fo's La Comune in Italy.

Monstrous Regiment and Joint Stock, while beginning from and continuing to explore Brechtian dramaturgy, also broke new theatrical ground. Joint Stock's experimentation has focused on the rehearsal period, which they expanded into a workshop process that came to include actors, playwrights, designers, and directors in research and improvisation that eventually led to playscripts. Monstrous Regiment's particular focus has been the analysis of gender issues. Churchill incorporated Brechtian devices into her process of experimentation, straightforwardly adapting and expanding upon Brechtian techniques in *Vinegar Tom* and *Light Shining in Buckinghamshire*, the first two plays she developed in collaboration with fringe companies. Later plays such as *Softcops*, however, use Brechtian techniques in ways that call attention to her differences from Brecht and critical attitude toward certain of his ideas. As important as Brecht in an overall view of Churchill's work is the combination of influences from Joint Stock and Monstrous Regiment, which gave her a unique access to means of theatricalizing socialist-feminist issues.

The plays examined in this chapter take an historical event or era as their starting point, but subject traditional versions of the historical phenomenon to critical revision. In compellingly unorthodox syntheses of images and action that challenge received perceptions of events and ideas, Churchill deals with witchcraft in *Vinegar Tom*, the English Civil War in *Light Shining in Buckinghamshire*, and methods of maintaining state power in *Softcops*. Sheila Rowbotham, feminist-socialist historian, has observed that 'the women's movement has made many of us ask different questions of our past'.[1] The questions Churchill asks deal not only with what has been said, seeking the untold side of accepted narratives of past events, but also with the process of telling, exploring how the present is constructed by the past and how the past is constructed by the present.

Churchill does not stop at questioning traditional accounts of history: by demanding active intellectual engagement, she attempts to empower audiences to participate in the process of reclaiming their own history. Her plays challenge the idea that existing representations of history – even those with the legitimacy of factuality – be regarded as sealed records not amenable to change in the present. Her work signals a rejection of the traditional function of the history play as a 'passive, "feminine" reflection of an unproblematically "given", masculine world'.[2] Instead, it asserts for itself the active role of intervention in the present. The idea of feminist artistic production as intervention receives broad support in current materialist-feminist theory. Judith Newton and Deborah Rosenfelt, for example, encourage an approach to writing or representing the history of women which defines it 'not as an assortment of facts in a linear arrangement, not as a static tale of unrelieved oppression of women or of their unalleviated triumphs, but as a process of transformation', and of the 'art or artifact of cultural production as an intervention in that process'.[3]

Churchill's history plays function structurally, as well as thematically, to stimulate re-examination of past and present from the viewpoint of women and other groups who have been marginal or invisible in traditional historical accounts. A crucial part of this formal revision is Churchill's experimentation with theatrical roles, which begins with *Vinegar Tom*. Of continuing importance is the technique, noted in earlier plays, of incorporating multiple points of view into the action, maintaining the strength of each through to the end. The before-during-after structure begun in earlier plays contributes further to Churchill's revision. This structure submerges the then-and-now dichotomy associated with traditional history plays in a continuum that gives the representation of history a life in the present and highlights its implicit paradigm of transformation. The sense of an on-going process, deliberately open-ended, empowers the audience to question and reformulate previously held assumptions. The active function of art exemplified in these plays reinforces the idea of reciprocity between the individual and society, articulated by Marxist theorists Rosalind Coward and John Ellis – that of 'a subject who is produced by society, and who acts to support or to change that society'.[4]

The three works discussed here, spanning eight years (1976–84), were written under quite different conditions. *Vinegar Tom* and *Light Shining in Buckinghamshire*, which emerged out of a single, intense period of creativity, share a common time period and many ideas. (A character originally intended for one play was even transplanted into the other.) However, despite these commonalities and the fact that both plays are considered collaborative in the broad sense, the processes by which they were developed differed considerably. *Vinegar Tom*, commissioned by Monstrous Regiment, was written first. After meeting with Monstrous Regiment and agreeing on the subject of the play, Churchill researched and drafted it on her own. After Churchill completed *Light Shining in Buckinghamshire* with Joint Stock, she returned to Monstrous Regiment to rehearse *Vinegar Tom*. During rehearsals, she refined the script, added a character, and worked out the songs, with suggestions from the acting company, the director, and the composer. Churchill has credited Monstrous Regiment with expanding her range of expression beyond that of 'personal pain and anger' to encompass 'a more objective and analytical way of looking at things'.[5]

Light Shining in Buckinghamshire was researched collaboratively in a Joint Stock workshop that included director Max Stafford-Clark, music director Colin Sell, and the acting company. Though the original focus had been the Crusades, early research redirected it to the period of the English Civil War, with an emphasis on the religious communitarian group known as the Ranters. 'Instead of glimpsing shadowy figures in armour', Churchill has written, 'we could hear vivid voices: "give up, give up your houses, horses, goods, gold . . . have all things common."'[6] Participants read and discussed relevant books and reported back to the group on observations of street people. They sang Psalms and improvised scenes related to the theme. One such improvisation required each participant to use a randomly chosen Bible verse as the basis of a speech attempting to persuade the others to take some unusual course of action. (One participant, according to Churchill, used the text of 'Suffer little children to come unto me', as the basis of 'an impassioned plea to lay children in the street and run them over with a steamroller'.[7]) Late in the workshop period, they visited a manor house in character as peasants.[8] Churchill found Joint Stock's approach congenial and stimulating: 'I'd never seen an exercise or an improvisation before and was as thrilled as a child at a pantomime.'[9] The project originally involved two writers, but only Churchill continued after the initial research stage. She wrote the play in the nine-week period between workshop and rehearsals typical of Joint Stock projects (and referred to by Joint Stock members as the 'writing gap'), but made major revisions during rehearsals. *Light Shining in Buckinghamshire* opened at the Traverse Theatre in Edinburgh in September 1976, only slightly more than a month before *Vinegar Tom*, directed by Pam Brighton, opened at the Humberside in Hull.

Softcops was researched and written by Churchill working alone in 1978. In this play she combined her own ideas on repressive state control with those in *Discipline and Punish*, Michel Foucault's study of the history, sociology, and philosophy of Western penal systems.[10] Churchill also incorporated material from the memoirs of two figures of the period – Vidocq, a famous detective, and Lacenaire, a thief who became a popular hero. Churchill 'put away and forgot'[11] this play until Howard Davies contacted her in 1984. She rewrote *Softcops* for Davies' Royal Shakespeare production, and worked with a choreographer and musicians, as well as the director and acting company, in its final development.

VINEGAR TOM

Churchill's first collaborative ventures began when companies approached her with their ideas for projects. Monstrous Regiment, a company dedicated to producing new work based on a socialist-feminist critique and creating substantive theatre roles for women, initiated the idea for a play about witchcraft, and Churchill responded with enthusiasm. She began researching the sixteenth- and seventeenth-century witch hunts in the spring of 1976. The previous work of Monstrous Regiment, a play titled *Scum* which focused on the 1871 Paris Commune through the experiences of Parisian washerwomen, encouraged Churchill to analyse the interaction of gender ideology and changing socio-economic conditions. Using this analysis as the primary motivating force gave *Vinegar Tom* an overtly political focus, as Churchill emphasizes in her introduction to the play:

I wanted to write a play about witches with no witches in it; a play not about evil, hysteria and possession by the devil but about poverty, humiliation and prejudice.[12]

Vinegar Tom accomplishes this aim with a series of twenty brief episodes, separated by songs, that dramatize the story of a village in which economic disparities combine with random misfortune to produce a witch hunt. Costumes and props suggest the historical period, while the set – a bare stage in the original production – makes no representational statement. Songs performed by the acting company appearing out of character and in contemporary dress, interrupt and punctuate the story, relating past persecutions to present-day oppression. The final scene, in a startling shift of mood, presents a stand-up comedy duo whose routine lays bare the ideological foundations of the oppression of women.

The play juxtaposes outward views of village life with glimpses of individual desire or suffering. An unknown gentleman who has copulated with Alice in a roadside ditch calls her 'whore' and 'witch' (137–8).[13] Jack and Margery, well-established tenant farmers who operate a dairy, worry about maintaining propriety and protecting their prosperity. Betty, the landowner's daughter rebelling against an arranged marriage, appears at the house of Jack and Margery pleading to be allowed to stay the night. Alice's mother Joan begs Margery for 'a little yeast' (143), but is turned away.

Drinking some meagre broth while Alice's child sleeps, Joan and Alice talk about hunger and loneliness. Alice and her friend Susan visit Ellen, the herbal healer, with their problems – Alice's desire for the man she was with in the first scene, and Susan's exhaustion from continual pregnancies. A doctor cures Betty's resistance with repeated bleeding. Jack demands slavish obedience and work from Margery, while he lusts after Alice.

Misfortune strikes Jack and Margery and sends them searching for someone to blame. Their cattle suddenly begin dying. Margery suffers debilitating headaches. Jack complains that he has lost his sexual organ and the use of his hand. Initially, Jack blames himself, seeing their afflictions as 'my sins stinking and swelling up' (152). Margery, however, disclaims responsibility, insisting, 'good folk get bewitched' (153). The two ask Ellen to confirm their suspicion of witchcraft, but she tries to keep peace between the neighbours. The arrival of a professional witch finder gives Jack and Margery the opportunity to accuse Joan and set in motion a hunt that also targets Alice, Susan, and Ellen. The witch finders subject the four accused women to tortures intended to exact confessions. Susan, tortured even more by guilt over the abortion she induced with a powder given her by Ellen, confesses and implicates the others. Eventually Joan and Ellen are hanged, while Alice and Susan await the same fate in prison. Alice, defiant to the end, dreams of revenge.

In the final scene, Kramer and Sprenger, two mediaeval theologians who wrote the misogynist classic, *Malleus Maleficarum, The Hammer of Witches*, appear as Edwardian music-hall comics. Speaking in turn and in unison, they explain that women's susceptibility to witchcraft is caused by their physical, intellectual, and moral inferiority. The final two songs, performed before and after the Kramer-Sprenger scene, address questions about their participation in patriarchy to women and men in turn, asking in the play's final moments whether or not the use of 'evil women' (178) as scapegoats is truly a thing of the past.

Churchill reclaims the history of the witch hunts, first of all, by referring to the work of revisionist historians, through which she expanded her own 'slight knowledge' beyond the portrayal, in 'films and fiction, of burnings, hysteria and sexual orgies'.[14] She credits Alan Macfarlane's thorough social-anthropological study of prosecutions for witchcraft, *Witchcraft in Tudor and Stuart England* (1970), with giving her an understanding of 'how petty and everyday the witches' offences were'.[15] She also built upon the work of feminist scholars which had, by the early 1970s, initiated the re-examination of such historical phenomena as witch hunts. In her preface to the play, Churchill mentions 'Witches, Midwives, and Nurses: A History of Women Healers', by Barbara Ehrenreich and Deirdre English (1973); this pamphlet links the witch hunts to suppression of female lay medical practitioners as the exclusively male medical profession gained ascendancy. The economic-class emphasis in *Vinegar Tom* has much in common with that of Sheila Rowbotham in *Hidden from History* (1973): 'Many of the women who were accused of being witches were old and poor. Disputes arose between neighbours and when misfortune came people looked for someone to blame.'[16] Rowbotham points out that 'scolds', or 'women who talked back', as well as midwives and 'wise' and 'cunning' women who dispensed 'ointments', were likely to become particular targets.[17] She also relates witch hunts to a seventeenth-century obsession with women's sexuality, quoting Robert Burton's *Anatomy* of 1621: 'Of woman's unnatural, insatiable lust what country, what village does not complain?'[18] By calling attention to some of her sources in the preface to the play, Churchill both allies her work with factual accounts and points interested or skeptical audience members or readers in the direction of further information.

Churchill borrows energy for *Vinegar Tom*'s vigorous reclamation of history from well-known Brechtian ideas and techniques. Brecht wrote:

> We need a type of theatre which not only releases the feelings, insights, and impulses possible within the particular historical field of human relations in which the action takes place, but employs and encourages those thoughts and feelings which help transform the field itself.[19]

He himself spent his creative lifetime working out techniques of historicization, alienation, and social gest through which to provoke questioning of social relations through the perspective of historical materialism. Churchill, who has similarly adopted historical materialism as an analytic tool, uses an episodic structure in which narrative and songs set up a dialogue between two distinct historical periods. Neither period stands on its own; each poses questions about the other. The songs addressed to the audience that break narrative continuity further serve to counteract the emotional exhaustion and passivity which could result from the harrowing story of the witch hunt. Churchill uses the social gest – a simple action that illuminates the power relations structuring a situation – to call attention to the interaction of economic and sexual oppression. Jack, whose status as a prosperous man removes him on two levels from the indigent, female Alice, brings her not one apple, but two as a token of his willingness to barter goods for sex. The two apples call attention to the finite but substantial nature of Jack's power and illuminate the dilemma of Alice, who could feed not only herself, but also her child, if she were to accede to Jack's wishes. *Vinegar Tom* is epic in the sense that it requires more from audiences than a passive suspension of disbelief. It asks for active engagement with the same questions the playwright dealt with in creating it and therefore 'arouses [the] capacity for action'.[20]

The primary dynamic in *Vinegar Tom* is that of oscillation. Alternation of scenes with contemporary songs sets up a pattern of comparison and contrast between the seventeenth century and the present. The dialogue created by this alternation not only emphasizes the persistence of misogynist attitudes, but also calls attention to the fact that the representation of history in *Vinegar Tom* has been influenced by questions contemporary women ask about their own lives. Through it, Churchill calls attention to the relationship between the creative process and the created work, exposing the contemporary origins of this history play and affirming the view that it is not possible to '"reflect" history in a simple mimetic moment'.[21] Janelle Reinelt has referred to this dynamic interaction between product and process as 'the relationship between history and consciousness'.[22]

The dynamic of alternation involves the audience in an analysis of 'the ways in which material conditions have historically structured the mental aspects of oppression'.[23] The material conditions of life during the seventeenth century – a time, as Churchill points out, of 'social upheavals, class changes, rising professionalism, and great hardship among the poor'[24] – are suggested by using the stage's material resources. Tangible objects, such as the churn, the empty bowl, or Ellen's mirror, provide reference points for the drudgery and deprivation of daily life. The use of realistic stage effects for Betty's bleeding by the doctor, the accused women's torture with long needles, and the hanging calls attention to the reality of harsh punishment for those who resisted the mandates of the established power structure. Dialogue reinforces the materiality of the pervasive sense of limitation by referring to specific desires, hungers, and frustrations. Material conditions frame Alice's statement, 'I hate my body' (146): she identifies her body with the limitation and pain structured by her position as a poor woman in the seventeenth century.

The songs, on the other hand, make no attempt to represent current material conditions. Instead, they address more general states of mind, such as fear of change, the desire to be loved, or a craving for security. Although they emphasize such body-based issues as menstruation, aging, beauty, and illness, the songs leave undefined the conditions that structure such near-universal behaviour as the attempt by women to conform to male-defined standards of attractiveness. The question is, however, finally made explicit in the song that immediately follows conclusion of the historical narrative. 'Lament for the Witches' asks, 'Who are the witches now?' and points the way to analysis of material conditions in its warning to 'Ask how they're stopping you now' (176).

As she did in *Traps*, Churchill changes tactics in the final scene of *Vinegar Tom*, thus breaking the pattern of alternation she has established and making it clear that the play's primary focus is an idea rather than a particular time period. Kramer and Sprenger, the master theorists of the witchhunts – played, as Churchill stipulates, by the two women just 'hanged' as Joan and Ellen – anachronistically assume the attire and stylized patter of Edwardian music-hall comics. In this scene, Churchill pulls back from the dual focus on seventeenth-century material conditions and contemporary consciousness to examine the ideology upon which oppression of women is founded. The book, *Malleus Maleficarum (The Hammer of Witches)* from which Kramer and Sprenger quote is an actual work of historical importance in the propagation of misogynist attitudes. The music-hall form reinforces the point that this ideology of gender has become, over the centuries, so ingrained that comedy acts traditionally play upon the familiarity of (but not against the inaccuracy of) these stereotypes for their humour. The introduction of another historical period as counterpoint to both the seventeenth century and the present further serves to invalidate a simplistic opposition between past and present in attempting to understand gender oppression.

After the emotional climax of the historical narrative, Brechtian distancing reasserts itself in the ironic detachment of the Kramer and Sprenger act. The playing of these roles by women (and male impersonation was an authentic music-hall specialty in the Edwardian era) sharpens the cynicism of their description of women as creatures of 'insatiable malice' and 'carnal lust' (178). It supplements the portrayal of collusion by Goody and Margery in the historical narrative by calling attention to the maintenance of patriarchy by male-impersonating women. The specified role doubling points to questions about defiance: Kramer and Sprenger's apparent defiance – the wearing of men's clothes – masks an actual submission to patriarchal ideology. This scene promotes a realization that the entire recorded history of women has been created in and through patriarchal ideology.

Kramer and Sprenger, however, do have one important commonality with the women accused of witchcraft in the historical narrative: marginality, the condition of being on the borderline of social acceptability. *Vinegar Tom*, in contrast to the radio plays, shows marginality to be a position of extreme vulnerability. Kramer and Sprenger create a privileged marginality for themselves, as do token women in a variety of political, economic, and cultural enterprises, by memorizing and repeating the patriarchal 'party line'. The marginality of the four women accused of being witches, however, results from a combination of economic and sexual factors, choice and necessity.

The play clearly shows that low value within the existing economic structure increases vulnerability. Joan, who is an economic burden rather than an asset to the village, is the first to be accused of witchcraft. Ellen's non-professional medical practice helps to maintain peace in the community, but her custom of accepting only 'gifts' as compensation threatens powerful economic interests. The desperate Susan evades her economic contribution, the primacy of which is indicated by her husband's coda to intercourse, 'Let's hope a fine child comes of it' (144). At the other end of the spectrum, Betty's usefulness as the glue in an economic alliance protects her from accusations of witchcraft, although the cruel medical treatment and forced marriage present her with inexorably grim prospects. Goody's willingness to do the most tiresome tasks of witch hunting in return for a good wage (which, she remarks with pride, is no less than that of Packer) places her solidly within the emerging institutions of capitalism. Margery's married status and domestic productiveness render her relatively immune to prosecution, although the lack of pleasure or security in her position is evident in the scene in which she doggedly but uselessly churns, chanting 'Come butter come, come butter come' (144).

The marginality and vulnerability of women is multiplied by any non-conformity that challenges their status in the sexual and economic hierarchy. Betty's rebellion cancels the terms of the relative privilege she has enjoyed as a member of the upper class, but her attempt to escape, even briefly, from her class is thwarted by the vigilant guardians of hierarchy, Jack and Margery. Alice, by frankly asserting her own sexual desire against that of Jack, sets herself up for blame. Jack cannot experience himself as masculine unless he can perceive the women in his own class or below as objects; therefore, when he loses his sexual potency, he accuses Alice of stealing his penis. Joan, by talking rudely to her well-established and proper neighbour Margery, defies the economic and social hierarchy. From the standpoint of Jack and Margery, these acts constitute extraordinary threats. Alice's refusal denies Jack the position of privilege which he identifies with his physical wholeness. Joan's impertinence deprives Margery of respect – one of the tenuous privileges of the middle position in the hierarchy she has worked so hard to preserve.

Marginality, in *Vinegar Tom*, thus does not constitute a position of special power, but rather one in which 'petty and everyday'[25] acts, perceived as extraordinary threats, bring dire consequences. The song, 'If Everybody Worked as Hard as Me', defines the place of women in the patriarchal order: 'the wife is what she is / to her man' (161). Husband, family, and country all depend on women's acceptance of this object position. Acceptance brings protection against the acknowledged dangers of marginality: 'So the horrors that are done will not be done to you' (161). The small acts of resistance that target the women for 'horrors' do not signify any degree of power, whether natural or supernatural. Joan's cat Vinegar Tom, who periodically trespasses in Margery's dairy, is no familiar. Alice's fashioning of a mud figure to represent the man she desires does nothing to contravene the limiting conditions of her sexual and economic status. Alice's verbal outburst at the end similarly makes no difference to the outcome of the narrative. However, on the level of the 'relationship between history and consciousness' that Reinelt found in the play, her anger does make an impact. As she watches the hanging, Alice vows:

> If I could live I'd be a witch now after what they've done. I'd make wax men and melt them on a slow fire. I'd kill their animals and blast their crops and make such storms, I'd wreck their ships all over the world . . . I'd make them feel it. (175)

The speech serves a political purpose: by 'speaking bitterness', Alice, like the Chinese peasant revolutionaries who originated the practice, breaks the silence that has aided her oppressors throughout history. Finally, by renouncing powerlessness even at the price of embracing an imagined evil, Alice offers a political response to the narrative from within that narrative.

Feminist-socialist empowerment in *Vinegar Tom* arises out of strong intervention in the player/role, narrative, and temporal elements of theatrical production. Churchill disrupts the stable player/role relationship which has served to reinforce the patriarchal patterns of gender division and opposition in three ways. First, the players alternate between roles as characters in the historical narrative and undefined performances as contemporary singers. Second, the two players 'hanged' as Joan and Ellen immediately reappear as Edwardian music hall comics. Finally, the roles within the narrative portion of the play, as the Monstrous Regiment note appended to one edition informs us, were cast against the expected physical type, to 'challenge those stereotypes' and allow members of the company 'to expand into parts normally forbidden to us because we were too young/old/thin/fat'.[26]

All three choices create a distance between player and role that limits the defining power of the role. The separation of player and role in *Vinegar Tom* disrupts the subject/object opposition that reifies patriarchy's masculine/feminine opposition. The alternating appearance of players in and out of period costume and character, combined with deliberate inconsistency in role doubling and mismatching of physical types, confounds perception of player and role as a binary pattern. It emphasizes the artificiality of these roles and makes a connection with the structure of society and the conflicting roles women often play within it. The play thus signals the possibility of freedom, rather than inevitability, in the assumption of roles.

The play similarly reorients narrativity and temporality. The alternation between a story of the past and contemporary voices questioning their own experiences opens the narrative into a dialogue that continually refocuses attention from the narrative product to the process through which such a product is created. It thus models a process through which the reclaiming of history may be continued. The before-during-after temporal structure takes the audience beyond the artificial closure of the hanging. It reminds the audience that neither the specific narrative that just unfolded nor the historical phenomenon of the witch hunts constitutes the final chapter in the story of patriarchy.

To a greater extent than any of Churchill's other plays, *Vinegar Tom* explicitly combats the male gaze. On the narrative level, the play focuses strongly on relationships between women, whether positive or negative. Its presentation of the female players in alternating historical roles and contemporary performances creates a consciously developed doubleness for women audience members. The final song, 'Evil Women', acknowledges the continuing power of the male gaze to create the 'movie dream' of fetishizing women, but asks men directly, 'Is that what you want?' (161) The undisguised rejection of male privilege in this play probably accounts for the disproportionate share of negative comments, compared to Churchill's other work, that it has received from male critics, who have referred to *Vinegar Tom* as 'graphic', 'shrill' and 'hysterical'.[27] Monstrous Regiment has acknowledged that 'some men in particular were upset by it', because they felt 'outside the experiences of the female characters' and 'accused by the songs'.[28] Although *Vinegar Tom* has proved its durable power in regular productions since 1976, the hostile criticism may have influenced Churchill to move away from the confrontational, and toward the more subversive comic style she has employed in later plays.

With two of its characters hanged and two awaiting execution at the end of the historical narrative, and an emphasis on oppression in the songs and music hall scene, the importance of play in *Vinegar Tom* may seem surprising. However, play is the key to *Vinegar Tom*'s assertion of the possibility of transformation. This emphasis on playing, which will be increasingly important in Churchill's later plays, creates a sphere of freedom and experiment. The role doublings enact a play of possibility that displaces the attitude of resignation that Brecht called 'the mark of the inevitable'[29] in traditional theatre and that Newton and Rosenfelt refer to as the 'tragic essentialism' in traditional constructions of history.[30] The anarchic and recuperative power of play points to a Brechtian 'way out'[31] for contemporary women.

LIGHT SHINING IN BUCKINGHAMSHIRE

Light Shining in Buckinghamshire continues Churchill's exploration of historical subjects and Brechtian staging. It originated in a Joint

Stock workshop addressing the question of 'why you would turn your life upside down' for an idea. Set within the period of the English Civil War, 1647–50, the play uses as its basis a variety of different materials, including contemporary historical accounts, primary sources such as pamphlets and written records, and the improvisational exercises of the workshop. Biblical psalms and nineteenth-century poetry set to music blend with the action. *Light Shining in Buckinghamshire* reverberates with the excitement of revolutionary upheaval and the 'millenial dream' of the mid-seventeenth century.[32] The opening lines, taken from the Book of Isaiah, set the mood of extremity: 'Fear, and the pit, and the snare are upon thee, O inhabitant of the earth . . . The earth is utterly broken down, the earth is clean dissolved, the earth is moved exceedingly' (191).[33]

Characterization and casting in this play extend methods employed by Joint Stock in its development and production (for which Max Stafford-Clark served as co-director) of David Hare's play about the Chinese Revolution, *Fanshen*. In Hare's play, each of the nine actors in the company played two to four roles. In *Light Shining in Buckinghamshire*, nearly thirty parts in twenty-one scenes are played by two women and four men, but the traditionally stable relationship between character and actor is replaced by a deliberate inconsistency in the assigning of roles. Characters appearing more than once are played by a different actor in each scene in which they appear. This way of distributing roles, which Churchill recommends for all productions of the play, negates the individuality of the characters. It widens the scope of the play so that it seems to encompass the stories of a great mass of people who found themselves caught up in the English Civil War. At the same time, it experiments with a more radical disjoining of player and role.

The general sequence of events conveys the shape of what Churchill calls 'a revolution that didn't happen'.[34] Initial episodes show how various participants are brought into the revolutionary struggle. Cobbe prays, revealing the conflict he feels over maintaining filial respect for a wealthy father whose greed and hypocrisy are evident. A servant whose child is dying of malnutrition receives cheerful assurance from his master, a wealthy vicar, that suffering proves his worthiness for heaven. Margaret Brotherton, a homeless woman, is sentenced to be whipped for vagrancy. Briggs joins the Parliamentary army when a recruiter convinces him that it will inaugurate the reign of Christ in England.

The initial victories of the Parliamentary forces give rise to 'the amazed excitement of people taking hold of their own lives'.[35] Hoskins, interrupting a sermon on predestination, asserts that God has 'chosen everyone', but is expelled and beaten for breaking the silence imposed on women in church. Claxton, who tends Hoskins' bruises, catches from her the spirit of defiance. Two women help loot a manor house, rejoicing in destruction of the land titles and family portraits which signified the lord's power. Briggs, recalling a battle in which he was wounded, voices faith in the imminent coming of Christ, saying, 'even when they moved me the pain was less than the joy' (208). The emerging sense of liberation reaches a climax when the company sings a passage from Walt Whitman's 'Song of the Open Road'.

Reaction begins when the leaders, in the interest of maintaining their own power, betray the common people who had turned their lives upside down for the Parliamentary cause. Act One ends with the Putney Debates: common soldiers bring to Cromwell their demands for civil rights and representative government, but a high-ranking officer argues that granting these demands would endanger property rights. Cromwell rules against the common soldiers. Act Two opens with reports that a group called the Diggers attempted to farm public land but were brutally repressed by the authorities.

The reactionary forces gain strength, defeating further progress toward revolution. A new generation of property owners replaces the old, forcing the tenants into even worse poverty. Incidents of individual defiance become increasingly isolated and desperate. Claxton advocates the Ranter philosophy of committing adultery or theft, to be 'free from sin' by rejecting the concept of sin (221). Briggs refuses to accompany the army to Ireland and writes a letter accusing army leaders of being 'as great a tyrant as the king was' (223). A butcher, incensed at the greed of his wealthy customers, refuses to sell meat to them. One witness describes the funeral of Robert Lockyer, an executed leader of the revolutionary Levellers, and another details the final defeat of the Levellers shortly thereafter.

As those who had brought the millenial dream to the centre of a society's consciousness are pushed back to its margins, the struggle ends with a grimly hilarious prayer meeting in a tavern. In bursts of speech that are sometimes incoherent, sometimes poetic, rousing, or vulgar, members of the ragged group refer to God as 'a bully', invoke vengeance for the deaths of the Levellers, curse Christ, and declare 'riches . . . the cause of all wickedness' (230–1). Briggs, the former Leveller, voices despair, but Cobbe, throwing his coat at Briggs' feet, insists that hope lies in living together with 'all things common' (234). The meeting concludes with a communal meal and the singing of verses from Ecclesiastes: 'The sleep of the labouring man is sweet . . . ' (239–40).

In the brief final scene, characters appear singly and make short statements about their lives after the Restoration. Hoskins says, 'I think what happened was, Jesus Christ did come and nobody noticed it' (240). Cobbe tells of his trial for blasphemy, and Brotherton speaks of stealing bread. The drunk remembers feasting 'the day the king came back' (240). Briggs has tried to alleviate the food shortage by gradually abandoning a conventional diet; now he eats only grass. Claxton, who has 'forsaken' the world, confesses, in the final line of the play, 'My great desire is to see and say nothing' (241).

Light Shining in Buckinghamshire combines a sense of accuracy with that of immediacy by keeping close to its origins in period documents and improvisational work. Many lines come directly from seventeenth-century pamphlets. Cobbe and Claxton are based on the preserved writings of Abiezer Coppe and Laurence Clarkson, two members of the Ranter sect. The Putney Debates in the play are a tight condensation of the actual debates, which took place in 1647. The regrouping of players in each scene incorporates into the scripted play a sense of the stimulating unpredictability associated with improvisation. Churchill's use, again, of game-playing strategies, together with her adaptation and acknowledgement of historical sources, signals the intent of empowering audiences both through active imagination and actual example.

Light Shining in Buckinghamshire, like *Vinegar Tom*, shows straightforward use of Brechtian techniques. The play is constructed in the form of self-contained episodes. Music separates the episodes and moves the action forward. The dark and ragged peasant costumes of the original production, as well as the props, which included a carefully designed table of scientific instruments, suggested social and material conditions of the period. Players not taking part in a given scene sit on either side of the stage observing the action, a Brechtian staging arrangement that interferes with theatrical illusion, ensuring that the 'representation . . . take[s] second place to what is represented'.[36] As in *Vinegar Tom*, the form demands more than passivity from the audience but simultaneously empowers them with a model of observing with 'the eyes fully open',[37] understanding, and participating in the action. The play employs the Brechtian technique of the social gest with great effectiveness to show awakening political consciousness. In one of the most potent of these scenes, a peasant woman who has taken part in the looting of a manor house describes to her friend the luxurious 'white linen sheets' and 'wool blankets' there for the taking. Dazzled by the wealth of possibilities, she could hardly decide 'what to take', but has brought out a broken mirror in which she and her friend see, for the first time, their own reflections. The first woman says, 'They must know what they look like all the time. And now we do' (207). The mirror that has imprisoned an upper-class woman by indicating how she should look, becomes a means of empowerment in the hands of these lower class women, who use it to discover how they do look. In this remarkable fusion of class and gender issues, Churchill gives tangible form to an insight expressed by Sheila Rowbotham:

> In order to create an alternative an oppressed group must at once shatter the self-reflecting world which encircles it and, at the same time, project its own image onto history. In order to discover its own identity as distinct from that of the oppressor it has to become visible to itself.[38]

The play adapts and extends Brechtian ideas, as well as going farther in the direction of player/role experiment, with the important structural innovation of assigning the roles of particular characters to different players for each character appearance. This technique produces Brechtian alienation by disrupting the audience's expected emotional identification with individual characters. It further serves to maintain the multiple viewpoint and direct attention to the overall shape of events rather than to individual story lines. Most notably it offers, to an even greater degree than did the disrupted player/role relationship in *Vinegar Tom*, a feminist model of engagement with and separation from roles which emphasizes the power of choice. Player and role function as separate signs in continuously reconfigured combinations that negate stable identity. Simple doubleness gives way to diffusion. A mobile range of meanings, rather than a static definition, comprises identity. Again, the revolutionary message of the theatrical form becomes the power of play.

Heightened language, in which Churchill fuses poetry and political analysis, enhances the play's overt revolutionary theme, the political potential of personal transformation. The short scenes show characters converted, transformed, caught up 'like a newborn child', in the words of Cobbe, 'picked up, put down, not knowing if you're good or evil' (236). As individuals find their own lives turned upside-down, they join with others to overturn previous categories of people, knowledge, and behaviour. Sheila Rowbotham, again, has described the Civil War as a period when 'imagination leapt out of material reality for a time, only to be forced back into proper circumspection'.[39] The force of imagination – the power to mentally project oneself beyond the constraints of material conditions – always potent in Churchill's plays, is intensified here by the multiple transformations the players undergo from one scene to the next as they move between passive and active roles, assume one character after another, and portray the change each character undergoes in the course of the scene.

This first play created through the type of collaboration Churchill has characterized as an exercise of the 'common imagination'[40] deals with the power of collective imagination. In the beginning, when that power increases and dominates the action, material conditions are only sketched in, notably in the scene where the well-fed vicar parts with an orange for his servant's starving child. The real focus of the early scenes is language, with its capacity for articulating injustice, rousing a group to action, and conveying visions of a better future. Sermons, speeches, and prayers – as well as the Psalms and the anachronistic poem sung by the entire company – inspire and unite the people who turn from the ordinary routines of their lives to seek a future they have just grasped the power to imagine. The Levellers translate the abstract language of fired imagination into more concrete political demands aimed at redistribution of power. In the Putney Debates which serve as the play's turning point, however, the symbolic power of language proves no match for the unchanged material strength of a power structure based upon private property.

As the revolution begins to falter, and a new generation of squires supplants the old, material conditions reassert their importance. Short scenes show a starving mother abandoning her baby and a butcher denouncing the wealthy for the amount of meat they consume. By the time people come together in the tavern scene, ideas must be given tangible form by an object, such as the apple passed around the circle by Hoskins as she testifies to the presence of God, or the coat thrown to the floor by Cobbe to demonstrate sharing. The dislocated and sparsely worded individual utterances of the final 'After' scene, with their emphasis on food, confirms not only the defeat of the millenial vision but also the death of the collective imagination in the face of yet more limiting material conditions.

Although *Light Shining in Buckinghamshire* deals, on one level, with defeat, 'a revolution that didn't happen',[41] it conveys an equally strong sense of what did happen, energizing audiences through its realization of collective power. The play shows that the dream of salvation, not just the desire for material improvements, motivates the revolutionary movement. While those caught up in it make few tangible gains, and their participation does not, in the end, redirect the course of history, it gives them access to the process of political change. The insurrection gives them their first experience of self-awareness, and they embrace it eagerly. The woman who steals the mirror from the manor house becomes visible to herself. Rainborough and the other Levellers, who at the beginning of the Putney Debates carefully announce their full name and position or function, project their images onto history. Participants in the prayer meeting have begun to analyse the ways in which the religio-political codes of ownership and sin interact to oppress them. Therefore, although the stage, and the world it represents, are dark at the end, the 'light shining' is the on-going potential of collective thought and action.

Light Shining in Buckinghamshire questions customary perceptions both of history generally and of the historical events which it presents. The before-during-after structure, as in *Vinegar Tom*, replaces the then-and-now opposition inherent in traditional perceptions of past events with a form that represents history as a process rather than an artifact. Dramatizing a well-known era in British history, the play suggests a more diffuse view of the upheavals of the Civil War period than 'the simple "Cavaliers and Roundheads" history taught at school'.[42] Although no standard-length play could present a really comprehensive view of the diverse and conflicting groups 'to the left of Parliament',[43] *Light Shining in Buckinghamshire* gives provocative glimpses of the different aims and philosophies of Ranters, Diggers, Levellers, and others in a wide-ranging, collage-like assemblage of scenes. The final meeting, in which each participant holds and responds to an apple passed around – until the drunk is passed the apple and eats it – exemplifies the play's incorporation of the diverse viewpoints that contributed to the near-revolution. This work revises the concept of the history play by offering an active spectacle of heterogeneous participation rather than the typically passive one based on a central figure characterized by unity and the 'timelessness' which Brecht ascribed to 'bourgeois' theatre.[44] Rather than focusing upon a single character, or even a particular group of characters, as representative of the period, the play expands the concept of representation by presenting a dense and varied collage of sometimes interchangeable, sometimes overlapping, sometimes conflicting images. By including a wide spectrum of men and women involved in the revolution, as well as through the further fragmentation of character by the inconsistent role assignments, *Light Shining in Buckinghamshire* disallows imposition of the final unity or resolution associated with traditional theatre. In its avoidance both of the specifically individual and the 'universal' or 'eternally human',[45] the play emphasizes interaction between people and their particular historic environment, and thus points the way toward change. Ultimately, it rejects a 'tragic'[46] view of history that affirms the inevitability of oppression, and allies itself with Brecht's intent that epic theatre help to overturn the conditioned acceptance of given social structures as natural or unassailable.

SOFTCOPS

After working intensely with Joint Stock and Monstrous Regiment in 1976, and contributing to *Floorshow*, a cabaret production put together by Monstrous Regiment in 1977, Churchill pulled back temporarily from involvement with collaborative groups. In 1978, she wrote *Softcops*, which she researched and wrote alone. According to Churchill's account, she had been thinking of writing a play 'about the soft methods of control, schools, hospitals, social workers, when I came across the Foucault book [*Discipline and Punish*], and was so thrilled with it that I set the play not here and now but in nineteenth century France'.[47] The play remained in Churchill's files until 1983, when Howard Davies asked her to write a play for production by the Royal Shakespeare Company in its small London theatre, the Pit at the Barbican Centre. Churchill rewrote *Softcops* for this purpose. Its production evolved into a different type of collaboration than Churchill had hitherto experienced, with the inclusion of a composer, choreographer, and group of musicians in the process. Incorporating complex choreography and the onstage presence of the Medici String Quartet into the action, the Royal Shakespeare production heightened nontextual elements of the play, pointing Churchill toward a broader conception of theatre. *Softcops* premiered at the Pit in January, 1984.

Written in one act, *Softcops* employs comic sketches, songs, dancing, and acrobatics to illustrate the changing methods used by the apparatus of the state to maintain control over the populace. Pierre, a hapless bureaucrat determined to eradicate crime, initiates the action and appears in most scenes. He stages an elaborate execution intended to teach the public a lesson, but when a condemned man defies him the crowd riots. Although the Minister who employs Pierre insists on the necessity of old-fashioned, brutal punishments that inspire fear, Pierre promotes the softer approach of moral education. He envisions a 'garden of laws' to educate the public about the consequences of crime (14).[48] Pierre himself receives some instruction from Vidocq, a criminal turned police informer, who cleverly demonstrates that certainty is more important than severity when punishment is intended to deter crime.

Vidocq goes on to prove that the best way to catch a criminal is to be one. The condemned criminals play a colourful and sometimes romantic part in the drama of state power. Lacenaire, a handsome petty thief and amateur poet, holds court in his prison cell for an assortment of publicity- and thrill-seekers. A boy condemned to serve on a chain gang pleads, screams, and struggles; yet the instant the iron collar is finally clamped on his neck, he begins cursing and boasting, then joins the other gang members in a wild revel celebrating the freedom of having nothing more to lose.

Softcops' turning point occurs with the appearance of an old man who turns out to be Jeremy Bentham. He demonstrates his invention, the panopticon, by placing Pierre on a bench and observing him from behind a curtain. After a few uncomfortable moments in this position, Pierre admits that the panopticon is 'more reasonable' than spectacles of punishment: 'It's a form of power, like the steam engine. I just have to apply it' (40). The final scenes show implementations of Bentham's concept. Pierre and the Minister, during their tour of a model reformatory, see the boy from the chain gang brought in and assigned a number, a monitor, and a

The Plays of Caryl Churchill

schedule that permits no time or thought for forbidden behaviour. Two conspirators meet, and neither can determine whether or not the other is a spy. Pierre takes a group of mental patients on an outing to the beach, assuring a curious passerby that the men are well supervised. When one of the patients lunges at him and is shot dead by an unseen guard, Pierre quickly restores calm to the group. Rehearsing a speech he is to give later, he explains 'how the criminals are punished, the sick are cured', and so on, but becomes increasingly confused about the categories of people he oversees. The play ends as Pierre proclaims: 'The sick are punished. The insane are educated. The workers are cured. The criminals are cured. The unemployed are punished' (49).

Constructed in the form of a revue, *Softcops* presents dual perspectives on history and the theatre through a series of gestic episodes. The revue form, which originated in nineteenth-century France, reinforces and reflects upon the sense of periodicity within the play. Use of this quintessentially popular form as the vehicle for arguments drawn from an academic treatise makes an ironic statement in itself. The disparity between form and content creates a distancing effect that allows the audience to view the play's situations critically. Revue has been used and championed by others interested in the Brecht-Meyerhold idea of 'theatre of situation', from Joan Littlewood to Dario Fo.[49] For Littlewood and Fo, an important aim of revue pieces has been that of attracting a working-class audience with the simplified situations and broad treatment typical of music hall or television comedy. In her use of revue, Churchill attempts to make Foucault's historical survey of evolving structures of state power accessible to an audience viewed and defined primarily in terms of their position as theatregoers.

In the play's first scene Churchill effectively encapsulates her subject – the authoritarian power of the state – through the device of a theatre within the theatre. The agent of the state is Pierre, an overworked, nervous, and apparently harmless stage manager who hopes his show will impress his superior, the Minister. As he arranges black draperies and placards, Pierre worries about how best to appeal to the reason of the spectators, but he loses control of his performance almost from the outset. Pierre's bumbling mismanagement does not prevent the first punishment from taking place; after speeches by the Magistrate and the condemned man, Duval's hand is severed and held aloft by the executioner. However, when the next prisoner, Lafayette is brought to the scaffold, he refuses to give the rehearsed statement of repentance on which Pierre's appeal to reason is predicated. Instead, he flaunts his lack of remorse over killing his boss. His defiance provokes conflicting emotions and actions among the spectators: some free Lafayette and beat the executioner, while others grab Lafayette and beat him. By the time they are dispersed by soldiers with fixed bayonets, the rioting crowd has demolished the scaffold on which the power of the state was to be represented.

Central to this first scene, and to the play as a whole, is the use of theatre as a metaphor for the capacity of a powerful central authority to project its image onto history. Churchill follows Foucault, but also seeks to make a strong connection between the play's statement and the theatre audience, by using this metaphor to highlight the opposition between the power of the government and that of the governed. Theatre brings together two groups of people; those who produce the drama and those who watch it. Of the two, the spectators appear less active but exercise equal power, because their presence gives the production its meaning. The various punishments depicted or discussed in the course of the play – from the hanging, drawing and quartering preferred by the Minister to the chain gang into which the boy is later impressed – all serve as spectacles in which the state exhibits its power to the general populace. Scripted speeches, role-playing, scenic structures, and special costumes contribute to the effects. All these spectacles, however, depend upon the willingness of the general populace to validate state authority by watching. The power that the audience thus exercises always constitutes a potential threat to the small elite which wields state power, as the riot that frees the murderer Lafayette proves.

The first part of the play presents competing ideas of which type of theatre best exhibits state power. Pierre, of course, advocates didactic theatre as the best means of deterring behaviour defined by the state as criminal. Churchill subjects Brecht to some pointed satire when she shows this dedicated but inept agent of the state proclaiming, 'Reason is my goddess' (6), hanging explanatory placards on the scaffold, and insisting on both the entertainment and instructional value of public punishments. The dream which Pierre indefatigably promotes is a 'Garden of Laws' with 'little theatres of punishment' giving spectators the pleasure of seeing the guilty suffer, along with the moral lesson of 'how the crime came about and how to resist any such tendencies in one's own life' (30, 38).

His carefully planned execution, however, transmutes itself into theatre of the absurd. The Minister, in contrast to Pierre, believes in a theatre of cruelty, maintaining that 'what brings a crowd, it's very simple, is agony' (11), and that fear, not reason, deters common people from defying state authority. Later, Pierre accepts the need for 'shock' and opts for traditional illusionistic theatre, raising the curtain on a device that simulates torture of a man paid to feign pain – and assuring Bentham, to whom he demonstrates the device, that 'what matters is that he's seen to suffer' (38). Vidocq takes a different approach entirely to spectacle. While dealing with serious criminals in private, he advises using theatre as a means to 'take people's attention off' (22) their potential power to challenge the state. Accordingly, Vidocq encourages the romanticization of the relatively harmless Lacenaire, because this diverts energy away from more effective resistance to authority.

The dependence of theatre on spectators, as Pierre eventually learns, imposes constraints on the definition of crime. This limitation makes theatre, regardless of the form in which it is presented, a very imperfect means of ensuring state power. The relationship between spectators and spectacle demands that a large audience focus on a small number of condemned criminals: therefore, using any form of theatre as a deterrent makes it necessary to define crime in narrow terms that exclude the general populace. Furthermore, bringing large numbers of people together for a single purpose carries the risk that they may recognize their power. Seeing criminals exhibited may allow them to realize the possibility or even the desirability of resisting state power. The pragmatist Vidocq scoffs at Pierre's idea of displaying a regicide in an iron cage as an example, because 'people follow an example' (22).

The potential alluded to by Vidocq – that theatre may stimulate people to act – points to an even greater disadvantage, from the state's point of view, to theatre as a form of control. Effective theatre sparks imagination. The imagination, once ignited, resists control, as the eruptions of the crowd at the execution and the ecstatic singing and dancing of the chain gang show. The indispensable place of imagination in the 'spectacle of physical punishment'[50] is revealed by the Minister's repetition of the word *dream* as he argues the need for theatres of cruelty. The Minister uses the word in three different contexts: first he cautions Pierre that 'people have vile dreams', but goes on to say that if they act on those thoughts, their bodies are punished severely, 'beyond their dreams'. Finally, recalling a famous execution by torture, he speaks of finding, in its aftermath, a 'lady . . . ready for hours of ingenuity beyond my dreams' (12). Allied not only to pain, but also to pleasure, imagination may ignite anarchy, rebellion, or revolution. Pierre seeks to make the spectators in his Garden of Laws mere passive recipients of his messages, but the wiser Vidocq understands that even a fairly passive exercise of the imagination – i.e., following an example – may ultimately threaten state power.

Bentham's panopticon principle reverses theatre's power equation and renders spectacle obsolete as a means of controlling behaviour. The populace is denied the opportunity to watch, but is itself watched by the elite group operating the machinery of state power. The panopticon's ingenuity lies in the fact that it allows one to monitor many; it therefore gives the state the power to broaden indefinitely its definition of crime, without any need for legitimation by the general populace. The common people, always suspect because of their capacity for resistance, become the focus of the panopticon's all-seeing eye.

Operating directly on the mind, surveillance takes away the capacity for imagination and choice, negating both reason and emotion in a system that objectifies the former spectator. Subjected to soft control that avoids extremes, either of pain or pleasure, and with their minds 'fastened every moment of the day to a fine rigid frame' (32–3), the former spectators lose the power to imagine anything beyond immediate material conditions. Marching in the synchronized ranks of those who 'like to do what we ought' (42), the watched populace becomes an extension of the will of the state. The stage manager is thus replaced by the monitor, and the collective imagination is destroyed by a pervasive and irresistible central authority.

Churchill, emphasizing the fact that surveillance and direct control by state authority affect ever-broadening groups of people, overturns commonly accepted categories of the criminal and the law-abiding. So central is the questioning of these categories to the theme of the play that she focuses on the issue in several different ways. First, she specifies that most actors play both 'cop' and 'robber' roles. The doubling again disrupts the traditionally stable player/role relationship, but here the disruption helps to make visible the artificiality of societal distinctions between the criminal and non-criminal. Second, she builds the questioning of distinctions into some of the characters and situations. Vidocq, the sometime robber, sometime cop, deconstructs categories on which such distinctions are based. So protean that he has forgotten what his original features look like, he assumes one disguise after another in order to move easily between the law enforcement and criminal worlds. A key factor in Vidocq's approach to crime is the close proximity of police 'to that criminal class', so that they can 'take informers from it, know it like itself'; furthermore, to Pierre's prediction that 'crime will be eliminated', he replies 'not entirely eliminated, no. It is my profession' (20). In the vignettes showing Vidocq at work, the players freeze in tableau each time he makes an arrest; the visual image is the same as if Vidocq were carrying out a robbery. Similarly, in the later scene between the two conspirators, each confesses to being a police spy, retracts the confession, and confesses again until the audience cannot possibly know which one, if either, is the informer.

Churchill further questions the distinction between criminal and non-criminal through her portrayal of the behaviour deemed by the state to be unacceptable. Duval stole a leg of lamb because he was starving. Lafayette strangled his employer in an angry reaction to the man's bad treatment of him. Luc receives punishment from the Headmaster because he vomits at the sight of Duval's hand being cut off. The boy brought to the model reformatory has been sent there because he does not 'sleep at home' (40). The mental patient described by Pierre as an interesting case is a union organizer. A final point about the artificiality of criminal and non-criminal categories is made in Pierre's rehearsal of his speech. Now responsible for control of a 'whole city', Pierre randomly and crazily juxtaposes the categories of people under his control; 'the criminals . . . the sick . . . the workers . . . the ignorant . . . the unemployed . . . the insane' (49). All are to be subjected to similar types of control.

The Holidaymaker who encounters Pierre on the beach, and whose comment about the 'lovely day out for them' concludes the play blandly – and blindly, as the audience should understand by that point – accepts the abrupt death of one of the mental patients because he does not feel personally threatened by state power. He perceives himself as belonging to a category separate from that of the patients. Churchill's strong questioning of such categorical divisions, however, aims to prevent audience members from making such comfortable assumptions. In a world where kings no longer hold political power, the 'notorious regicide' sought but never seen on stage may be any member of the audience who resists the authority of the state. While Foucault writes about revolts against the model prisons, Churchill does not; she knows that resistance against an authoritarian system's 'very materiality as an instrument and vector of power'[51] must come from the spectators rather than from the spectacle.

Softcops emphasizes the static and hegemonic character of state power over the last hundred years of history by employing an all male cast. Asked about this choice, Churchill has stated that 'it would have been almost contrived to have included women because of what the play's about, a system of power operated by men'.[52] Peopling the stage exclusively with men (who were, in the original production, dressed identically in black tuxedos except when wearing the uniforms of prisoners or schoolboys) visually communicates the monolithic nature of state authority and indicates its potential power to reduce the diversity of voices and images in society. This play does not address gender explicitly, but does offer women, specifically, a possibility of empowerment. Leaving women out allows them a presence apart from the oppressor/victim pattern shown in the play. In the only 'role' given them – the inherently powerful one of spectator – women, even more than men in the audience, can construct their own relationship to the system of power represented.

In its disconnected and non-sequential episodes, *Softcops* questions a diachronic or progressive view of history. It raises the realistic spectre of modern authoritarian states which define criminality in ways that prevent political opposition, and in which all individuals are subjected to monolithic control and eventually denied the capacity for choice. At the same time, it empowers the audience through its suggestion that their use of imagination in their position as spectators arms them against authoritarian power. Ultimately, the play validates an inherently political function of theatre – and, by extension, all art forms.

Churchill's three 'history' plays initiate a dialectic between the human imagination and the material conditions of capitalist-patriarchal society. The powerless challenge social structures that oppress them by projecting their imagination beyond the limiting conditions under which they live. This imaginative potency takes different forms in each of the plays: armed rebellion, law-breaking, or simply voicing desire. Each of the plays testifies to the potential of collective imagination for catalyzing resistance, even in the face of overwhelming odds.

That the disruptive potential of creative imagination, often a theme in her previous work, re-emerges with even greater emphasis in this set of plays is probably related to the beginning of Churchill's involvement with collaborative groups, particularly Joint Stock. With these companies she worked in the outer fringe of the arts establishment, rehearsing in cheerless borrowed spaces of which one stage manager remarked disdainfully that even 'a Labour Party branch would have suspended standing orders and decamped to the local pub'.[53] Here she immersed herself, for the first time, in a collective process of creation. The collaborative process empowered Churchill to move beyond her individual boundaries of experience and perception. This process of exploration and discovery, which brought exhilaration and 'intense pleasure',[54] was one she attempted to duplicate for the audience. The plays deal with history, and with theatre itself, in a way that empowers the audience to go beyond the limitations of their individual experience, involving their minds in the momentum of collective events, ideas, or cycles as they take place on stage, in order to question them from a fresh perspective. The access to participation is reinforced, in all three works, by the before-during-after movement which encourages audiences to extend their own imaginations beyond the ending of the play.

Although Churchill's remaining plays do not directly focus on questions of history, her strong interest in re-examining historical images surfaces in the frequency with which she incorporates fragments of the past into plays set in the present. The first act of *Top Girls* assembles a group of women from history and mythology. Victorian colonialists play out their sexual attitudes in the first act of *Cloud Nine*. Ghosts from the past drift in and out of *Fen*. A scene from a Restoration play introduces the action of *Serious Money*. Thus, the relation to history continues to be an important preoccupation, though a subordinate theme, in later work.

6

Sex and Gender

Going from revision of history to a consideration of gender and change in contemporary relationships, Churchill abandoned the Brechtian terrain of the history plays, though not without taking from it some valuable freight, and set off in new directions prompted by her continuing impulse toward theatrical experimentation and expression of feminist insights into contemporary society. While originating structures and techniques, as well as combining those of diverse theatre periods and styles, Churchill remained close to the Brechtian spirit of encouraging the audience to actively criticize institutions and ideologies they had previously taken for granted, both in theatrical representation and in society itself. In *Cloud Nine, Three More Sleepless Nights*, and later plays which include the final version of *Softcops* discussed in Chapter 5 and the collaborative *A Mouthful of Birds*, Churchill links personal change with large-scale societal change, underscoring her belief in ordinary individuals' capacity to effect significant changes in themselves and their society.

CLOUD NINE

Cloud Nine explores the Victorian origins of contemporary gender definitions and sexual attitudes, recent changes in societal regulation of personal relationships, and some implications of these changes. It brings together issues of gender, sexuality, and power which had interested Churchill for many years, and which she continued to pursue in later work. *Cloud Nine* originated in 1978, with a three-week Joint Stock workshop. This workshop, like the previous one for *Light Shining in Buckinghamshire*, changed direction in the early stages: Max Stafford-Clark originally recruited Churchill for a play about emigration to America that was to be produced co-operatively with Joseph Papp's Public Theater in New York.

When funding for this project fell through, Churchill proposed the focus on sexual politics.[1] To research the subject, Churchill and Stafford-Clark decided to begin with personal experience. Workshop participants were therefore selected on the dual basis of acting experience and sexual perspective; the resulting group included male and female representatives of various heterosexual and homosexual lifestyles. Some members of the group had previously worked with Gay Sweatshop or other fringe companies on shows intended to promote sexual-political awareness; others were not initially familiar with the concept of sexual politics. During the research period, in addition to hearing guest speakers and sharing books, each member of the workshop took a turn to tell her or his life story and answer questions about personal sexual experiences. Led by Max Stafford-Clark, the actors participated in improvisations based on social status and social norm-breaking.

Cloud Nine gave Churchill her first experience of solid (though certainly not unanimous) critical acclaim. Opening at Dartington College in February of 1979, it toured and played in London that March at the Royal Court. A revival co-produced by the Royal Court and Joint Stock occurred in 1980. In 1981, the American director Tommy Tune mounted a New York production at the Theatre de Lys. Churchill, who attended rehearsals, agreed to some textual changes for this production, which subsequently won one of Broadway's Obie awards. *Cloud Nine* has been produced widely since, in various European countries, Australia, New Zealand, Japan, and Brazil.[2]

Cloud Nine challenges norms of consistent linearity through a theatrical manipulation of past and present. The first act is set during the height of the Victorian era, in an African country colonized by the British. In a manipulation of time similar to that in Virginia Woolf's novel *Orlando*, the second act takes place one hundred years later, in present-day London, but characters from the first act continued into the second age only twenty-five years. As Churchill explained in a 1983 interview, two important themes which emerged from the workshop formed the background of these choices:

> We explored Genet's idea that colonial oppression and sexual oppression are similar. And we explored the femininity of the colonized person . . . . Also people had talked in the workshop about their childhoods and what they had expected they would

be like as grown-ups . . . . Each person felt almost as if he or
she had started from a Victorian perspective and had, in their
lifetime, discovered possibilities of change.[3]

Sex and race reversals, in part a necessity given the particular
workshop group with which Churchill was working, contribute a
visual element to the play's explication of the ways in which gender
and colonial ideologies perpetuate themselves. In the first act, Betty
is played by a man; this cross-casting makes gender visible by separating feminine gender from the female body. Joshua, an African
devoted to his colonial masters, is played by a white; in this case,
the reversal exposes the rupture in Joshua's identity caused by his
internalization of colonial values. Edward, a little boy who attempts
to elude traditional role expectations, is played by a woman, and
here the cross-casting illuminates the role of socialization in the
formation of gender identity. In the second act, there is only one
example of cross-casting. Cathy, the preschool-aged girl, 'is played
by a man', to quote Churchill's introduction to the play, 'partly as a
simple reversal of Edward being played by a woman, partly because
the size and presence of a man on stage seemed appropriate to the
emotional force of young children, and partly, as with Edward, to
show more clearly the issues involved in learning what is considered correct behaviour for a girl'.[4]

The play begins with a song,'Come Gather Sons of England', a
spirited evocation of British imperialism. Clive, the paterfamilias,
then introduces (in rhymed couplets) the members of his household.
Betty, his wife, describes herself in this way:

> I live for Clive. The whole aim of my life
> Is to be what he looks for in a wife.
> I am a man's creation, as you see,
> And what men want is what I want to be. (251)[5]

Similarly, the house-servant Joshua ends his introduction with the
statement, 'What white men want is what I want to be' (251).
Edward echoes this desire to please Clive, saying, 'What father
wants I'd dearly like to be. I find it rather hard as you can see'
(251). The rest of the household, presented with an encompassing
wave of the hand by Clive, includes the governess Ellen, Clive's
mother-in-law Maud, and the daughter Victoria, who is 'played'
by a doll.

Action begins when Clive's arrival home after a day of touring native villages brings Betty in haste to take off his boots, soothe his weariness, and complain that the servant Joshua refuses to pay her the proper respect. Clive reports that an old friend, Harry Bagley, is coming to visit them. A neighbour, Mrs. Saunders, arrives unexpectedly just as Harry does, seeking refuge from a native uprising. In the relative safety of this compound patrolled by Joshua, who has been armed with a gun by Clive, the assembled individuals pursue personal predilections, social antipathies, and sexual affinities. Edward covertly plays with his sister's doll, but keeps getting caught and lectured about manliness. Maud gives unwanted advice to Betty and snipes at Mrs. Saunders, the independent widow. Betty is infatuated with Harry and the adventure of his jungle explorations; her desire, however, clashes both with Harry's idealization of her and with the demands of being a good wife, mother, and daughter. Harry has casual sex with Joshua and continues a guilt-ridden sexual relationship with Edward, who insists to his 'Uncle Harry' that he wants 'to do it again' (270). Clive incessantly pursues Mrs. Saunders, claiming her presence causes him to suffer a perpetual erection. Ellen, when not scolding Edward or displaying Victoria, yearns after Betty. Joshua observes everything and reports much of it to Clive.

While the group contrives to hold a Christmas picnic in spite of the danger, hostilities mount both inside and outside the compound. Acting on hints that his own stable boys have become involved in the rebellion, Clive has them flogged. Caught playing with the doll again, Edward screams a defiance he quickly retracts when his father appears. Joshua informs Clive of the tryst between Betty and Harry at the picnic, and Clive confronts his wife. When Clive approaches Harry on the same subject, the latter inadvertently reveals his homosexuality. Outraged, Clive demands that Harry redeem himself through marriage. Together they enlist the unhappy Ellen as the bride. Clive, meanwhile, is placed in an embarrassing position when British soldiers kill Joshua's parents. Joshua refuses sympathy, saying to Clive, 'You are my father and mother' (284). He then gives Clive his latest intelligence – that Ellen loves Betty – but Clive refuses to believe it and orders Joshua out of his sight. The wedding, though disrupted by accusations of theft and a fight between Betty and Mrs. Saunders, joins the two reluctant partners. As Clive toasts the bride and groom, Joshua aims a gun at him, while Edward covers his ears, and a stage blackout engulfs this final tableau.

Act Two begins on a radically different note, with Cathy chanting a scatological rhyme and brandishing a toy gun as she plays in the park. Cathy's mother Lin chats with Victoria, who has come to the park with her (always offstage) son Tommy. Vic, now a middle-class professional whose husband 'helps with the washing up' and Lin, a working-class lesbian, form a relationship that transcends their often conflicting perspectives (291). Vic's brother Edward, who works as a gardener in the park, has a lover named Gerry. Their mother Betty has just divorced Clive. All are involved in working out sexual and relationship problems and exploring new options.

In scenes that maintain the texture of everyday life, adults confront or comfort one another, children get lost or injured – and treated, at different times, with tenderness, impatience, or indulgence – and personal changes multiply, punctuated by music. Lin and Vic become lovers. Edward adjusts to Gerry's abandonment of their exclusive relationship, then becomes involved in a *ménage à trois* with Lin and Vic. Martin, who has put great pressure on Vic for personal and sexual perfection, accepts her decision to live apart from him and co-operates with Edward and Lin in taking care of Tommy and Cathy. Betty initially experiences great anxiety about her new independence, but grows to appreciate it. Having rediscovered her own sexuality, she recognizes the unorthodox sexual choices of her children, and finally makes a first attempt at initiating a new relationship – though she mistakenly directs it toward the gay Gerry.

Victorianism has not been entirely laid to rest, despite all the evidence of sexual liberation: its ghosts drift through the second act. In the midst of a mirthful invocation of a mythical goddess staged in the park after hours by Vic, Lin, and Edward, Lin sees her brother who was killed in Northern Ireland. As Betty sheds the restrictions of Victorian attitudes, spectral figures from Act One appear and admonish her. In a final statement of her desire and strength to face the future, Betty of Act Two wordlessly embraces the spectre of her Act One incarnation.

Several versions of *Cloud Nine* exist. The major variation is in the placement of Betty's monologue in Act Two. For the first American production directed in New York by Tommy Tune, Churchill permitted the monologue to be moved to the end, just preceding the final Betty/Betty embrace; this version of the script is found in the French's acting edition. As Churchill observes in her introduction to the 1984 Methuen edition, this change provides the play with 'more of an emotional climax' appropriate to the 'broader . . . more emotional' style of that production.[6] She has also noted that it emphasized 'Betty as an individual', rather than 'the development of a group of people'.[7] In the most recent editions, Churchill has expressed preference for the original placement of the monologue: 'On the whole, I prefer the play not to end with Betty's self-discovery but with her moving beyond that to a first attempt to make a new relationship with someone else.'[8] For this analysis, the most recent Methuen edition of the play, with earlier placement of the monologue, will be used.

Doubling of roles is an important component of *Cloud Nine's* conception. A single company performs the entire play, members being given different roles for the first and second acts. Characters are, in fact, constructed in such a way that they cannot be played by the same actor in both acts. In addition, one actor usually plays the roles of both Ellen and Mrs. Saunders in Act One – a doubling that sharpens the comedic edge of the scene where Harry asks first Mrs. Saunders, then Ellen, to marry him. Connections between a player's Act One and Act Two characters develop with whatever combinations are used for doubling. Churchill, while suggesting various possibilities, states that, as long as the cross-casting requirements are observed, 'the doubling can be done in any way that seems right for any particular production'.[9]

Cloud Nine empowers through a multi-leveled paradigm of change. Crucial to this paradigm is the two-act structure that emphasizes discontinuity through contrasting dramatic styles, different time periods, and partly different casts of characters. Act One relies on the British tradition of a farcical clash between outrageous physical vitality and a rigid behavioural code.[10] In *Cloud Nine's* first act, the Victorian moral code is given substance in the language, music, use of space, and form of action. Speech is stiffly formal, with minimal use of contractions or shortened names. Accents, except for Joshua's, are upper-class, resulting in a uniform sound for nearly all dialogue. Martial and sentimental music points up the interplay of family, religion, and nation in the given order. Space divides sharply into inside and outside, with the veranda serving as a bridge. Action similarly splits into categories of work and play. Comedically colliding with these rigid social forms are the incongruous visual images and unbridled vitality of the characters as they pursue outrageous desires, overstep the bounds of game-playing, and attempt to outrun retribution for their transgressions. Action moves at a breakneck pace, drawing together the various subplots relating to the native rebellion and frustrated love interests. The climactic marriage scene fuses the related issues of colonialism, gender oppression, and sexual repression in its final moment. The first act takes place within the enclosed world of the Victorian household, framed in the idealized unity of the opening tableau. Clive, who governs by patriarchy's and colonialism's divine right, constitutes the stable sun at the centre of this microcosm. His desire is law. He has the power to coerce Mrs. Saunders into having sex with him and then condemn Betty for a flirtation with Harry. He reviles Harry's homosexuality but simply refuses to acknowledge Ellen's. When Clive's affair with Mrs. Saunders becomes obvious, he shifts the blame for it onto her, ordering her to leave and embracing Betty with renewed affection, while Maud gloats, 'one flesh, you see' (287). Thus, Clive defines sexuality and sexual standards in the way that best serves his own sexual desires; everything else is deviant.

Wielding the patriarchal sceptre of linguistic authority, Clive controls the language of sexual desire. He pursues Mrs. Saunders with an outpouring of words dramatizing the 'appalling physical suffering' her 'disgustingly capricious' refusals cause him (263). Mrs. Saunders' monosyllables, whether 'stop' or 'don't stop', enable her only to respond, never initiate (and are consistently overruled by Clive). Harry's access to power gives him the language to approach Joshua directly to 'go in a barn and fuck' (262), and Joshua almost wordlessly complies. Harry's sexuality, however, remains locked in the subject/object pattern established by Clive – and hidden in marginal spaces such as the barn – until Clive seems to construct homosexuality as central to the given order in his words about a special relationship 'between men' (282). When Harry's action in response to this apparent definition brings a shocked demand for clarification from Clive, Harry can only repeat Clive's own words back to him.

Lack of ability to express sexual desire directly characterizes those with little power. Edward lacks the vocabulary of sex, as well as the means to command, but still communicates his desire to Harry in fairly direct terms: 'You know what we did when you were here before. I want to do it again' (270). Betty, who is less powerful than her son, can only express her desire indirectly, as a function of male desire for her: 'Please want me' (261). Her wish that Harry would 'stroke my hair . . . put his arm around my waist . . . kiss me again' shows that objectification defines even her experience of sexuality (271). The lesbian Ellen can express her desire for Betty only by attempting to place herself in the imaginary space created by Betty's fantasy of Harry. Her attempts to communicate are misinterpreted as joking, friendship, or mental confusion by Betty and denied access to meaning by Clive.

Clive's language of power enforces the opposition between subject and object on both women and colonized people, as is evident in parallels between patriarchal concepts of woman and Western European concepts of Africa in his speech. Clive compares Mrs. Saunders to Africa: 'You are dark like this continent. Mysterious. Treacherous' (263). He links suspicions of Betty's infidelity with threats from the natives, saying to her, 'This whole continent is my enemy . . . I sometimes feel it will break over me and swallow me up . . . we must resist this dark female lust, Betty, or it will swallow us up' (277). To Harry, Clive declares, 'There is something dark about women, that threatens what is best in us' (282). This identification divides women and Africans both from each other and within themselves, because they have been taught to hate the image of the other projected onto themselves.[11] Betty disowns and promises to resist her sexual desire. Joshua, who confirms a connection between women and Africa in the myth about a mother goddess he tells Edward, rejects Africa in the hatred of women shown both in his treatment of Betty and his stabbing of the doll. The tension between Betty and Joshua serves Clive by preventing any internal coalition against his power.

With the household patterned on and participating in the larger construct of Empire, ideas of duty conflate loyalty to Clive and loyalty to the Empire. Sexual non-conformity thus implies covert resistance to authority. Clive informs Betty that if she were unfaithful to him it would be his duty to expel her from the family. Harry's guilt over betraying the ideals of family and Empire through his homosexuality has sent him 'into the jungle to hide' (283). Clive attributes the fall of the Roman Empire to homosexuality, and urges Harry to get married for the sake of England. When Ellen begs to stay with Betty, she is told, 'Women have their duty as soldiers have. You must be a mother if you can' (281). Edward explicitly links his effeminate behaviour to rejection of his father, when he shouts, after being caught with the doll in the wake of the floggings, 'I don't want to be like papa. I hate papa' (275).

As father both to 'the natives here' and his 'family so dear' (251), Clive exercises two types of authority, illustrating the difference between establishing control and maintaining it. Little force is used against the women and children, and it tends to be symbolic, as when Maud slaps the doll as an example to Vicky and declares, 'There, now she's a good baby' (275). Women require only the 'soft' methods of control because their socialization inculcates patriarchal ideology and because the system allows them a degree of power over servants and children. Edward's curiosity about the adults' agitation at the end of scene four activates the household's internal power hierarchy. Ellen says, 'Go inside, Edward. I shall tell your mother,' and Betty immediately follows this threat with, 'Go inside, Edward at once. I shall tell your father' (285). The self-denial to which women condition themselves and their children stands out in Betty's scolding of Edward: 'You're a horrid wicked boy and papa will beat you. Of course you don't hate him, you love him' (275). Africans, however, have not yet been 'tamed' by imperialist ideology. Clive wants to 'bring them all to be like Joshua', who has internalized oppression, but relies on violence in the meantime.

Clive's authoritarian control, while never totally effective in eliminating deviant desire, enforces its standards on public behaviour and denies suspect individuals the opportunity for privacy. Betty, suspect because of her gender, has great difficulty finding a moment alone with Harry, and even then is spied upon by Joshua. As Harry explains: 'You are a mother. And a daughter. And a wife' (268). Only in a game of hide-and-seek can she momentarily elude the roles that hem her in. Collusive agents within the household extend Clive's control. Edward is monitored constantly by mother, grandmother, and governess – all of whom forbid him to play with the doll.

Adult males, who share in Clive's privilege as long as they acknowledge his dominance and maintain proper behaviour in public, have the most privacy in which to pursue forbidden desires, as Harry and Joshua show. Joshua loses his position of relative privilege when he dares to speak the unspeakable. When it becomes apparent to him that Harry has abused his privileges, Clive first reacts with fear of the 'contagious' element that has penetrated his private domain. Clive soon recovers his sense of power and immediately begins to treat Harry differently, demanding that he cover his homosexuality with the public ceremony of marriage and proposing for him a mate who will limit his privacy – someone, Clive suggests, to 'go with you on your expeditions' (283). The contagion Clive fears has, however, taken root in his household, and Clive's troubles multiply. It is the ultimate futility of monitoring all private behaviour that threatens to destroy Clive's personal empire by the end of the first act.

The enclosed world of the first act disallows explicit questions within its context. The presentation of that world, however, demands a critical response from the audience. Clearly, an important element in this presentation is the cross-casting which challenges assumptions that gender and social definitions are natural concomitants of physical differences. The inconsistency between Betty's gender and sex sets up a reciprocity between player and role that exposes every gesture and speech to question, as each gesture or speech becomes a gest of gender construction. The ambiguity of Betty's pairings with other characters extends the questioning to sexuality. Betty and Harry may be viewed as either a heterosexual or homosexual couple, depending on whether one perceives Betty in terms of gender or biology. Clive (played by a man) tenderly embraces Betty (played by a man), but pulls away in revulsion from the embrace of Harry (played by a man). He thus indicates a rejection less of Harry's maleness than of Harry's non-subordinate role. These interactions accentuate the part played by power relations in constructing sexual identity and sexual relationships.

The use of space within the first act suggests further questions regarding power and sexual attitudes. Most activities, whether sexual or non-sexual, take place in open spaces – on the veranda of the house or on the grounds of the compound. The one visible example of confinement in an enclosed space occurs in scene three, when all the women (except Mrs. Saunders) remain inside a room with the blinds drawn, while the males carry out the flogging of the stable boys. The enclosure thus functions primarily to segregate the women under the guise of protection, excluding them from viewing or understanding the exercise of control. Mrs. Saunders, of course, leaves the room, determined to appropriate for herself the power of knowledge. Betty, on the other hand, later demonstrates her inability to control Joshua when she issues an order to him but is met with sexually insinuating insults until she turns the task of enforcing the order over to Edward.

Comedy serves a crucial function in eliciting questions from the audience while creating enjoyment. The 'comic attitude', according to Alice Rayner, 'takes any object for its material and inverts our perspective on it'.[12] When the object taken by the play is gender, or any given power configuration, the comic attitude is inherently analytic, serving to unsettle habitual perceptions. Comic analysis in *Cloud Nine* reveals what had been hidden and empowers audiences to overcome ingrained habits of acceptance. Comedic dialogue and action throughout the play reinforce the questioning of stereotype initiated by the cross-casting. Betty's introduction explaining the split image of her appearance: 'I am a man's creation as you see', encourages the audience to see with freshly critical eyes during and after the performance (251). Informed that Ellen is unhappy, the elderly Maud who has long been relegated to the ranks of the sexless and invisible, observes acidly, 'Young women are never happy. Then when they're older they look back and see that comparatively speaking they were ecstatic' (261). In a game of catch at the picnic, Betty claims to be unable to throw a ball, despite the competent display of skill she has just given. Abandoning all pretense of dignity, Clive chases and begs Mrs. Saunders, but emerges from under her skirt to immediately resume his role as enforcer of tidiness and decorum.

Questions, finally, arise out of the pain that is inseparable from humor in this comedy. Referring to rehearsals for the original production in her introduction to the play, Churchill states that 'we were initially taken by how funny the first act was and then by the painfulness of the relationships – which then became more funny than when they had seemed purely farcical' (246). Beyond the mixups and misdirected passion lie the unbreachable walls of propriety which ensure that first-act characters find more frustration and shame than pleasure in their attempts to stretch its limits. Even Clive seems able to achieve only momentary relief from an oppressive sex drive. While his fantasy of sex with Mrs. Saunders involves an extravagant scenario of poisoned arrows, his actual experience of it produces only the matter-of-fact observations, 'I came . . . I'm all sticky' (264). Of course, the less powerful characters show an even stronger element of pathos. The continual lies and subterfuge to which they must resort in the attempt to reconcile their sexuality with their roles call those roles into question. Breaking the sentence of simple generic categorization, the painful/funny characters and situations confound identification at the same time that they demand it. At the end of the first act, genuine tragedy does threaten to engulf the comedy, as the walls of propriety close in to solidify the new union of Harry and Ellen. In the very moment they achieve the frozen representation of unity, however, they dissolve.

As the second act begins, changes in time, place, and attitude come alive immediately in the language of the oversized Cathy, chanting, 'Yum yum bubblegum. Stick it up your mother's bum' (289). The emphasis on role playing in the presentation of Cathy by an adult male affects perception of the more realistically presented adults, allowing maximum distance and conscious playfulness. The playground setting – a space doubly encoded with the openness of play – has fluid boundaries that accommodate an ever-changing mixture of styles, activities, and personal choices. A variety of accents and verbal rhythms, some carrying forward the legato speech of the first act, some with the staccato rhythm and slangy, obscenity-laced flavor of London street talk, jostle each other in the realistic conversational exchanges. The casually joyous 'Cloud Nine' song which drifts in and out of Act Two celebrates freedom and diversity through its overlapping voices. Questions about definition and authority pervade this contemporary world of the play and are asked explicitly, both in moments of conflict or reflection, and in moments of comedy perceived as such by other characters on stage – such as when Cathy makes one of her outrageous remarks. The slower pace of Act Two, evident from the beginning in the frequent pauses and meandering conversation, gives audiences time to consider the more difficult and complex issues of choice raised by the action.

The relationship between characters and social forms reverses that of the first act, with the new freedoms challenging characters to overcome their inertia. Cathy brings into this act the farcical energy that animated the first one, and with it she frequently disrupts the realistic interactions of the other characters. The soldier who interrupts the invocation of the goddess with his outburst of barely coherent anger – and who is played by the same actor playing Cathy – similarly dislocates the jocular, but realistic, proceedings, with his disturbing and ambiguous presence. At the end, spectral visitors from Act One bring into the world of present-day realism their messages and their determination not to be forgotten. The final image – an embrace of the realistically imagined and the playfully invented characters of Betty – uses an unexpected theatrical combination to ally the defiant energy of the first act with the greater possibilities of the second.

By juxtaposing a strong contemporary image against vivid images of the past, Act Two focuses on changes in the structure of power and authority, as they affect sex and relationships. Churchill, in a reflection upon the values within her play, states in the introduction to *Cloud Nine* that 'all the characters in this act change a little for the better'.[13] Definitive alteration of power relations, however, proves neither easy nor predictable for these representatives of contemporary life. In a world devoid of the stable centre provided by Clive, and without the threatening nearness of a vast region of the unknown, freedom engenders uncertainty. Only Lin, the lesbian mother who reverses the position of Ellen in Act One, seems able to make decisions without constant questioning; the other characters seem stymied by their very wealth of possibility. Cathy's restless indecisiveness in the first scene, as she responds to her mother's activity suggestions with 'no . . . already done that . . . I don't want to paint', sets the mood for much of the exploration and questioning that takes place within the second act.

With its setting in the public space of a park emphasizing the degree to which sexuality and sexual choices have been brought into the open, the second act presents progressively stronger examples of sexual taboo-breaking, as it tests the limits of the new freedom. In the first scene, Lin tells Vic that she is lesbian and straightforwardly initiates a relationship with her. Later, both Gerry and Betty explicitly describe previously hidden sexual behaviour – for Gerry, homosexual sex with a stranger in a train compartment, and for Betty, masturbation. By the end of the act, Lin, Vic, and Edward have entered into a sexual relationship with one another. This three-way relationship which is simultaneously homosexual, heterosexual, and incestuous, takes its participants near the boundaries of contemporary tolerance as it evokes possibilities beyond any simple pairing based on 'difference, antagonism, and exchange',[14] and challenges perhaps the most pervasive taboo, which has also been linked with the 'exchange of women'.[15]

Language expands, in this contemporary world, to name previously unthought desires. Ability to communicate sexual desire follows a pattern contrary to that of the first act, with the women and gay characters expressing themselves more freely than the male heterosexual, and the others adapting their language. Lin asks Vic directly, 'Will you have sex with me?' (296). Gerry and Betty, in their monologues, vividly convey the different ways in which they find sexual excitement and pleasure. Edward appropriates language, humorously but effectively, and uses it to communicate his particular meaning when he says, at the end of scene two, 'I think I'm a lesbian' (307). In her series of questions to Lin – 'Would you love me if I went to Manchester . . . if I went on a climbing expedition in the Andes mountains . . . if my teeth fell out . . . if I loved ten other people?' – Vic struggles to define a relationship free of the patriarchal patterns of domination and objectification, whether hetero- or homosexual (302). Martin, by contrast, expresses his desire only through reference to the response of his female partner, insisting to Vic, 'My one aim is to give you pleasure. My one aim is to give you rolling orgasms like I do other women' (300). At the same time, Martin feels so threatened by talking about sex, referring to it as 'taking in technical information', that he loses his desire (300).

In contrast to the inhibiting influence of societal condemnation in the first act, the norm-breaking of the second occurs against a social background in which neutral acceptance predominates. Of course, the spectre of Clive in Act One dress appears at the end to voice disapproval of Betty's independence and connect her rebellion against Victorian sexual mores to a predicted 'communist' sweep of Africa, but he is now barely even marginal to the lives of the Act Two characters. Even Martin accepts and supports Vic's sexual liaison with Lin and Edward. Edward, the only character to show a fear of condemnation, initially worries that he will lose his job if it becomes known that he is gay, despite Lin's dismissal of the risk, but his worries only impose a hush-hush quality on his conversations with Gerry. Gerry speaks openly and directly in his monologue, and Edward loses his inhibitions as the act progresses. That the norms themselves are changing is obvious in the socialization of Cathy: Lin equips her with a toy gun and encourages her aggressiveness.

Increasing casualness about varieties of sexual behaviour, while offering greater range for personal pleasure, tends to dissociate sexual non-conformity from political resistance. When Vic, Lin, and Edward playfully drag Martin into participation in the 'orgy' through which they drunkenly invoke a mythical goddess, he reacts with relief: 'If all we're talking about is having a lot of sex there's no problem' (310). Location of the action in a place intended primarily for children's recreation, warns that the changes taking place concern an area of life that has been devalued as it has been accorded greater individual discretion.

The persistence of relationship patterns from the first act strengthens this note of warning. Martin, like Clive before him, seeks to define women to fit his needs. He is 'writing a novel about women from the women's point of view', and attempts to control Vic in insidious ways, such as implying that her sexual unresponsiveness makes him unhappy and complaining that her indecisiveness over a proposed job change hurts his image of himself. The always absent Tommy, like the doll Victoria, serves adult needs by his non-presence. Cathy, despite (or because of) her untraditional rearing, wants dresses, earrings, and a 'perm'. In an attempt to protect her, Edward and Vic conceal from their mother the truth about their sexual choices, just as Clive concealed knowledge of the rebellion in the first act. All of the characters, as Churchill states, make changes in their personal lives, but they all emphatically acknowledge the difficulty of doing so. Late in the act, as he argues with Lin about the child care responsibilities he has assumed, Martin insists, 'I work very hard at not being like this,' and she replies, 'It's hard for me too' (318).

In fact, while sexual patterns show themselves somewhat resistant to change, patterns of societal power are yet more resistant, proving the adaptability of the prevailing power structure in the process of maintaining itself. Lin has gained the freedom to express lesbian desire without being sanctioned for it, but remains limited to the low-level jobs, such as clerk in a clothing store, open to a working-class woman. While working-class people take an active part in the social reconfigurations of the second act, even the symbolic black person of the first act has disappeared. Cultural representation of female power, which is seen in the futile attempt to invoke the fertility goddess, remains marginal, referred to only in the after-dark and alcohol-assisted rite. Even then, despite the aura of impossibility that comes to pervade the scene, the mythical goddess does not appear. Instead, the invocation only attracts the attention of Martin and provokes the appearance of the unidenti-fied and unsubstantiated British soldier who testifies to England's continuing, if reduced, capacity to dominate and oppress.

Within the context of a group of people adjusting to the amor-phous perplexity created by the absence of an external authority figure, Betty provides the most dramatic example of change in the second act. Now played by a woman because, as Churchill states, 'she gradually becomes real to herself',[16] Betty divorces Clive at the beginning of the act but nevertheless retains the strongest ties of any character to the past. In spite of leaving her husband, Betty at first seems unable to overcome her patterns of dependency. Each new situation calls forth her feelings of inadequacy and her fear of being alone. Disadvantaged by the helplessness she had cultivated as a sign of femininity, she says, 'I'll never be able to manage. If I can't even walk down the street by myself. Everything looks so fierce' (298). Her previous conditioning shows up, furthermore, in her comment to Lin that 'I've never been so short of men's company that I've had to bother with women' (301) and in her refusal to acknowledge the real nature of the relationship between Lin, Vic, and Edward. Betty's empowerment over the circumstances in her life begins when she starts to earn money. Announcing that she has been working as a receptionist in a doctor's office, Betty shows Cathy her money and later buys ice cream for the others. Having indicated her growing independence by sending the others off so that she can be alone, Betty describes her experience of masturbating for the first time since childhood. She concludes by relating this previously forbidden pleasure to a new sense of herself:

> I felt triumphant because I was a separate person from them. And I cried because I didn't want to be. But I don't cry about it any more. Sometimes I do it three times in one night and it really is great fun. (316)

Betty's recognition of her value as a 'separate person' leads to a new plane of activity, in which she tries new patterns of relating. First, she offers Vic acceptance and acknowledgment of her sexual choices, proposing to buy a house in which their entire alternate family could live together. Lin is willing to consider this arrangement, but this time it is Vic who seems reluctant to change established patterns, protesting, 'But mummy we don't even like each other' (317). Betty's wistful, 'We might begin to' gets swallowed up by a crisis as Cathy comes in crying with her nose bleeding. In her next speech to her mother, however, Vic does call her 'Betty' rather than 'mummy'. When Gerry comes along, Betty initiates a conversation with him and discusses the pleasures of living alone. She invites him to her flat, vaulting over the confining walls of decorum by reasoning, 'if there isn't a right way to do things you have to invent one' (319). Though embarrassed when she understands that Gerry is gay, she remains open to initiating future relationships. Betty's attempt to pick up Gerry, while not wholly dissimilar to her hopeless infatuation with Harry in Act One, indicates, in its directness and unromanticized expression of her desire for companionship, an increasing ability to assert her own needs in forming new relationships.

The second act ends with the embrace of Betty from Act One and Betty from Act Two. While this is the final image of the play, it would be inconsistent with the theme of change and the process of open-ended questioning to view this embrace in terms of traditional closure.[17] It occurs in the wake of the two rejections by those with whom Betty has attempted to establish a new type of intimacy, and after condemnations by the spectral figures of Maud and Clive from Act One. The embrace does not integrate past and present or the two characters. Rather, it shows that Betty of Act Two now feels herself, for the first time, to be separate from her Act One self, but acknowledges as well their continuing oneness. The embrace evokes Luce Irigaray's characterization of female sexuality as simultaneously one and more than one:

> A woman 'touches herself' constantly without anyone being able to forbid her to do so, for her sex is composed of two lips which embrace continuously. Thus, within herself she is already two – but not divisible into ones who stimulate each other.[18]

Touch transmits the consciousness of a reciprocal relationship between past and present. Just as the past continues to live on in the present, in the form of held-over attitudes and patterns of relating, so the seeds of present change were contained in the little girl masturbating 'under the kitchen table' or the 'man's creation' that was Clive's wife (316, 251). The double image of the embrace breaks apart the unitary patriarchal construction of woman and creates an empowering moment of theatrical doubleness for women audience members.

Because of the magnitude of Betty's shift in attitude, and because for her the issues of sex and relationships have remained an integral part of her place in society, the change she undergoes is far-reaching in its symbolic significance, both for Betty as an individual and for the society around her. For Betty, sexual change is fundamental change; her difficult and deeply experienced struggle, unlike Martin's limited accommodation, leaves no area of her life untouched. Her attainment of greater sexual freedom follows the achievement of economic independence, supporting Vic's glib but significant statement that 'you can't separate fucking and economics' (309). Her new openness, moreover, overrides class distinctions: she tries to pick up the working-class Gerry. That Betty, the most repressed Act One character, takes control of her fate and moves in radically new and positive directions offers a statement of hope. The suggestion that even in Act One Betty contained the seeds of resistance and the capacity for change additionally encourages the reclamation of history, including the often invisible or misrepresented women of the past. The play thus structures a reciprocal relationship between the individual and society, challenging, as does Brecht, 'the traditional belief in the continuity and unity of the self',[19] apart from environmental or historical circumstances, by showing individuals in two very different historical contexts and exploring the ways in which they constitute and are constituted by these societies.

In discussing the play with interviewers, Churchill has transferred some responsibility and credit for sexual and societal change to older and non-middle-class women who may not have associated themselves with feminism. She tells this story of an unexpected participant in the workshop, a woman who ran the snack bar in the building where the company met:

> She wanted us to sit down and drink our tea and not stand about making a lot of noise. But she gradually became friendly. And finally she came forward, voluntarily, with amazing braveness, and did what each of us had done in turn – which was to sit on a chair in front of everybody else and talk about her childhood and her life. She had come from a large, poor family, had married at sixteen, and had a very violent and unhappy marriage, with no pleasure from sex at all . . . and after thirty years she had remarried. She told us in quite a bit of detail how she and her new husband gradually got their relationship together. Finally she said: 'We may not do it as often as you young people, but when we have our organisms [sic], we're on Cloud Nine.'[20]

Basing the title of the play in the authority of this woman's (and her husband's) experience gives evidence of Churchill's recognition in all people, even those not possessed of education or a high-status job, the potential for personal empowerment and change through the enjoyment of sexual pleasure previously denied by societal constraints.[21]

Cloud Nine shows Churchill in a different relationship to historical material than in her history plays. The farcical misery and sometimes bizarre fictions of the first act make for a deliberately artificial construction of the past. Churchill originally conceived of the entire play as occurring in the present, then seized upon the idea of setting the first act in Victorian times as a means of dramatizing the idea of Victorian restrictions on sex and relationships. Therefore, the entire first act serves as a reference point within the second, rather than an episode preceding it.

In *Cloud Nine*, Churchill uses the discontinuity of dream, rather than a logical progression of events, to represent change, creating gaps – including that left open at the end – which can only be bridged by imagination. The contrasts between the first act's farcically painful dilemmas and the second's contemporary quandaries, as well as the variety of perspective, image, and style evident in the second, defy reduction to a single viewpoint or clear conclusion. The radical time shift between the first and second acts similarly disrupts the development of plot or character through a unified narrative.

Lack of completion characterizes the end of both acts and of the play itself. In the first act, closure of the forced marriage is interrupted by Joshua's aiming of the gun, followed by the stage blackout, which signals the imminence of – but also does not complete – the destruction of the Victorian way of life. The second act's final image is that of Betty embracing her Act One counterpart, but this image both celebrates Betty's breaking away from old restrictions and evokes the autoerotic pleasure of the self touching the self. Both in the two-act structure and in Betty's second-act transformation, the play offers 'before' and 'during' movements, but ends there. It thus invites the audience, which has imaginatively bridged the gaps within the play, to go beyond the patently artificial ending of the Betty/Betty embrace, initiate its own experimentation with roles, and imagine its own 'after'.

While it deals frankly with the subject of orgasm, and offers a great deal of discussion about it, *Cloud Nine* does not represent the experience (though it comes closest when Clive obtains a measure of satisfaction while hidden under Mrs. Saunders' skirts). A necessarily personal release into the 'cloud nine' of non-objectified and non-objectifying pleasure would probably be inhibited, rather than enhanced, by such a representation. Instead, the play empowers audiences, through its communicative density and its deconstruction of theatrical doubleness, to go beyond the theatricality of the ending and the artificiality of the play to discover new areas of possibility for themselves. The fusion of opposing styles and viewpoints in the first act makes it possible to understand the characters and situations both as farcical symbols of Victorian attitudes and as painful examples of human dilemmas. The stylistic inconsistency and multiple viewpoint of the second act makes accessible to audiences the potential of the unexpected and undirected insights that may arise out of improvised play. Thus, historicized constraint is shown in a reciprocal relation to the inherent capacity to analyse, challenge, and re-create. The cross-casting promotes conscious awareness of the doubleness of the theatrical representation: exposing this usually hidden assumption inverts its function. Rather than serving as an instrument of repression, the exposed doubleness allows the audience to ask explicit questions about the true or false sexualities and roles presented in varying combinations. The continuation of this exposure in the second act, through the cross-casting of Cathy, provokes a complex of questions about the future. Far from being a reassuring reification of patriarchy's construction of subjectivity, Cathy's role exhibits a caricature of contemporary masculinity. Cathy, like the other cross-cast combinations (and the final Betty–Betty embrace) presents a choice of two opposites that can neither stand alone nor be synthesized. Instead, these double images create an imaginable space for representing what has not yet been represented and demand an 'after' – an as yet uncreated alternative to the 'man's creation' of gender division.

For Churchill, an interest in the interaction of private sexuality and public behavioural norms went back as far as her earliest radio plays. *Cloud Nine*, however, reverberates with a polyphonal intensity clearly derived from the workshop. It incorporates the immediate experience, the multiple viewpoints, the sometimes conflicting voices, and the creative energy of the different people brought together for it. The limiting factors of writing roughly equal roles for a particular group of people and meeting a tight schedule interacted with the expansive element of the workshop, as Churchill makes clear in her discussions of working with Joint Stock, to both inspire and challenge her. Though *Cloud Nine* deals with a central issue of feminism, it is not a women's play in the sense of being based solely on the experiences and perspectives of a woman. Churchill insisted upon including the viewpoints of both men and women; for example, when Max Stafford-Clark suggested that perhaps a woman should direct the play, she asserted that his stake in the subject of sexual politics was as great as hers.[22] Churchill's vision of empowerment through non-exploitative pleasure thus addresses similar capacities and needs among homo- and heterosexuals, men and women.

THREE MORE SLEEPLESS NIGHTS

Soon after *Cloud Nine*, Churchill wrote a short play titled *Three More Sleepless Nights*, in which she continues the exploration of sexual politics in three traditional, heterosexual relationships. Written without the collaborative input of a workshop, it was directed by Les Waters and produced early in 1980 by Soho Poly, a small fringe theatre which had earlier adapted Churchill's radio play *Perfect Happiness*. Later in the same year, *Three More Sleepless Nights* was presented as a visiting production at the Royal Court Theatre Upstairs. Its proximity to *Cloud Nine* in terms of when it was written, its similar subject matter, and its brevity all combine to suggest that *Three More Sleepless Nights* represents spillover – things Churchill perhaps wanted to say but could not fit into *Cloud Nine*. This play, to a much greater extent than *Cloud Nine*, acknowledges the difficulty of change within intimate relationships.

Three More Sleepless Nights takes place in three scenes, in three different bedrooms. The set remains simply a double bed. The first scene focuses on a late-night quarrel between Frank, a working-class man, and his wife Margaret. She is angry that he has come home late again and accuses him of having been with another woman. He interrupts her with surly commands to 'shut it', claiming to have been at the pub (1).[23] Though they set the alarm and turn off the light, the two continue quarreling rather than going to sleep. Margaret berates Frank for his personal habits, reproaches him for limiting her to housewifery when she 'could have been a model, could have been a hairdresser, could have been a shorthand typist', and disparages the other woman (2). Frank complains that Margaret is sexually unresponsive, does not care for him, feels sorry for herself, and mismanages the household money. As their feelings intensify, each finds more things for which to blame the other. Frank finally admits that he did spend the evening with the other woman, but says, 'I don't even like her, don't know why I keep seeing her' (7). Margaret thinks aloud about violently attacking this unnamed woman, while Frank reiterates, 'Shut it. Shut it' (7). Margaret bitterly heaps blame on the other woman, while Frank sighs, 'It's not her. It's not you' (7).

The second scene begins with Pete and Dawn settling down for the night. Dialogue at first consists entirely of monosyllables, with Churchill supplying subtext in the form of stage directions. For example, 'Pete asks how Dawn is', is rendered as 'Mm? Mmm?'

and 'Dawn is fed up with the night', is conveyed by 'Ugh' (8).
Dawn cannot sleep. In response, Pete begins to recount for her
the plot of a science fiction movie. Dawn's words and actions
increasingly point to a disturbed mental state, but Pete continues
to react as if nothing were wrong. She dials the telephone several
times, dresses up elegantly and announces she is going out, then
undresses again, and toys with a knife. She voices thoughts about
death and twice tells him, 'I'm frightened' (11–12). He reads a book,
gets some food to eat, turns on music, and continues describing the
plot of the film. After the snack, Pete settles back in bed, reverting
to monosyllabic communication to ask Dawn if she is all right.
Dawn murmurs affirmatively, but under the sheets she cuts her
wrist with the bread knife. As blood soaks through the sheet, Pete
sighs comfortably and turns off the light without seeing it.

   The third scene takes place between Margaret, from the first
scene, and Pete, from the second. As becomes clear in their duologue, Margaret has moved in with Pete, a teacher she met at
the school where she worked as a teacher's assistant. The scene's
opening breaks in on a conversation between them about how they
have changed. Margaret says her job allowed her to throw off the
dependency that destroyed her relationship with Frank, saying of
her previous role, 'I was just his wife, I wasn't a person' (13). Both
agree that their former spouses are better, or at least no worse off,
without them. Pete acknowledges the problems of communication
that destroyed his previous relationship: 'I'd got with Dawn so
I didn't know what to say to her' (14). Over and over, the two
assure themselves and each other: 'We've both changed . . . we
have learnt' (13, 14).

   After a silence, however, persistent patterns begin to emerge.
Margaret, because of funding cuts, has lost her job and, though Pete
encourages her not to worry, she feels 'a bit frightened' about her
lack of prospects, need for money, and the isolation of being at home
(14). Pete turns off the light and, in the darkness, makes a comment
about microchips. Abruptly, Margaret begins to quiz him about
when and where he last saw Dawn. Between long silences, their
talk meanders across impersonal areas until Margaret demands, 'Is
it us? You keep being unhappy . . . what's the matter?' (16). Getting
only an 'I don't know' in answer, she unleashes a verbal torrent
of suppressed insecurity, as Pete sits up and turns the light back
on. When she finishes, Pete admits that he does not know what to
say, struggles against old patterns, saying 'I've stopped being like

this', but finally begins describing to Margaret the plot of the film 'Apocalypse Now' (17).

Three More Sleepless Nights, in contrast to *Cloud Nine*, focuses on the repetitive, undramatic patterns of everyday life. In place of *Cloud Nine*'s theatrical inventions, startling time shifts, and extraordinary transformations, it offers a realistically dramatized view of common people coping with ordinary circumstances and dealing with issues of sex and relationships within the material confines of a double bed. Against such a background, change is measured on a much smaller scale, both in terms of time frame and scope of expectations. Even so, the characters find it extraordinarily difficult to alter habitual patterns of relating.

The first two scenes serve to establish a sense of the personalities and habits of interaction the four people have developed. Frank and Margaret, though they show evidence of affection for each other and ability to communicate some of their needs, have failed to create a bond of respect and trust. The viciousness with which each partner attacks the other in the course of their quarrel reveals the low self-esteem at the basis of this lack of trust and respect. Pete and Dawn, the middle-class couple, have a very different set of problems. Though concerned about Dawn, Pete cannot deal with her intense emotions and escapes into the impersonal fantasy world of film plots. Dawn needs help and support, but, as Pete later observes, depends on him too exclusively. Most obvious, of course, among Dawn and Pete's destructive patterns, is their inability to communicate with each other.

In the third scene, both Pete and Margaret indicate that they have understood and tried to alter the basic condition that contributed to the failure of their first relationships. In her statement, 'I've got some idea of myself', since getting training and working at a job, Margaret shows that she has learned to value herself as a person. She compares her increased self-esteem to that of her former husband, remarking that seeing him was like 'seeing a ghost', and declaring, 'I don't want to be like that any more' (13). Pete reinforces her sense of self-worth when he says, 'I think you're wonderful' (13). For his part, Pete recognizes his failure to communicate with Dawn and assumes part of the responsibility for her suicidal act: 'I didn't know what to say to her. And she couldn't talk. It was me killing her. If we'd stayed together she'd be dead by now' (14). Margaret reciprocates Pete's emotional support, sympathizing with the position in which he was placed by Dawn's demands and assuring him that he is no longer out of touch with his feelings.

Certainly, by the third scene, both Margaret and Pete have initiated what most would view as major changes in their lives, including leaving their former spouses, living together without formal marriage, and entering an intimate relationship with someone of a different class background. In addition, Margaret has been employed outside the home, and Pete has accepted her children into the household. Both offer explicit recognition, in their references to housework, and implicit recognition, in the discussion of dependency and self-esteem, that a relationship should be built upon equality between the partners. Initially, the pattern of their dialogue echoes the changes they have effected: neither dominates the conversation, and both prove able to share personal concerns and respond to the other's needs.

Perhaps, in a different play, Pete and Margaret could go on providing support for and avoiding conflict with each other throughout all their wide-awake, daytime hours together, but Churchill presents them in the transition period between waking and sleep – a time in which both vulnerability and the capacity for intimacy are greatest. It is after the light is turned off that they begin to have problems. In contrast to Frank, who touched Margaret in the dark, Pete distances himself from her with his talk of microchips. She explores the idea that a renewed relationship with Dawn might be the cause of this lack of intimacy, but does not get very far. When, however, Pete attributes his sleeplessness to worry about Fascists, Margaret can no longer accept the situation as it is. Physically tired and emotionally uncertain as they are, neither Margaret nor Pete can prevent old patterns of behaviour from reasserting themselves. In their final speeches, she becomes again a dependent, demanding, accusatory malcontent, and he resumes the role of insensitive escapist.

Clearly, the implications of this couple's failure to securely establish new patterns of intimacy, despite their strong desire to do so, extends beyond their individual personalities. As individuals, they are contending against behavioural models which have attained archetypal status within Western culture – those of the emotional, dependent woman and the detached and uncommunicative man. Such models have given rise to habits that resist conscious control. For example, manipulation of the only really variable element of the stage environment – the light switch – illustrates ingrained habits of dominance and passivity. Only once in all three scenes does the woman turn the lights off or on, and that is when Dawn, in her extremity of need, seeks recognition of her reality from Pete. He, of course, reacts with protest, reorients the environment by bringing in food and turning on music, and eventually turns the light off again.

The straightforward message of *Three More Sleepless Nights*, then, is that apparently major modifications in personal circumstances – for example, changing who one sleeps with, to refer to Lin's line in *Cloud Nine* – may actually serve to mask fundamental stasis. The heterosexual bias emphatically overturned in *Cloud Nine* is reintroduced in this play as the assumed norm, along with that of the nuclear family. Traditional forms of male-female relationships, based as they are upon prevailing power relations, tend to re-assert themselves in new situations. The factor of economic constraint exerts a similarly important influence in this play: Margaret's independence and confidence are undermined by the fact that she has lost her job, due to employee cutbacks. *Three More Sleepless Nights* suggests, therefore, that those who seek to establish egalitarian forms of intimacy within traditionally structured relationships may actually be attempting a change much more difficult than the playful taboo-breaking in *Cloud Nine*.

From the standpoint of structure, *Three More Sleepless Nights* is quite similar to *Cloud Nine*. It deals with a group of people who 'change a little for the better', as Churchill says of her *Cloud Nine* characters. The difference is that, while *Cloud Nine* emphasized the 'better' aspects of its characters' changes, *Three More Sleepless Nights* emphasizes the 'little' dimension. This play, like the earlier one, contains a 'before' and a 'during', but not an 'after' movement. It thus invites the audience to construct one – to envision a future and further changes for Margaret, Frank. Pete, and Dawn. *Three More Sleepless Nights*, of course, promotes a much more explicit awareness of the obstacles posed by habit and material conditions. This stress on limitation points to Churchill's direction in her next group of plays, which would focus much more heavily on material conditions than had previous work.

While *Three More Sleepless Nights* uses situations and characters closely related to those of the radio plays *Abortive* and *Identical Twins*, and seems, in its reliance on dialogue, to revert somewhat to the radio form, it contains one stylistic innovation that would prove important in Churchill's subsequent work – the use of overlapping dialogue. In the first scene, where Margaret and Frank quarrel, their lack of respect for each other is conveyed in part by the fact that they speak simultaneously, interrupting, contradicting, and ignoring each other. From a chronological perspective, this is the first piece in which Churchill uses overlapping dialogue. The technique serves as one of the hallmarks of her later stage plays *Top Girls, Fen, Serious Money,* and the collaborative *A Mouthful of Birds.* Identifying the origin of the technique helps in establishing the intention of overlapping dialogue in these later plays.

The fusion of dialogue functions to de-authorize the narrative. The simultaneous presentation of both sides of an argument prevents an audience from hearing the points of reference (or even hearing the coherent combinations of words) on which meaning depends. The result is that each side cancels the other. This cancellation deconstructs the meaning of the conflict – that central parameter of meaning imbedded within and definitive of written drama since the early Greeks invented the *agon*. By deconstructing this central element of dramatic narrative, Churchill absents herself from the author's patriarchal position as the voice of meaning. There is no single narrative voice. Narrative is redefined as the intermingling of related and equally non-definitive voices.

In *Cloud Nine* and *Three More Sleepless Nights,* perhaps the best- and least-known of her recent plays, Churchill both consolidates experience gained in writing previous plays to reach a new plane of skill within her chosen genre, and insistently pushes on to experiment with the conventions of this genre. In *Cloud Nine* she exploits the ability of theatre to present the literally impossible in the techniques of cross-casting and inconsistent time shift. She combines and juxtaposes, with great confidence, a variety of styles, including those of farce, traditional realism, and epic theatre, reinforcing through this inconsistency her established pattern of multiple perspectives. She shows, in both plays, an ability to use the various possibilities of stage space as an important element of the action, with the inside and outside spaces of *Cloud Nine*'s Act One denoting relative oppression and freedom, the open-sided shelter in its second act denoting a corresponding freedom from coerced confinement, and the double bed in *Three More Sleepless Nights* suggesting psychological confinement. In *Three More Sleepless Nights,* Churchill, attempting to convey the multiple monologues of self-involved individuals who seem unable to listen to others, introduces a new pattern of dialogue in which characters acknowledge or briefly answer others without losing the train or rhythm of their own narratIve.

Churchill uses imagination as a powerful, and often the only, force opposing the material conditions of women's oppression. What is a dialectic between imagination and material conditions in other plays becomes almost a tug of war in these two. With *Cloud Nine*, Churchill can be seen to extend the power of imagination indefinitely, as Betty comes to terms with her tragic-farcical past and takes charge of major issues in her present. Though Betty is still en route to 'cloud nine' at the end of the play, she has taken the first steps, and audiences are invigorated by her example. *Three More Sleepless Nights* is weighted more heavily in the opposite direction, making it clear just how difficult it is for individuals to alter their habits of relating to intimates, even when they have a strong desire to do so. As will be seen in subsequent plays, the dialectic between imagination and material conditions is one which resists synthesis. It continues to energize Churchill's work and contributes, perhaps more than any other single factor, to the open-ended quality of her plays.

7

Labour and Capital

Having, with *Cloud Nine*, established a secure base for her work within Joint Stock and the Royal Court, Churchill moved into a yet broader range of social critique. *Top Girls* (1982), *Fen* (1983), and *Serious Money* (1987) show Churchill building upon techniques introduced in *Vinegar Tom*, *Light Shining in Buckinghamshire*, *Cloud Nine*, and *Three More Sleepless Nights*, extracting elements from both the epic and personal areas of theatre, reshaping traditional devices, and melding all of these factors into a truly original style. Max Stafford-Clark has referred to *Top Girls* as 'a domestic epic',[1] and the fusion of theatrical forms implied in that description seems to characterize all three of the plays discussed in this chapter. Thematically, Churchill takes on a range of questions addressing the social-economic effects of policies instituted since Margaret Thatcher became Prime Minister of England amid a general upsurge in political conservatism. These plays, accordingly, reveal a declining optimism and increased recognition of limitations on action, compared to earlier works, but they also show the strength of Churchill's continuing effort to question existing arrangements within society, model patterns of resistance, and elicit energy and commitment toward change.

TOP GIRLS

Top Girls, compared to the plays developed through workshops, evolved over the relatively long period of three years. Rather than focusing on a single issue, Churchill brought together several different ideas which had presented themselves to her at various points while she was working on the play. As she told an interviewer:

> The ideas for *Top Girls* came from all kinds of things. A lot of it went back a really long way. The idea for Dull Gret as a character

I found in some old notebook from 1977 or 78. There'd been the idea of a play about a lot of dead women having coffee with someone from the present. And an idea about women doing all kinds of jobs. It was also that Thatcher had just become prime minister; and also I had been to America for a student production of *Vinegar Tom* and had been talking to women there who were saying things were going very well: they were getting far more women executives, women vice-presidents and so on. And that was such a different attitude from anything I'd ever met here, where feminism tends to be much more connected with socialism and not so much to do with women succeeding on the sort of capitalist ladder.[2]

Despite the fact that the play was not workshop-developed, the Joint Stock style of company participation affected its rehearsal: Churchill reports, for example, that the actors debated for hours the question of whether there could be 'right-wing feminism',[3] or whether the term was an oxymoron. Directed by Max Stafford-Clark, the production opened at the Royal Court Theatre in August, 1982. It transferred to the Public Theater in New York as part of a British-American exchange. Like *Cloud Nine*, it won an Obie and returned to the Royal Court for an additional run. *Top Girls* has since been widely produced all over the world.

Top Girls analyses the relationship between women and labour at opposite extremes of the possibilities available to working women, both in today's world and in the past. It argues against replacement of the concern for and care of others, which formed the central orientation of traditional women's work,[4] with an orientation toward competition. In exploring the theory and practice of an opposition between caring and competitiveness, *Top Girls* juxtaposes the mundane and the literally impossible, uses an all-female cast of sixteen characters played by seven women.

The play's inventive density shows a combination of techniques developed by Churchill in previous work. It shares with *Owners* a dual thematic emphasis – in this case, non-traditional work possibilities for women coupled with an exploration of the meaning of feminist empowerment. The use of theatrically effective but realistically impossible combinations evident in many of her plays, from the shifting realities of *Traps* to the cross-cast images of *Cloud Nine*, here manifests itself in a dinner party attended by women from history, literature, and art. The before-during-after plot movement is present but deliberately wrenched out of order: with Marlene's party in the first scene as the 'during' movement, the 'after' happens over the following three scenes, and the 'before' action of Marlene visiting Joyce occurs in the final scene, thus increasing the dramatic impact of the revelation it contains. Finally, this play nearly matches the scenic diversity of *Owners* in the four different settings, three of which – a restaurant, an office, and a kitchen – are places associated with women's work (the fourth, a makeshift shelter in a backyard, denotes the children's work of play).

The play begins with a celebration of Marlene's promotion to managing director of the Top Girls Employment Agency. A colourful group of friends assembles at a restaurant. It includes Lady Nijo, a thirteenth-century Japanese courtesan who became an itinerant Buddhist nun; Lady Isabella Bird, a nineteenth-century Scottish woman who traveled to remote parts of the world; Pope Joan, the apocryphal church leader; Dull Gret, a figure in a Breugel painting who leads a charge through hell; and Patient Griselda, the obedient wife in stories by Boccaccio, Petrarch, and Chaucer. The women talk about their extraordinary lives, overlapping one another in a cacophony of accents that contrast as vividly as do their appearances. Their initially festive mood gradually turns bitter, with the growing realization of what each has lost in her struggle to survive and succeed. By the end of the scene, with Nijo sobbing, Joan vomiting, and Marlene drinking heavily, the party has turned into an outpouring of pain and anger.

Subsequent scenes show Marlene and those related to her in various ways carrying out their responsibilities in the realistically delineated world of everyday work. At the employment agency, Marlene briskly deflates a young woman's hopes and sends her to a clerical job with a lamp shade manufacturer. In a small town north of London, Marlene's niece Angie and her friend Kit exchange confidences and teasing challenges inside the backyard shelter they have built out of junk. Angie, a sixteen-year-old school dropout, tells Kit she plans to run away to London and see her Aunt Marlene, whom she believes to be her mother. When her mother Joyce calls her inside, Angie defies and threatens her.

Act Two opens on Monday morning in the employment agency. Two of Marlene's co-workers chat about their weekend activities and discuss the impact of Marlene's promotion on Howard, another co-worker who wanted the position. When Angie arrives unannounced, Marlene attempts to dispose of the girl with her usual efficiency. However, this interruption is compounded by the sudden appearance of Howard's distressed wife, who tries to persuade Marlene to step aside for her husband. Marlene orders the woman out and deposits Angie – who has witnessed the scene with delight – at a vacant desk, returning to her appointments. During lunch break, the news comes that Howard has suffered a heart attack. One of Marlene's co-workers refers to Angie, who has now fallen asleep in her chair, as a 'nice kid'. Marlene, however, dismisses her as 'a bit thick . . . a bit funny', and – in the line marking the chronological end point of the play – comments, 'She's not going to make it' (602).[5]

The final scene, jumping backward to the previous year, occurs when Marlene visits Joyce. Awkward, defensive, and out of touch with each other, the two sisters converse about Angie (who invited Marlene without telling Joyce) and recent changes in their lives such as Joyce's separation from her husband and Marlene's new job. Their discussion reveals that Angie is an illegitimate child born to Marlene and left with Joyce when Marlene went to London. The sisters' differing views – Joyce identifying with her working class background and Marlene expressing admiration for Margaret Thatcher – surface and finally culminate in a bitter and personal quarrel. The sisters retire without being able to bridge their differences. From the next room, Angie comes in murmuring, 'Mum? Frightening. Frightening' (623).

While rejecting the patriarchal axiom that certain types of work cannot be performed by women, *Top Girls* shows how the gender-based division of labour has constructed an opposition between an ethic of caring and an ethic of competition. The ethic of caring informs the interpersonal responsibilities that have traditionally comprised the private, uncompensated labour of women. The ethic of competition has structured the individualistic striving associated with the more public and remunerative labour traditionally performed by men. Accordingly, patriarchal-capitalist hierarchies award power to the competitors and deny it to the carers. The way in which power is defined renders it least accessible to those whose labour is that of nurturing and caretaking. While she shows, through the all-female cast and the incorporation of actual historical figures into the text, that women can compete, Churchill emphasizes, through the classic use of dramatic irony as something hidden to the characters within the play but apparent to the audience, that the price of winning such competitions is abandonment of the responsibilities and relationships central to the caring ethic. The last scene, with its strong image of Marlene's cold dismissal of her terrified daughter, provokes anger and energizes a revisioning, as well as a redistribution, of power.

Through focusing on the personal and societal costs of the competition to reach the top, Churchill asserts the difference between personal acquisition of power and socialist-feminist empowerment. Marlene, like the prime minister she admires, proves that women can be even more competitive, ruthless, and successful at climbing to the top than many men. Her rejection of Angie, however, makes the emphatic point that acquisition of power by a woman who has no concern for the powerless does not constitute a feminist victory. Empowerment does not mean the traditional accumulation of influence within the given system, but rather a dispersion of choice in relation to the system.

The vision animating *Top Girls* is a fusion of power and nurturing, like that at the end of *Moving Clocks Go Slow*, which has the capability of fundamentally redefining the world. This play, like the earlier one, does not represent this vision. Instead it ends with an unresolved argument that denies vindication to both sides and testifies to an urgent need for alternatives to the existing opposition between caring and competition. Churchill, who has stated that she 'meant the thing that is absent to have a presence in the play',[6] thus creates a space of possibility in which the audience member can construct her or his relation to the system.

The structure of *Top Girls* reinforces the dichotomy between power and empowerment. The vividly impossible gathering of the first scene, the twists of time in subsequent scenes, and the dynamic of displacement in the role switching all stand in opposition to the consistent image and character of Marlene. While Marlene controls the action, she does not participate in the theatrical transmutations that signal possibility beyond the realm of represented action. In the context of the role displacements going on all around her, Marlene as a stable player/role dyad seems oddly and rather sadly limited by her traditionally powerful quality of immutability. She has gained power but must use all her energy to defend it; she has not empowered herself to participate in a shared, diffuse, and expanding access to possibility.

Scene One of *Top Girls*, the gathering which defies reality, seems at first to hold out a promise of empowerment, but gradually reveals itself as only a replication of familiar forms of power. The excitement communicated through Marlene's preparations and the arrival of the first colourfully costumed guests stimulates anticipation of a unique celebration of women's potential. The appearance of women from the past suggests that a panorama of progress may unfold. This impression gives way, as the unorthodox procession of historical icons continues, to the still more enticing hope that the gathering may offer a grand synthesis of these women's trans-historical experiences, strengths, and strategies of resistance as inspiration to the struggling women of the present.

The dinner party does begin by celebrating achievement in very diverse areas of endeavour. The assembled women recount to one another the travels, intellectual accomplishments, and love affairs that have made them 'top girls'. Marlene's toast to all of their 'extraordinary achievements', however, marks a turning point (549), after which they increasingly reveal instances of suffering and loss. Pope Joan's pretense of being a man was undone by a pregnancy which she, having always denied her femaleness, did not recognize for what it was; the disastrous public childbirth brought her death by stoning. Nijo gave up the three children fathered by lovers other than the emperor whose official concubine she was. Political intrigue at the emperor's court, furthermore, denied her the privilege of seeing her father when he lay dying. Gret lost children to a murderous invading army: 'My big son die on a wheel. Birds eat him. My baby, a soldier run her through with a sword' (564). Isabella's travels prevented her from forming close relationships and alternated with bouts of 'agony' caused by the type of neurasthenic ailment that was one response to the demands of Victorian femininity.[7] Griselda, a peasant taken in marriage by a marquis, was forced to prove her loyalty to him by giving up her children to what she thought was death and renouncing all the privileges of her position, before her husband fully accepted her. The varied forms of triumph the women had originally seemed to represent is, by the end, reduced to a single chord of misery and anger, with only Isabella insisting on ending her narrative with a flourish.

The anticlimax of the final victory stubbornly described by Isabella calls attention to the irony that has subtly pervaded the entire celebration. Just as her greatest moment is the doubtful one, from a feminist standpoint, of being 'the only European woman ever to have seen the Emperor of Morocco' (565), so have all the women based their lives on imitation of and obedience to masculine authority. Joan pretended to be a man. Nijo followed her father's advice to 'enter holy orders' if she fell out of favour with the emperor, and justifies her decision to travel by remarking, 'Priests were often vagrants, so why not a nun . . . I still did what my father wanted' (539). Isabella, who describes her father as 'the mainspring of my life', tried to please him by devoting herself to Latin, needlework, 'charitable schemes', and illnesses in which she 'spent a great deal of time on the sofa' (539, 540). Griselda obeyed her husband without question. Gret took up a sword and the armour of a man and went into battle. In the end, all the women demonstrate that the toughness Marlene will evince in later scenes does not indicate a new potential in women, since even the obedient Griselda must be recognized as tough. Their toughness, however, has served to validate rather than challenge patriarchal power.

Instead of the expected celebration or expansion of opportunities, the first scene of Top Girls shows a group of women who, despite the heightened possibility suggested in the theatricality of the gathering, fail to come together in a moment of collective imagination that might allow them to come to terms with their common oppression. The difficulty of such an act is recognized, from the beginning, in the women's differing class backgrounds – a factor evident not only in the different accents with which they speak, but also in how much they speak. The titled Isabella and aristocratic Nijo, who are known today because they wrote their own narratives,[8] dominate the conversation, frequently interrupting and overlapping others. The humbly born Joan and Griselda, known through stories told by men, speak only in answer to questions. Gret, the uneducated peasant known only in a pictorial representation created by a man, speaks very little. The two contemporary women present show an even greater contrast: Marlene directs the progress of the dinner, while the waitress serving the party does not speak at all.

The women prove unable to communicate and identify with one another, despite attempts to understand and sympathize. One often repeats a word uttered by another in the course of her personal narrative (such as 'father' or 'poetry' for Nijo and Isabella), but then uses this word as an entry (or re-entry) point into her own individual narrative, rather than as a community-building link. Similarly, one often defines another's experiences in terms of her own, as when Nijo says of Joan's flight from home with a friend, 'Ah, an elopement' (544), but this type of appropriation leads to absurdity rather than understanding. Joan vents her strongest emotions in a long, incomprehensible recitation of Latin verse. All of the women remain locked in their own, singular perspectives, unable to see the relationship between the choice to obey or imitate masculine models of competition and their painful personal isolation. Of course, they (and the audience) eventually do perceive a commonality in their dead lovers, lost children, and angry response to injustice. This commonality, however, is intrinsically negative because imposed on them by oppression.

Having staked out a position in the fantastic presentation of the dinner party, Churchill goes on to argue it in the realistic representation of contemporary work. The employment agency for which Marlene has just been appointed the managing director also seems, at the beginning, to hold out possibility: though clearly a commercial venture, it might offer a positive combination of caring and competition through its function of finding jobs for people. Irony again replaces possibility, however, as Marlene defends the power base she has acquired by patronizing, intimidating, and further narrowing the options of women who come seeking opportunity.

In their interactions with each other and with clients, Marlene and her co-workers in the employment agency demonstrate their commitment to the ethic of competition integral to the masculine model of success. Marlene's co-workers reveal the male bias under the surface of their apparently liberated attitudes when they endorse her promotion in preference to Howard, because, as one says, 'Marlene's got far more balls than Howard' (582). Negating any expectation of a sisterly concern for other women, they automatically look for men to fill the 'high-flyer' sales jobs. Shona, the hyper-aggressive young working-class woman, bluffs her way into an interview for one of the 'high-flyer' positions through imitation-macho braggadocio, though her actual lack of experience dooms this imitation to ludicrous failure. Those who follow feminine models, however, never receive even the chance of such an interview. Jeannine, who hopes for an interesting job, is advised by Marlene that her marriage plans constitute a serious detriment to her prospects. Mrs. Kidd, the loyal, if genuinely irritating, wife who appeals to Marlene for help, receives a quick and harsh dismissal. To advance themselves, women at the agency promote society's bleak set of givens, always urging clients to accept rather than challenge. In their internalization and support of patriarchal values, the supposedly liberated women who work in the employment agency are merely the most up-to-date examples of what *Cloud Nine*'s Act One Betty acknowledges herself to be: 'a man's creation'.

The limited success that Marlene has purchased with her competitive striving means little if she cannot progress yet higher in the hierarchy. Her future prospects, however, seem questionable in light of the interview with Louise, the middle-aged middle manager seeking a job change. Though she has managed to 'pass as a man at work', has never mixed with 'the girls', and has 'worked in the evenings' during her twenty-one years with her current employer, Louise has lost repeated bids for promotion to upper-level management (588). In the course of an interview that robs her of dignity and evokes the chord of misery in the first scene, she admits that her motivation to move is that her company 'will see when I've gone what I was doing for them'. She is told that the only alternative positions are ones where she will 'be in competition with younger men' and is advised to enter a field 'easier for a woman', like cosmetics (588). Louise, like the other women in the play, has remained a 'girl' despite her earnest efforts to make it to the top.

The office environment, like the dinner party, brings people together without creating any bond of community among them. Nell and Win, Marlene's co-workers, view this job as one of many stations on the road to success. When Angie, with her claim to familial affection, arrives, Marlene chooses to ignore the obligations of this personal bond in favour of the demands of the office routine. She treats Angie with the same impersonal efficiency accorded clients and the unfortunate Mrs. Kidd. Marlene describes her niece in terms of the same bleak set of givens she uses for her clients, predicting a future as a grocery packer at a supermarket. Placing no value on Angie's adoration of her or on Win's sympathetic attitude toward Angie, Marlene callously dismisses the girl in her presence, despite the possibility that she may be awake or half-awake and listening. This disregard for Angie demonstrates that Marlene views other people only as a means to her own success.

The contrasting scene in Joyce's home testifies to Joyce's passionate commitment to community, but highlights the limitations of the work through which women have expressed this commitment. Joyce has remained within traditionally feminine patterns, living in the house where she grew up, caring for Angie, maintaining contact with her institutionalized mother, and cleaning houses for a living since the departure of her husband. Unlike her self-involved sister, Joyce identifies with other people – not just family, but also other workers. However, she does not think beyond immediate material conditions; her anger, rather than directing itself toward structures of power, centres on the 'dirty dishes with blanquette of fucking veau' of the women for whom she cleans house.

This final scene, like the others, begins with a positive impression which is then ironically overturned in the course of the scene. At first, as she showers Angie with presents and tries to sustain a pleasant conversation with Joyce, Marlene seems to care about these two members of her family. However, when the conversation reveals that Angie was born to Marlene but has been cared for by Joyce, the six-year gap between visits takes on a much more negative meaning. The revelation also makes evident the fact that Marlene's rise to the top has been founded upon Joyce's willingness to take upon herself, without compensation, the 'messy', female-identified tasks Marlene does not even want to talk about. Marlene's labour in the public marketplace, like that of a traditional husband, depends on Joyce's labour in the home for its profitability. Marlene shows her further dependence upon Joyce for emotional support, in spite of long absence and lack of communication, in her crying and seeking of maternal comfort. Joyce, who is torn between affection and anger, says little until Marlene compounds exploitativeness with betrayal by praising Thatcher and condemning the working class as 'lazy and stupid' (622). Joyce then responds by defining Marlene as 'one of them', and making it clear that their relationship is at an end (622).

The situation of the two sisters illustrates the way in which the traditional allocation of responsibilities separates women's strength from societal power. Marlene has increased her power by cutting herself off from her mother, sister, and daughter. Although she has, in the process, acquired toughness, she has little personal strength – as her inability to deal with familial relationships, her self-pitying tears, and her pseudo-capitulation when she claims, 'I didn't really mean all that', show (622). In fact, Marlene's reliance on Joyce recalls the need expressed by Isabella in the first scene for Hennie, 'the dear, sweet soul waiting at home' to justify her journeys (547). Joyce, in contrast, shows strength in her consistent attention to Angie and her mother, the determination to support herself despite lack of opportunity, and her resolute refusal to submerge her passionately held political beliefs under a show of amicability. She tries to dissociate her caring for Angie from the undeniable advantage it has given Marlene by insisting that she does not want financial support from her sister. Joyce's choices within a current socio-economic system which still enforces a gender-based division of labour have, however, cut her off from power. The inability of the two to embrace at the end of their argument emphasizes the unbridgeable division between them. Significantly, it is Joyce who refuses the embrace: she realizes that the competitive inevitably exploits the caring.

Theatrically, the two sisters provide a doubled doubleness that, instead of invoking an opposition between self and other, makes visible two unacceptable others. The naturalistic style of this scene places the double vision of contrasting roles in the foreground. Patterned on the patriarchal opposition between masculine and feminine, these roles offer no new choices to contemporary women, despite the fact that both are played by women. The player/role doubleness, however – with a measure of estrangement created by the non-realistic images of the first scene, the non-sequential time shifts, and the role changes – remains an area of possibility, despite its mutedness in this scene. The protracted argument between the two sisters, with its dense, overlapping dialogue, means that neither side of the argument stands alone: its only meaning lies in the angry alternation between the two voices, the two opposing points of view. Not being permitted to identify with either sister, audience members must create for themselves an alternative to the on-going dialogue of the exploiter and exploited – a narrative with which they themselves can identify.

Angie does not participate in the argument, but is its source. Not yet a worker, Angie engages in the alternating play and sleep of the child. At the same time, she is not really a child, and certainly not the sentimentally appealing figure usually associated with representations of childhood. In fact, the sullen, defiant, and awkward Angie exhibits the least attractive face of dependency. Furthermore, as Joyce recognizes, Angie's personal limitations allow her few options: she is, indeed, 'one of those girls [who] might never leave home' (578). Angie may indulge in the fantasy of being able to move objects 'by thinking about them without touching them' (570), but she probably faces a future of being manipulated by forces she does not clearly perceive. Clearly, 'she's not going to make it' (602) in a competitive world.

Angie's situation, however, does not preclude empowerment. When first seen, Angie and her friend Kit are inside the backyard shelter they have constructed out of junk. The shelter provides a visible symbol of the girls' freedom to create alternate structures through play. Their friendship, the closest relationship in the play, and one that has persisted despite an age differential, parental disapproval, differences in intelligence and outlook, and even sharp conflicts, suggests an alternative to traditional patterns of relating. Although the two do inflict pain on each other at times (intentionally and unintentionally), they show an honesty and loyalty toward each other that is not undermined by irony.

Angie and Kit, as emblems of the future, offer ambiguous hints about the future of women, work, and power. Kit, seen only briefly in two scenes, is suspended between current limitation and future potential. As she assures Joyce, Kit 'loves' the larger and older, but socially backward Angie, even though Angie bullies her. A good student – perhaps a future intellectual – Kit worries about nuclear war, but seeks power over her fears by stating the ambition to be a nuclear physicist when she grows up. For the present, however, Kit holds to her birthright of relatedness: she emphatically rejects the values represented by Angie's visiting Aunt Marlene, pronouncing her perfume 'horrible' and ignoring the proffered chocolates. Angie's strengths potentially complement Kit's: she has failed to do well at school, but indicates, in her gesture of tasting Kit's menstrual blood, an innate strength to deal with the 'messy' issues Kit fears (and Marlene cannot tolerate). Unfortunately, Angie rebels against Joyce, who has cared for her, and lets herself be seduced – though already abandoned – by the glamour of Marlene's competitive position. Angie's final lines reveal her as stranded between her own 'frightening' powerlessness and Marlene's power to be 'frightening' (622). This final presentation of two unacceptable alternatives constitutes Churchill's plea for a radical restructuring of the world of work to re-allocate and perhaps redefine both the personal costs of caring for society's dependents and the rewards of economic productivity.

In *Top Girls* Churchill insists upon the inseparability of feminism and socialism. By focusing specifically on women, she allows men – another unrepresented absence in the play – a heightened freedom to situate themselves in a new relation to the division between caring and competition mandated by patriarchy and capitalism. By focusing on work, she makes a strong connection with what is potentially the most important form of empowerment for the individual. As currently structured, however, different categories of work denote either power or servitude. The challenges to attach genuine economic and political value to the work of nurturing, extend the ethic of caring beyond the confines of work specifically related to dependents, and encourage non-competitive strength prove much more difficult than that of increasing women's access to employment outside the home. In showing how contemporary economic disparity forces women (and men) to choose between work that builds relatedness or work that offers access to power, Churchill strongly rejects any hint of progress. She demands recognition of the needs of that great majority of women (and men) in society who, like Angie (or Howard), have no chance of rising to the top. Ultimately, she implies the need for a redistribution of economic and political power, rather than a simple accommodation of the individualistic aspirations of a few women.

FEN

In a review of *Fen*, which followed *Top Girls* to the Public Theater in New York, Frank Rich suggested that this play could appropriately be named 'Bottom Girls'.[9] The characters of *Fen*, a play inspired by Mary Chamberlain's oral history, *Fenwomen: Portrait of Women in an English Village* (1975), do indeed represent a group even more politically powerless and economically deprived than grocery packers – the category of workers to which Marlene disdainfully assigns Angie in *Top Girls*. In a cast of six, doubled to play twenty-two roles, five are women. As home workers and day labourers on farms, the women of *Fen* occupy the unpaid and lowest-paid ranks of the labour force. Their lives refute two common assumptions: that farm work is based upon a close union between land and labour and is thus less alienated than work in industry or commerce, and that the simpler social organization of rural areas subjects women to relatively little stress over conflicting roles.

In her introduction to *Fenwomen*, Mary Chamberlain gives this description of the Fens:

Black fen they call it round here. Black – for the dark peaty soil; black – for the mood of the area, for its history and for its future. Black fen, reclaimed marsh from Cambridge in the south, Wisbech in the north. Flat, flat land, extending as far as the eye can see with no distinguishing characteristics which for a stranger would separate one monotonous stretch from another.[10]

To acquaint themselves directly with this fertile but bleak region, Churchill and director Les Waters decided to conduct the first part of the workshop there.

This Joint Stock workshop, then, was split between the Fens area and London. The company spent two weeks in the village of Upwell, observing daily life and talking with people in their homes, work settings, or the pub. A group of participants spent a day picking apples at an area orchard. During the second phase of the workshop, in London, the group concentrated on improvisation. Work exercises included one in which each actor was given a bucket of water and told to 'move up and down the floor dabbing each wooden block' and another in which they were required to 'iron a shirt, peel potatoes, sweep the floor, fold a sheet, feed a baby, settle a miserable child, and give a man his tea' within a ten-minute period.[11] Les Waters set up particular relationships as the basis of improvised scenes. For example, 'one exercise involved a farmer and a farmworker. The worker wanted a wage increase but the farmer insisted on paying the worker in kind. The more gifts he received, the more guilty the worker became about asking for more money'.[12] The result of this workshop was a more integrated, densely woven play than Churchill had previously written – set in the present but with the pervasive presence of the past.

Fen opened in January, 1983, at the University of Essex in Colchester (near the Fens area where it had originated), toured briefly, and played at the Almeida in London the following month. One observer of the play in its London premiere perceived an integral relationship between it and its venue:

> The Almeida Theatre, still in the process of refurbishment, hosted the London run. Bare walls, freezing temperatures and a mist that slowly engulfed the auditorium were conditions that would not have suited many plays . . . but they were splendidly apt for *Fen*. At the press night, there were screams – not at the axe murder (two gasps, one 'Oh my God') but at the appearance of the victim's ghost seconds after the body had been locked in a wardrobe. It was, in all senses, a chilling evening.[13]

To the surprise of many in the Joint Stock company who had thought it unlikely that audiences would be interested in its subject, *Fen* was an immediate success. After its initial run at the Public Theater, it was recast with American actors and continued in New York while the original cast returned to London to play at the Royal Court. The play won the Susan Smith Blackburn Prize, an international award for outstanding plays by women.

A tightly bound – but, again, realistically impossible – collage of images from the daily life of rural women and men, *Fen* examines the conflict between hope and despair evident in the fatal love affair between Val and Frank. In twenty-one scenes, played without an interval, the play presents a sense of the rapidly changing structure of farm ownership and financing, together with the unchanging limitations of work in houses and fields, and the timeless endurance of the labourers. The set of the original production, a potato field in a kitchen, designed by Annie Smart, visually merged the domestic and agricultural environments of rural women's work.

As the audience enters the theatre, a ragged boy from a century ago shouts and chases crows away from a misty field, while lighting suggests the passage of a day. The stage goes black, and out of the fog steps a Japanese businessman explaining the history of this rich agricultural region and the complex structure of its current ownership – 'Baxter Nolesford, Ltd. which belongs to Reindorp Smith Farm Land trust, which belongs 65% to our company' (55).[14] At the conclusion of the businessman's loquacious introduction, the farm workers soundlessly begin to move up and down the rows picking potatoes. Shirley breaks their extended silence by starting to sing a children's song, but suddenly Val stops working and announces she has to leave.

Val, who quits work early because she feels she must talk to Frank, thus initiates the action by articulating her desire. Val wants Frank to go away with her to the better life she envisions in London, but despite his evident dissatisfaction with his present situation, Frank cannot break away from it. He persuades Val to move in with him, although she has to give up her children to do so. Her dream of happiness, conveyed in a romantic dance sequence with Frank, fades when Val finds that she cannot reconcile to being away from her children. She vacillates between them and Frank, as her desperation mounts. Family and friends offer their advice on coping with the conflict. Val's mother May, who has willingly taken on the care of the two girls while their father works, shames her for giving in to desire. Her friend Shirley counsels perseverance and recommends hard work as an antidote to unhappiness. Angela suggests to Val that she 'get some valium' (81), and Alice invites her to a prayer meeting.

Scenes of village life intersperse various moments of conflict, cruelty, limitation, dream, and the palpable presence of the past among the unremitting realities of constant work. Angela abuses and humiliates her teenaged stepdaughter Becky. Becky and her friends, Val's daughters Shona and Deb, torment Nell, the village non-conformist. During a quiet time with their grandmother May, Deb and Shona ask her to sing for them, and their request causes her evident distress. Tewson makes an agreement with a city real estate agent to sell his land and remain as a tenant; immediately afterward, he encounters the ghost of a young woman who turns from her field work to speak bitterly of continual starvation. While the work crew packs onions, Nell tells a story from her father's youth about a man who killed his wife and her lover with a pitchfork, escaped with his savings, and cleverly avoided suspicion by pretending to be dead. Shirley fixes a meal, cleans her house and tends a grandchild – and describes the great hardships she has endured. Val's children join in celebrating the ninetieth birthday of their great-grandmother, and the elderly woman talks of union organizing in her youth.

Both Frank and Val are driven by their insoluble dilemma to contemplate suicide. Sitting alone at the pub, a grim Frank resists being drawn into conversation by Nell and Angela. In the next scene, Angela sarcastically reads aloud some poems Becky has written in private, then composes an impromptu rhyme of her own reporting Frank's attempt at suicide. Val meets Shona on the street and has a poignantly affectionate conversation with her. That evening, Val shows Frank a mark she has made on her body and asks him to stab her there with a knife. He refuses the knife, then suddenly kills her with an ax and puts her body in the wardrobe.

Val comes back a ghost, and suddenly the stage fills with phantasmic figures amid swirling fog. Val tells of a desperately ill young girl who wished only to see spring, then died when the first spring flower was picked. Becky appears, having nightmares about Angela and pleading to wake up. Angela confesses that she inflicts pain on Becky to feel that she exists. Nell crosses the stage on stilts – as did the ancient fen people before the marshes were drained – and speaks with poetic defiance. Shirley, ironing the field, says that people long ago maimed animals when things became unbearable. Frank voices his regret and anger over Val's death. In the final image, May stands, with closed mouth, and sings.

Fen recognizes constant, back-breaking labour and economic deprivation as the material conditions limiting the lives of agricultural workers. The play thus consists of a continuous progression of episodes, 'scenes following with hardly a break'.[15] The action of the crow-chasing sequence occurs before the play formally begins, emphasizing that work on the land extends back before the beginning of what we in the present day structure as narrative, and suggesting the inadequacy of any representation to capture the ceaselessness of farm work. Use of a single set and the same furniture and properties call attention to the relatively unchanging conditions, over time, of agricultural and domestic work.

As the pre-opening action of scaring crows, the potato-picking scene, and subsequent enactments of work emphasize, daily life for most of the women portrayed in the play has not changed significantly from that described in the eighteenth-century poem by Mary Collier, quoted at the beginning of *Fenwomen*:

> When Ev'ning does approach we homeward hie
> And our domestic Toils incessant ply;
> Against your coming Home prepare to get
> Our Work all done, our House in order set . . .
> . . . Early next morning we on you attend;
> Our children dress and feed, their Cloths we mend;
> And in the Field our daily Task renew
> Soon as the rising sun has dry'd the dew . . .
> Our Toil and Labour's daily so extreme,
> That we have hardly ever Time to dream.[16]

Hard work, of course, is not in itself necessarily oppressive. What oppresses the people of *Fen* is the alienation that results from having no control over the land, the production in which they are engaged, or the products of their work. Marxist-feminist theorist Nancy Hartsock defines alienation as the process by which 'the life activity of the workers separates them from their human potential', so that 'the worker's own activity destroys what he could become, separates each human being from all others, and creates the domination of the non-producer over the product'.[17] By maintaining, through their hard work, the system that forces division of their labour and their potential, the characters cripple themselves and negate the possibility of collective power. That alienation governs the lives of the farm workers is made clear in the early scene where the Japanese businessman describes the complex structure of ownership that profits from the land and the labour of agricultural workers. Since even the former landowner has become a tenant, as a later scene reveals, many layers of control separate the worker from the land. As a result, the fens area exports food but denies its own people the basic sustenance of autonomy, choice, and the ability to dream.

Through generations of alienation, farm workers have internalized the powerlessness that prevents them from seeing any alternative to this way of life. Their self-division cuts them off from their own desires. Unlike the 'wild people', the 'fen tigers' of the past (55) the present-day characters have largely lost the capacity for defiance. In an extraordinarily effective social gest, Frank's imagined conversation with his boss, Mr. Tewson (in which Frank takes both parts) shows the operation of internalized oppression. As Frank, he humbly asks for a raise; then, as Tewson, he patiently explains that times are hard for him too, carefully reminds Frank of past favours, and describes their long-standing relationship as 'like family' (59). Frank concludes the conversation with, 'I hate you, you old bugger,' and hits Tewson – 'that is he hits himself across the face' (59). Frank's long dependence on Tewson has caused him to internalize Tewson's attitude. Since Tewson's viewpoint has become part of his own viewpoint, Frank hurts only himself with his anger and cannot conceive either of leaving the farm to take a factory job or of going away to London with Val.

Domestic labour, while not as markedly alienated as day labour in the fields, adds to the women's burden of self-estrangement. May, who takes loving care of her daughter Val's children, refuses to admit that her life has lacked satisfaction; but when one of the girls asks her to sing, she claims that she cannot, even though, at one point, 'she seems about to sing' (66). Shirley cares for her daughter's baby, irons and mends her family's clothes, and prepares her husband's dinner – each of her tasks serving someone else. That Shirley's relationship with her husband is oppressive becomes clear when Geoffrey arrives home. He conveys an expectation of Shirley's subservience in the demand, 'Dinner ready?' with which he greets her and in the following conment, 'Could do with some dinner' (77). He then sits down and eats, while she continues to work.

Work tests both the strengths and limitations of the play's characters. Within this context, the primary characters show a variety of responses to oppression. Shirley's response typifies the predominant one of acceptance – a choice which, in the lack of responsibility or conflict it implies, offers a degree of contentment. She throws herself into the work of picking potatoes and still has energy to sing. The song she chooses in the first scene – a topical reference to a children's television program – connects her firmly to the present, reinforces the rhythm of the stoop labour which has not changed in the centuries of agricultural production, and indicates her child-like status in the system of production she has accepted. While working through the storm, she sings an old Christian hymn that expresses pride in her ability to endure suffering – a pride she further emphasizes by continuing to work when the others quit in deference to the weather. Shirley sympathizes with others but counsels them to accept oppression. To Becky who shakes with cold in the storm, she says, 'You'll get used to it' (80). She comments to her infant granddaughter, 'Nothing's perfect is it, my poppet?' (77). Shirley mediates when conflict arises. She urges the defiant Nell, in the first work scene, to 'get on with it', and assures Tewson in the second, 'She's a good worker . . . she don't do no harm' (58, 80). Although Shirley does not condemn Val for leaving her husband and children, she does object to the 'fuss' of Val's indecision (77) and urges her to make a choice and stick to it. She has been trained in perseverance, as is evident when she tells Val about her first job as a house servant: 'I was fifteen and I hated it . . . but I didn't want my mother to think she'd bred a gibber. Stayed my full year' (76). At fifty the oldest of the women still working in the fields, Shirley remembers the isolation and hardship of 'living right out on the fen', and, by comparison, remarks, 'It's easy living here like I do now' (77–8).

Angela exemplifies an externally destructive reaction to the repression of her own feelings: she has become senselessly cruel to one even less powerful than she. As Churchill eventually makes clear, Angela's abuse of her stepdaughter Becky is an attempt to counteract her own numbness and thus feel that she is still alive. The pattern of her abuse is to elicit a response from Becky, punish it harshly, elicit the opposite response and punish that too, blaming the girl constantly, whatever she does. Angela's first words to Becky, in a scene where she compels the girl to stand still and drink a cup of very hot water, are, 'You shouldn't let me treat you like this' (61). When Becky finally accedes to her demand to apologize for an unnamed offense, Angela begins to stroke her hair, then jerks it brutally and accuses the girl of having 'no stamina' (62). Anyone else's pain stimulates Angela, as can be seen when she puts aside conflict with Becky for a moment of enjoyment improvising a comic, rhyming description of Frank's suicide attempt. Angela's sadism has the unconscious design of inducing in Becky the same kind of numbness she experiences, as the girl represses her capacity for feeling in order to survive.

Nell is the only character who uses her strength to defy authority. Even she does not fully understand this choice, as she tells Frank:

> I just can't think like they do. I don't know why. I was brought up here like everyone else. My family thinks like everyone else. Why can't I? I've tried to. I've given up now. I see it all as rotten. (88)

Her own experience of unjust treatment by the company that laid her off has made Nell the advocate of other workers and the opponent of all bosses. In the first scene, she demands that Mrs. Hassett pay Val for the potatoes she picked. In a later scene she suggests to Tewson that he 'top himself' – commit suicide – like another landowner in the area has done, then adds, 'Best hope if they all top themselves. Start with the queen and work down and I'll tell them when to stop' (80). The story she relates as she grades onions, while susceptible to varying interpretations – as funny or not, and as urging self-indulgence or self-abnegation – begins with the anti-authoritarian act of running away from home. As a loner and non-conformist, however, Nell is frequently accused of making trouble, considered by some to be 'funny in the head' and subjected to more than her share of ridicule (80). Her marginalization within the community is indicated by the girls' view of her as a 'morphrodite' (63) – someone who may not be quite human.

Nell herself indirectly acknowledges the futility of her defiance in the story, which awards freedom to the perpetrators of a clever deception rather than to a claimant of justice. At the same time, her personal work of hoeing her own garden indicates less alienation in her domestic life than is the case for the others. Furthermore, only Nell, of all the workers, shows some ability to analyse her situation. She asserts to Frank that the sentiments Tewson advertises in the 'Buy British Beef' window sticker on his car are contradicted by the car itself, which is foreign-made (89). Nell vehemently expresses the anger Frank feels but cannot voice when she brushes aside Shirley's protestation that she does 'no harm' and growls at Tewson, 'Don't I though. Don't I do harm. I'll do you some harm one of these days, you old bugger' (80).

Val, while not explicitly defying authority as Nell does, violates the community's unwritten code of self-denial by making her desire visible. Asserting her desire in a way the others find incomprehensible, she stops working, first by leaving the potato field and later by leaving her children. Val's action, however, proves no match for the combined force of material conditions (the small sum she has saved for her escape to London) and ingrained defeatism (Frank's inability to imagine himself living in London). Her assertion of desire, in a context which denies it as a matter of individual and collective survival, only subjects her to a more fundamental division that can only be bridged by violence. Val's vacillation between Frank and her children makes her painful division visible to everyone, thus confirming the predominant view in the community that people should not 'expect too much' (77). Shirley advises her not to be 'so soft', and other friends offer her the opiates of valium or religion. The strongest reaction, however, comes from Val's mother, who has fiercely repressed her own desire to be a singer. May demands harshly, 'How long is this nonsense going to last?' (67). Overriding Val's objection to talking 'in front' of the children, May continues: 'What you after? Happiness? Got it, have you? Bluebird of happiness?' (67). She thus warns the girls, at the same time that she attempts to convince Val, that they should not look for happiness. Significantly, in her last conversation with her younger daughter, when she is hurried but alone, Val says, 'Shona, when you grow up I hope you're happy' (13). Val remains the one character able to envision a better life, but her individual strength is insufficient to sustain such a vision for herself, her children, or her community.

The girls in *Fen*, much the same as Angie and Kit in *Top Girls*, represent potential for the future. Their situation, which, as Linda Fitzsimmons notes, receives visual representation by the rabbit hutch in which Nell briefly imprisons Shona,[18] offers them few options. Just as the adults have internalized oppression, the children have internalized limitation. The 'Girl's Song' expresses very meagre ambitions for the future: 'to be a nurse . . . to be a hairdresser or perhaps a teacher . . . to be a cook . . . to be a housewife.' The teenaged Becky's schoolgirlish attempts at creativity are subjected to Angela's brutal ridicule. The younger girls' capacity for play has been perverted by their acceptance of oppression: just as they colour rather than draw, their game of teasing Nell helps enforce conformity rather than expanding possibility in any sense. While they do not hear Nell's story of the ill-fated lovers and the clever escape, they look on as Val's dream of escape turns into an actual trap. Val's death and reappearance serves as a catalyst that finally unleashes on stage the power of collective imagination. The workers who do not, as the Collier poem asserts, have 'time to dream', suddenly have a space in which a fusion of life and death empowers them to experience and articulate pain, desire, joy, and strength. This dream-like sequence of transformative possibility makes resistance to oppression conceivable. Val herself, by connecting with the story of the young woman who wished to live until spring and only got her wish, recognizes in herself the same pattern of exchanging life for hope. Becky releases her pent-up pain and anger, then refuses to allow herself to be tortured any longer. Angela begins to 'feel something' and concludes, 'I must be here if it hurts' (97). Nell, with the strength to challenge even the most potent authority, crosses the stage on stilts, as the ancient 'fen tigers' are said to have moved, and declares, 'The sun spoke to me. It said, "Turn back, turn back." I said, "I won't turn back for you or anyone"' (97). Shirley, fusing the two spheres of her labour as she irons the field, understands that she had 'forgotten what it was like to be unhappy' and begins to question her attitude of acceptance with the statement, 'I don't want to' (97). Frank affirms Val's right to desire, but wishes she had desired 'something different' (98). May – in a climactic and impossible moment that fuses imagination and material conditions – mutely sings: 'she stands as if singing and we hear what she would have liked to sing . . . something amazing and beautiful.'[19]

Despite the unchanging set, the repetitive tasks, and the maimed consciousness of the characters within the narrative framework of the play, the audience has been prepared for this final moment by the theatricality of the multiple transformations of players into many different characters that calls attention to the human potential for empowerment. With the episodic structure offering a collage-like view of the experiences of an entire community, the doubling serves to communicate multiple reciprocities between individuals and the surrounding community, as the various individualities alternately stand on their own in a dominant actor/main character relationship and merge with the group in a variety of actor/minor character relationships. As in other Churchill plays, doubling involves the audience in an active perception of the distance between actor and role on stage, and thus encourages them to question arbitrary roles assigned people in their actual lives. Juxtaposing representational episodes such as the confrontation between Nell and the girls, presentational episodes such as the lecture given by the Japanese businessman, and simple images, such as Frank and Val dancing, halts the smooth flow of narrative. This structure exposes abstract ideas that would be hidden in a traditional dramatization. Such unlikely combinations as a Japanese businessman standing in a potato field that is also a kitchen, and which was a moment before occupied by a boy from the nineteenth century, expand the field of perception and demand more than a passive exercise of the audience's imagination. Expanding the range of viewpoints from the dichotomy of *Top Girls*, *Fen* offers a spectrum of unsatisfactory relationships to power, again giving the audience the responsibility of constructing satisfactory alternatives.

In *Fen*, as in *Top Girls*, Churchill insists that society itself, not just women's place in society, needs changing, both in Britain and throughout the world. The women characters of *Fen* can be seen to represent poor women in industrialized countries and the Third World women who have largely been ignored in the reformist orientation of feminists who seek to enter public workplaces and participate in production on an equal basis with men. 'Far from being excluded from production', as Sheila Rowbotham says generally of poor women in the nineteenth century, *Fen*'s women lead lives of 'unceasing labour' in fields and homes.[20] To them, the idea of conflict between 'career' and family seems arcane; they combine family duties with work outside the home as a matter of survival. By focusing on workers at the lowest end of the economic spectrum, *Fen* questions all workers' acceptance of oppression. She suggests that in Thatcher's Britain the workers have lost the fierce spirit that characterized them at times in the past. They carry on their lives as individuals, not a community, and fail to offer one another support. Aware of the ways in which they cripple themselves, they nevertheless persist in self-crippling patterns. They accept severe limitations and do not, until the end, recognize their own unlimited potential. The revelation of that potential in the dream sequence at the end places May's singing, which expresses a hope for something better, against Shirley's singing at the beginning, which only testified to a hope for nothing worse.

SERIOUS MONEY

With *Serious Money*, Churchill turned from consideration of labour to an examination of capital. According to Churchill, 'Max Stafford-

Clark had been thinking for several years of doing a play about the City',[21] the international financial centre located within the walls of the old City of London. In September of 1986, Stafford-Clark organized a Royal Court workshop similar to those he had led for Joint Stock, and invited Churchill to participate. With a company of eight actors, Churchill and Stafford-Clark, as well as musical director Colin Sell, spent two weeks visiting City offices and institutions to gather information and impressions. They observed trading in the different markets – the stock exchange, the metals exchange, the futures exchange, commodities markets – and talked to traders, brokers, an American lawyer, a 'fraud squad' member, and others.[22] What they encountered was surprisingly theatrical to those who had previously seen the City as 'synonymous with boring', including sessions in which youthful, adrenalin-fueled traders in vari-coloured blazers threw themselves into what appeared to be 'an incomprehensible sport' in a place called LIFFE – the London International Financial Futures Exchange.[23] Participants in the workshop read *The Financial Times* each day: for Churchill, it was the beginning of several months' close acquaintance with the salmon-coloured financial daily. At the end of the two weeks, the workshop group produced a short, improvised piece, which they performed in the City.[24]

Written over a period of several months, the play presents the view Churchill gained of the City as 'amoral and greedy in a curiously detached and cheery way, as if it was a game with prizes, risks and the thrill of winning and no obvious consequences beyond the green screens'.[25] Following in the wake of months of headlines trumpeting changes and scandals in the City, *Serious Money* opened at the Royal Court in March, 1987, sold out its initial run, and then transferred to Wyndham's Theatre in the West End. It won, among other distinctions, the Olivier Award for best new play and Churchill's second Susan Smith Blackburn Award.

Serious Money opens with a period staging of a brief scene from *The Volunteers, or The Stockjobbers* by Thomas Shadwell (1692). Hackwell inquires about new stock issues, and two jobbers report to him on various 'undertakings', from mousetraps to Chinese rope-dancers. Brushing aside questions from his wife and one of the jobbers regarding the usefulness or legality of such endeavours, Hackwell propels the play into the present with his comment that the only object of dealing in stocks is 'to turn the penny' (13).[26]

In the contemporary financial environment of computer screens and banks of telephones, a day of dealing begins with a single stockbroker on one phone and builds to a melee of trading that is suddenly cut short by a power failure. The assorted dealers of futures, commercial paper, and gilts range from the upper-class Scilla Todd, who loves working on the floor of LIFFE 'because it's like playing a cross between roulette and space invaders' (54), to school dropout Grimes who speaks with the obscenity-laced argot of a Cockney street trader. Jake Todd, Scilla's brother, is, according to Grimes, 'the only public school boy what can really deal'; and Jake says, 'That's because I didn't go to university and learn to think twice' (21).

Zac Zackerman, American investment banker and enthusiastic spokesman for capitalism, amiably narrates much of the action. He introduces the scene depicting a corporate shuffle that transferred him to London. He conducts a guided tour of the financial centre, including a riotous session on the floor of LIFFE (that culminates in the 'Futures Song' at the end of the first act) and a meeting of the London Metals Exchange (improvised by the actors) that quietly builds to an instant of frenzy. Zac, who is orchestrating major changes in the City, enjoys London because 'I go to the theatre, I don't get mugged, I have classy friends' (25). At a weekend hunt with his classy friends, Zac tries desperately to control his horse, but he easily takes control of City institutions that have not yet adjusted to the end of England's 'cartel', the British Empire. Frosby, an old friend of the Todds displaced from his stock exchange job by the changes Zac has initiated, decides to get revenge by reporting Jake's insider dealing to the Department of Trade and Industry (DTI).

With a forward jump in the action, Zac phones Marylou Baines, international cocaine dealer and 'one of America's top arbitrageurs' (35), to tell her Jake has been found shot, an apparent suicide. From this point, the action moves on a double track, intertwining the aftermath of Jake's death with Billy Corman's attempt to take over the Albion Corporation. Convinced that Jake has been the victim of foul play because of what he could tell the DTI, Scilla sets out to find his murderer. Soon, however, her quest changes directions, as she realizes Jake was 'making serious money' (53) and determines to track down the cash. Her search starts with her father, progresses to Corman, and eventually takes her across the Atlantic to confront Marylou.

Meanwhile, Zac has been helping Billy Corman in his maniacal obsession with taking over Albion, a manufacturing firm run by the benign but befuddled Duckett. Acquiring enough shares to complete the bid has tested the ingenuity even of Zac and the unctuous British broker, Mrs. Etherington. Duckett, with his 'white knight' Biddulph, has begun to fight back. The desperate Corman makes deals with Peruvian copper (and cocaine) magnate Jacinta Condor and Ghanian cocoa importer Nigel Ajibala for their support. Marylou Baines has been involved from the outset, but to Corman's utter rage, double-crosses him in order to dissociate herself from Jake's death. An investigator from the DTI does arrive, at a highly inopportune time. Ajibala walks away with two million pounds advanced to him. Compounding Corman's troubles is a revenge takeover of Corman Enterprises by Missouri Gumballs, engineered by the man edged out in the corporate shuffle at the bank with which Zac is associated. Corman tries to complete his bid with a final push, but is stopped by the news that a cabinet minister has requested to see him.

The play's conclusion unfolds in the course of several brief scenes. The cabinet minister orders Corman to drop the takeover bid to avoid embarrassing the Tories just before an election, assuring him that his 'services to industry will be recognised' (113). Zac and Jacinta, who have been trying to make a date throughout the takeover, finally get together, but are too exhausted to do anything but sleep. Greville makes plans to work for charity, and Frosby contemplates suicide. Scilla meets Marylou, who hires her. Zac narrates once more, speculating on who killed Jake, reporting the Tory victory, and describing his new assignment of financing a sixteen-billion-dollar satellite. The other twenty-four characters (played by the seven actors, who hop in and out of a line-up as their different personae) give one-line descriptions of their eventual fates: among them, Scilla becomes a Wall Street star; Zac and Jacinta get married; Corman, now financing a tunnel under the English channel, is knighted and made chairman of the board of the National Theatre; and Marylou Baines runs for president of the USA. All join in the song 'Five More Glorious Years', a rousing anthem to Thatcherism.

Serious Money deals with misplaced energy and misdirected revolution. While celebrating the energy, intelligence, and spirit of its divergent group of traders and dealers that includes women, blacks, and representatives of both working-class Britain and third-world countries, the play shows how their potential has been channeled into striving for personal success within new, but equally destructive, patterns. The palpable absence in this play is any shared ethos that could transform the group of individuals into a collective and stimulate their latent potential for empowerment against a system based on exploitation.

The play's characters at first appear to exercise an exhilarating degree of personal autonomy, as they throw themselves into the free-wheeling action or explain it to the audience, but the verse dialogue within which this action is contained firmly subordinates their autonomy to the system they support with their work. In the trans-national world of finance, the traders and dealers who seem to exercise power and discretion ultimately prove themselves just another commodity for exchange. They, like those in the middle of the power hierarchy in other Churchill plays, collude in their own oppression as they oppress others. Moreover, the promise of wealth which they pursue with single-minded disregard of all decency eludes them within the context of the play: Albion's takeover is never completed, and Jake's treasure is never found. Still, intoxicated with an illusion of power and wealth, *Serious Money*'s characters continue to embrace a cleverly disguised form of enslavement. At the end, they all sing a song of praise to Thatcher, but they have actually been marching to her tune all throughout the play.

Churchill renders the complexities of financial institutions and their activities understandable through a combination of presentational and representational techniques. *Serious Money*, to a greater extent than most of her plays, relies on the use of plot and suspense. The double plot lines – Corman's bid to take over Albion, and Scilla's detective-story and treasure-hunt quests for her brother's murderer and his money – twist around each other tantalizingly as they develop, and are joined by a third line – the Tories' bid for re-election – at the end. Narration takes over at times, to compress the action within its twenty-four hour time span, and to interpret for the audience the 'incomprehensible sport' in which, as Scilla explains, 'you can buy and sell money, you can buy and sell absence of money, debt, which used to strike me as funny' (54). Something of the actual excitement of the exchanges is transmitted in the realistically acted or improvised scenes of telephone selling, dealing on the floor of LIFFE, and trading in the London Metals Exchange. (The accuracy of these scenes was endorsed by financial editor Neil Collins, who praised the 'technical detail' and 'authentic atmosphere'²⁷ in the review he wrote for the *Daily Telegraph*.) The element of plot, with its individual protagonists, predominates at the beginning of the play, but ultimately the sheer force of the energy generated in the boisterous trading sessions overwhelms the fragile plot lines. The takeover bid dies with a whimper, and the mysteries of Jake Todd's death and money are left unsolved, but neither of these things matters in the end. 'What really matters', according to Zac, in his final monologue, is that the screens continue to glow, the phones to ring, and the exchanges to roar with activity as 'massive sums' of money continue madly circling the earth (109).

The episodic structure, which jumps forward and backward in time and skips as easily across oceans, continents, and time zones as from one dealing room to another, provides a rapid overview of London's financial centre, as well as offering glimpses of the wider arena of global finance. The breakneck pace, with episodes continually overlapping as the action accelerates, gives audiences a taste of the competition-fired velocity of traders who travel in 'the fast lane' and learn not to 'think twice' (25, 21). The movement of the play conveys the sense of a Britain no longer the powerful centre of an empire but merely a small part of an expanding world, as subject to takeover as the significantly titled Albion Corporation.

Serious Money projects a resolutely consistent range of viewpoints. The assortment of colourful individuals from England, the United States, South America, and Africa comes together through the device of the takeover plot – and through reliance on the information provided by everybody's insider, Jake Todd. Their only real commonality consists of a single-minded determination to make money and ignore the cost. Temporary alliances may form, but loyalty, let alone community, hardly merits a thought. Durkfeld, in the corporate shuffle at Klein-Merrick, fires the man who promoted him. Jacinta, who has no qualms about using the plight of her country's 'poor drug-addicted children' (76) to extort a greater share of the profits from Corman, certainly does not hesitate to sell against Corman's interest when the price is right. Jake speculates with money advanced to Ajibala by Corman for the purpose of buying Albion stock. Marylou sells her Albion stock to Corman's competitor to dissociate herself from Jake's death, and sells Corman stock to the revenge-bent banker to increase her profits.

Legality does not greatly interest most of the dealers either. When Etherington assures Corman that she is capable of treading the fine line between the legal 'fan club' and the illegal 'concert party', he insists, 'Tread in the shit. Tread where you need to tread' (40). Even the fear of prosecution carries little weight. Jake, already under investigation by the DTI, hesitates only a moment before pushing on to the next deal, reasoning, 'Greed's been good to me. Fear's a bitch' (65). Threatened with jail by Scilla, Marylou replies coolly, 'I'll take the risk. I'm a risk arbitrageur' (108). She describes Boesky's highly publicized arrest as 'the biggest insider deal of all': the fact that he was allowed to sell his colossal holdings before the arrest made 'paying a hundred million dollar fine . . . pretty minimal', a slap on the wrist Marylou considers 'great, because he overstepped some regulations, sure, but the guy's no criminal' (45).

The statement of Boesky's philosophy approvingly quoted by Marylou – 'Greed is all right. Greed is healthy. You can be greedy and still feel good about yourself' (45) – epitomizes the determinedly positive attitude of all the characters in *Serious Money*. If they consider the impact of their actions on others at all, it is only in positive terms. Marylou refers to arbitrage as 'a service to the community' (44). Zac, though he prefers not to live in Hong Kong, where he would have to 'turn a blind eye to the suffering' and feel 'wrong', makes even broader claims for the benefits of his work: 'the third world doesn't need our charity or aid. / All they need is the chance to sit down in front of some green screens and trade' (25, 64). He adds that, with the AIDS scare, money can be made by buying into rubber. Jacinta, who shows a downright sensual appreciation for Eurobonds, sells her country's natural resources and barters its debt in deals that give a huge advantage to foreigners, in order to raise money that she invests in the safe and profitable European economy. Ajibala blithely insists that third world countries will simply have to 'accept restricted diets' in order to pay their debt to Western banks (68). Greville admits that his primary reaction when he heard that Sadat had been assassinated was concern about possible effects on the surplus of gold bullion he happened to be holding at the time. Scilla sums up the general denial of culpability when she brushes aside the accusations against Jake, 'If it was just insider dealing,/ It's not a proper crime like stealing' (35).

The new City welcomes and mixes those of either sex, any social background, and every nationality, but only on its own terms. For the women, this means accepting sexual humiliation. A young woman working as a runner on the floor of LIFFE for the first time, is told to deliver a message to 'Mike Hunt'; when she asks one of the men to help locate this individual, he whoops, 'She's looking for her cunt' (60). Another young woman comforts her with the assurance that this joke is played on all new women. Scilla, who has internalized misogynist values, insults her father by accusing him of 'trading like a cunt' (89). The Eton-educated Nigel Ajibala denies association with anything African, stating delicately, 'one's mostly based over here' (68). The 'barrow boys' from the working class have made the new City their own: within its context, being 'tough as a yob' is a proud claim (108).

Of course, the play does not advocate the sentimental longing for the past epitomized in Frosby's memory of the days when 'the stock exchange was a village street' (29). Frosby's own betrayal of an old family friend reveals the hollowness of the friendliness he recalls. The new City has simply removed a veneer of pretence. As Corman shouts at his takeover team when the deal moves into high gear, 'Put your family life and your sex life on hold' (47), so the City undisguisedly demands subordination to the primacy of profit. So immersed are they in business that when they have time to pursue personal desires, they can only do so in the language and metaphors of their work in the City. Jacinta, for example, tells Zac, 'I'm almost as fond of you as I am of a Eurobond'; he replies, 'I thought we'd never manage to make a date. You're more fun than a changing interest rate' (104).

The rhymed verse reinforces the deliberately narrow focus of the play, providing a rigid form that contains and directs the energy of the characters. Speaking the often extremely complicated lines without missing a beat chains the actors – and hence the characters they portray – to the driving pace of the action, making their actual position contrast ironically with the 'freedom' and power they claim to have gained through their work. The frequently outrageous rhymes (for example, Greville says of Marylou Baines, 'She set out to make whatever she wanted hers / And now she's one of America's top arbitrageurs') at the same time lend the text a sportive quality that heightens the sense of risk-taking in its action (35). The impact of the irrepressibly energetic and often obscenity-laced dialogue on the formal structure of the verse produces a farcical collision, evident in a cleverly versified scene at Albion in which the bewildered Duckett follows his would-be 'white knight' around the office, echoing the final phrases of each of her lines. This verbal farcicality broadens the satire of pointed two-liners such as Zac's unforgettable, 'England's been fucking the world with interest but now it's a different scene.

/ I don't mind bending over and greasing my ass but I sure ain't using my own vaseline' (25).

While the monolithic context of the action shuts out explicit questioning within the play, a variety of techniques used in structuring it invite audience members to challenge the values *Serious Money* portrays. Primary among these are the Brechtian concepts of historicization and alienation, used here with a uniquely theatrical twist. Breaks in the dominant style of presentation provide brief conceptual spaces that offer a way out of the unidimensional world of the City. The theatricality of role switching, as in previous works, signals the possibilities of transformation. In *Serious Money*, this sense of possibility is enhanced by the intense energy infused into the reciprocal relationship between player and role.

Historicization of the basic situation presented in *Serious Money* results from the strong current of topicality that calls attention to the play's conceptual origin in the actual news-making events of the previous year. The Big Bang, a recent and highly publicized change in British stockbrokers' mode of operation, from face-to-face trading among a tightly knit coterie of established brokerage concerns to a more open, computerized system, forms part of the background for a conflict between old and new styles of making money. Privatization, the issuing of shares in previously government-owned corporations such as British Telecom – a highly visible accomplishment of the Thatcher government – receives attention when the stockbroker Etherington notes: 'The British public's financial education / Is going in leaps and bounds with privatisation' (41). Dialogue refers to both the Guinness and Boesky scandals, as well as to such current topics as AIDS, cocaine, the CIA, MI5, and the Contras. Corman receives a summons from the cabinet minister to meet him during a performance of 'Lear at the National' (99), an actual production of which was running concurrently with the first production of *Serious Money* (and for which the cabinet minister in the original production carried a large programme no doubt familiar to many in the audience). Most important, the Tory victory referred to in the play parallels the outcome of the general election that was in progress as the play went into production. This insistent topicality produces the play's unusually strong sense of contact with a specific and changeable, if contemporary, world.

References to various theatre traditions throughout the play further serve to combat the perception that the British economic system under Thatcher is natural, self-justified, or impregnable. Churchill subtitles *Serious Money* 'a city comedy' – a genre associated with the Jacobean theatre. She thus associates her play with these satiric treatments of greed and miserliness popular in the early 1600s. The brief introductory scene from Shadwell's *The Volunteers, or The Stock-jobbers*, locates *Serious Money* within a continuing tradition of resistance through satiric representation. The focus on Shakespeare's *King Lear* in one episode throws an oblique emphasis on themes of betrayal, family disloyalty, and division of property that power brokers in the City would do well to note (of course, Corman and the cabinet minister both reveal that they do not value or understand the play). In terms of contemporary drama, *Serious Money* itself could well be placed in a tradition-spanning category defined by Maureen Duffy, in an introduction to her play *Rites*, as 'black farce, a style of drama derived from the mediaeval morality where the devil and all his works were often funny at the same time as fearful'.[28] While Churchill identifies the theatre with the capacity to resist profit-making empires, she tempers her confidence with caution in the final note about Corman – that he has become 'chairman of the board of the National Theatre' (110).

Alienation, the presentation of familiar situations in such a way that they appear strange, and prompt analysis, takes both unexpected and classic forms in *Serious Money*. For most audiences, the strangeness of the play's experience would probably derive simply from seeing the arcane world of high-stakes finance presented in the familiar territory of a theatre – and from feeling the pull of its specific and very real magnetism. Observing an imitation of the ordinarily hidden action within this world and beginning to understand the reality on which it is based empowers the audience member to analyse its function within the capitalist system and its relation to him or her personally. Such genial characterizations as those of Zac and Jacinta deflect anger from the easy target of an individual villain to the more important one of the economic structure and its supporting ideology. The satirically joyous music of the final 'Five More Glorious Years' (which consciously or unconsciously echoes the song 'Fifteen Glorious Years' in Peter Weiss's *Marat/Sade*) unsentimentally focuses attention on the inverted morality, growing strength, and power for harm of those who have the greatest access to financial resources. The driving pace of the play gestically communicates threat. In its often outrageous portrayal of City insiders, the play attempts to elicit from outsiders a stronger response to the attitudes and activities of the City than the customary shrug.

Breaks in the play's dominant style of presentation point to possibility – to the Brechtian 'way out' for characters and audience. While nearly all of the play's forty-eight scenes use rhymed dialogue, a few episodes break from this pattern to point to a breakdown of form during moments of extremity. The trading scenes, with their overlapping hubbub of speech, are not rhymed. In these scenes the game of making money reaches a peak of seeming life-or-death intensity. The only other non-rhymed scene is the flashback in which Jake tells Scilla that he is under investigation by the DTl. Here Jake, who has been thrown out of the game, faces for the first time the life-or-death reality the trading games attempt to deny. Prose intrudes briefly in several speeches – for example, when Frosby vents the bitter resentment he feels toward Greville and his children for allying themselves with Zac, and when Duckett panics in the face of the takeover attempt. These breaks momentarily displace the City viewpoint that the only important reality lies in the vast sums of money being transferred from one computer screen to another. They inform audience members that the City, and the system it epitomizes, are not impregnable to disruption and change.

Hovering over the entire play – as Marylou Baines, in the original production, hovered over the trading arena from an office positioned high over it – is the sense that a new style of no-holds-barred competition imported from America has come to dominate Britain's financial institutions. Accordingly Zac, the chief proponent of American capitalism in the play, is constructed as the only stable player/role dyad. He, like Marlene in *Top Girls*, represents a dead end that denies possibility. The other nineteen characters are doubled by seven actors. It is their enormous transformative energy, persisting even in the final line-up of characters after the Tory victory is announced, that suggests the possibility of empowerment and of altering one's relation to the capitalist system.

In the three plays discussed in this chapter, Churchill has infused her critique of the socio-economic structure of Britain in the 1980s with unexpected yet powerfully evocative images of the winners and losers in this contemporary structure. The pointedly ironic contrast between the ruthless winner, Marlene, and the plaintive loser, Angie, in *Top Girls* questions a system based on competition and extremely disproportionate rewards. The submissive attitudes compelling the system's losers to accept and perpetuate a system which offers them so few rewards are explored in *Fen*, and ultimately questioned through the images fusing imagination and material conditions in the final, dreamlike sequence. *Serious Money* parodies the current frantic race for almost unimaginably large winnings, thereby questioning participation in a system of enslavement in the belief that 'money buys freedom' (109). The spectrum of winners and losers presented within these plays have in common their support of and exploitation by a system that they could change if they ever understood and built upon that commonality to change the power structure.

None of these plays represent empowerment; in each of them, that potential lies more in what they are than in what they say. Each presents a process in which theatricality challenges the limiting material conditions and oppressive power relations that are realistically recognized and compellingly represented. *Top Girls*, *Fen*, and *Serious Money* exemplify the best of Churchill's work to date – plays which combine controversial ideas and effective theatre, plays which simultaneously entertain and challenge. Churchill has, at this juncture, begun to accomplish the task she set for playwrights of the future at the beginning of her career in 1960 – confronting audiences with plays that are 'not ordinary, not safe'.

8

Revising Myth

The revision of myth constitutes a major element of feminist writing; it is within this culturally powerful arena that women come to terms with the images and narratives accepted as timeless vessels of universal human experience. As Alicia Ostriker writes, the material of myth is assumed to be 'not only true but important'.[1] Ostriker, who has written mythic poetry, points to three reasons why women writers might want to use the material of myth: 'to be taken seriously as a writer', 'to get at something very deep in herself', and 'to release an imprisoned meaning' not yet discovered in previous versions of the myth.[2] For Churchill, this exploration of mythic dimensions in contemporary life indicates a renewed interest in the fusion of personal experience and political analysis and a recognition of the inseparability of reason and emotion.

A MOUTHFUL OF BIRDS

With *A Mouthful of Birds*, written and produced in 1986 (just before the Royal Court workshop that resulted in *Serious Money* began), Churchill moves into the territory of myth. This Joint Stock project developed out of an interest in Euripides' *The Bacchae*. The twelve-week workshop included two writers, Churchill and David Lan, as well as director Les Waters, choreographer Ian Spink, and a mixed ensemble of actors and dancers. The workshop's five-week research period included such activities as visiting a spirit medium, undergoing hypnosis, attending a show featuring drag acts and male strippers, talking with women in the disarmament camp at Greenham Common, and sampling the experience of sleeping outdoors. Unlike previous Joint Stock projects with which Churchill had been associated, this one provided for no 'writing gap', in which the writers would work alone preparing a script. Instead, exploration of *The Bacchae*'s themes through improvisation and movement

172

exercises went on continuously, and text was written and given to the actors from day to day after the initial five weeks. Churchill has described the period of writing as 'quite strange' for Lan and herself, 'because it meant that parts of the play were being worked on before we'd ever had a chance to sit down and look at it as a whole'.[3] *A Mouthful of Birds* opened at the Birmingham Repertory Theatre in September of 1986, toured, and had a three-week run at the Royal Court.

Several factors make *A Mouthful of Birds* unique among Churchill's works to date. First, it is her only co-authored stage play, though it is worth noting that she has been open to collaboration in previous work: *Light Shining in Buckinghamshire* began as a project with two authors, and *Floorshow*, the Monstrous Regiment cabaret to which Churchill contributed in 1977, used several writers. Extracting and separately analysing the particular episodes of *A Mouthful of Birds* written by Churchill could be attempted, but would seem to do violence to the work, which combines, in its overall conception and execution, the work of three people – Churchill, Lan, and Spink. Second, *A Mouthful of Birds* shows the influence of performance art – influences in part derived from her participation in the performance art piece 'Midday Sun' in 1983,[4] and in part from her admiration of the cross-genre work of Pina Bausch combining movement, light, music, and text.[5] Finally, it takes as its starting point a classical myth as dramatized by an earlier playwright.

Churchill and co-writer David Lan brought to the project somewhat different responses to *The Bacchae* of Euripides. The image of violent women caught Churchill's attention, and she saw in it a challenge to the 'traditional view . . . that women were peaceful and men were violent', and a means through which to question the recent politicization of this 'conventional stereotype' by women protesting war.[6] Churchill has defined her approach to the question of women and violence in this way: 'If we are to avoid the danger of a static polarization of women as peaceful and men as violent (and, therefore, men just continuing to be violent), it's perhaps important for women to recognize their capacity for violence, if men are also to recognize their capacity for peacefulness.'[7] To Lan, who is both a playwright and an anthropologist, *The Bacchae* presented an example of spirit possession, a phenomenon he had studied among the people of Zimbabwe. He was interested in the ecstatic state as 'an act of resistance' to established orders such as church or government, and in the individual and societal implications of this 'abandonment of control'.[8]

With Churchill's challenge of a gender-based stereotype and Lan's identification of possession as a form of resistance, both were interested in addressing contemporary issues suggested to them by the central image of the myth – the dismemberment of Pentheus by the Bacchants. From the experience of those members of the company who spent a day or two out of doors, without the security of shelter or ordinary routines, 'came the idea of the "undefended day" in which there is nothing to protect you from the forces inside and outside yourself'.[9] Lan and Churchill then agreed on a structure that would tell the stories of seven people, introducing them in their everyday surroundings, taking them through the 'undefended day' in which they experience possession, and giving them a final speech in which they describe changes in their lives. Woven in and out of the seven stories, connecting them, is the myth 'that bursts from the past into these people open to possession, first the voice of an unquiet spirit telling of a murder, finally the murder itself happening as the climax to all their stories'.[10]

The fragmented process through which *A Mouthful of Birds* was created is, as will be seen, an extension of the theme of the play. Given its composite nature, with thirty-one episodes, forty roles, mix of dance and drama, fusion of classic and contemporary, and juxtaposition of two distinct writing styles, the play needs the textual links Lan and Churchill provide between the various parts of the seven central stories. Each character has a line of dialogue indicating his or her attitude before possession; Paul, for example, says, 'That way we make more profit.' Each character opens his or her introductory scene with the line, repeats it during this first scene, and again opens the possession scene by it. Though these verbal clues tend to get submerged in the multiplicity of transitions, emphasis on movement results in a rhythmic cohesion arising out of the repeated physical patterns. The total experience of the play combines a core of primitive energy, some scenes of poetic clarity, and a pervasive sense of the mysterious world of dream and trance.

The play begins with the visually ambiguous presence of Dionysos, the Greek god of wine and theatre. Played by a man with long braided hair, dressed in a white petticoat, Dionysos performs, in silence, a delicate and enigmatic dance. Part One introduces the seven main characters, in brief sketches. Lena recoils from skinning a rabbit. Marcia juggles work and private life at a telephone switchboard. Derek, who is unemployed, lifts weights at a gym. Yvonne, an acupuncturist, tries to get a client to face the anger that prevents him from sleeping. Paul computes his profit on 'fifty thousand tons of beef' (21–2). Dan, a vicar busily arranging items for a jumble sale, announces, 'I don't believe God is necessarily male' (22). Doreen, who has left home, pleads for peace and quiet. The 'undefended day' for all the characters begins with 'Excuses', a rapidly accelerating sequence of telephone conversations in which scheduled commitments are broken.

Part Two focuses on experiences of spirit possession for each of the seven main characters. A demon torments Lena with her inadequacies and orders her to kill her baby. Marcia, the Trinidadian switchboard operator, holds a seance in which she calls 'Baron Sunday', but instead becomes possessed by the spirit of a white, upper-class woman who wrings from Marcia the story of Baron Sunday's brutal death. Dionysos splits into two incarnations, one of whom is Dan, now wearing a woman's slip in addition to his clerical collar. Dan/Dionysos dances to three people in turn, and each 'dies of pleasure' (37). When placed in prison, Dan/Dionysos confounds categorization as a man or woman; after a sequence of peaceful, mysterious deaths inside the prison, officials quietly free him/her. Paul abandons his business when he becomes infatuated with the Pig. He makes a desperate attempt to prevent the Pig's slaughter, but arrives too late. Cradled by a grieving Paul, the Pig magically revives; Paul and the entire company wordlessly enact moments of 'extreme happiness' (46–9). Derek encounters Herculine Barbin, a hermaphrodite 'played by a woman but dressed in the clothes of a Frenchman of the nineteenth century' (51), who tells Derek the painful story of her life and gives him objects associated with her past. Derek changes places with Herculine, repeating her words as his own and giving the objects back to her. The acupuncturist Yvonne paces her room in a housecoat, trying to overcome her craving for alcohol. Doreen, suffering from a headache on a hot night in a crowded house, confronts a neighbor and slashes the other woman's face, then discovers that she is free from pain and can move things by means of psychokinesis.

Bits of *The Bacchae*'s imagery, enacted as dance-mime during and between episodes concerning the seven primary characters, highlight a collective dimension in these stories of spirit possession. Dionysos appears to Doreen and Derek, who become possessed by the spirits of Agave and Pentheus, speaking of their parts in the action of *The Bacchae*. The entire company performs the 'fruit ballet', a wordless depiction of tearing apart and eating fruit. Doreen and the other women, as Agave and the Bacchants, abandon themselves to ecstasy, and Derek/Pentheus sets out to subdue them. At this point, *The Bacchae* takes over the play. Pentheus is brought into the centre of the company dressed as a woman, while the others re-enact moments of violence and extreme happiness. Agave and the other women ritualistically dismember Pentheus, while Paul/Dionysos and Dan/Dionysos watch. Realizing what they have done, the women begin edging away, recalling various reasons to be elsewhere. Agave, however, decides to remain on the mountain, and the other women turn back and stay with her.

In Part Three, the play's final movement, the seven main characters briefly describe how they have been transformed. Lena now works in a nursing home, and acknowledges the pleasure of taking or supporting life. Yvonne, the former acupuncturist, has become a butcher, using her 'feel for the strengths of the body' (70). Dan labors to convert desert land into productive fields. Marcia has returned to Trinidad and lives alone on a boat. Paul, no longer in love and without a job or family, spends his days drinking and hoping for another chance at love (70). Derek, now a woman, takes great pleasure in her new body. Doreen, the last to speak, expresses only anguish:

> I can find no rest. My head is filled with horrible images. I can't say I actually see them, it's more that I feel them. It seems that my mouth is filled with birds which I crunch between my teeth. Their feathers, their blood and broken bones are choking me. I carry on my work as a secretary. (71)

In the final, wordless, sequence Dionysos dances.

If myth embodies the human longing for truth, in *The Bacchae* this truth is found in a vision of fragmentation rather than wholeness. Taking as its starting point the dual images of the mother's divided psyche and the son's shattered body, *A Mouthful of Birds* centres on the rediscovery of complexity and multiplicity through the dismemberment of the artificial wholeness of patriarchal subjectivity. At the same time that it finds within *The Bacchae* a primary point of contact for contemporary socialist/feminists,[11] the play questions and revises both the Euripidean version of the myth and the predominant form in which myth has been constructed in patriarchal culture. It further questions the political myth-making conventions of contemporary theatre which Brecht compiled, worked with, and named epic theatre.

A Mouthful of Birds' overall theme of spiritual regeneration through breaking open artificial structures that have imposed patriarchal order on the disunity of nature confirms the revolutionary spirit of Euripides' play. Emphasis on the power of the irrational to disrupt the organization of society and change the attitudes of individuals comes directly from the original. As does *The Bacchae, A Mouthful of Birds* portrays the disruption of a male-dominated system that has repressed and marginalized the feminine, and supports the demand for a more diffuse pattern of power. Both plays show a multi-leveled transition from coerced wholeness, either of the family, the individual, or the state, to a freer and more organic disunity. In its contemporary validation of these important facets of the Euripides play, *A Mouthful of Birds* confirms the power of theatre's origins in a Dionysian ideal of overturning established order, and thus asserts for theatre an intrinsically revolutionary function.

Churchill and Lan, however, revise *The Bacchae* in a number of ways. First, they expand its concept of possession as divine intervention in the lives of humans to encompass not only the African belief in possession by supernatural or divine spirits, but also such non-conscious states as 'memory . . . fear . . . anxiety . . . habit'.[12] Their multifaceted use of the concept of possession means that no single or unified meaning governs the presentation of the action. Possession takes varied emotional, spiritual, and physical forms, none of which is definitive. Reinforcing the sense of multiple meanings, players enact three different states in their primary role, as well as numerous minor roles as subordinate characters in the other narratives. The actor playing Marcia, for example, enacts her ordinary state as a switchboard operator, her possessed state as a spirit medium, and her possessed state as a Bacchant – also taking the parts of Paul's friend, Yvonne's mother, Doreen's neighbor, someone who succumbs to the deadly dance of Dan/Dionysos, and a number of unnamed characters. This communicative density insures that the play can be understood only through what Ostriker refers to as 'plural vision' – the use of the imagination to 'see many contradictory things simultaneously'.[13]

The action of *A Mouthful of Birds* occurs among people marginalized within contemporary British society – black women, working-class women, unemployed men, and those who do not conform to society's sexual norms. These characters, who are from that segment of society always perceived by Churchill as containing the strongest potential for resisting authoritarian control, define the theatrical world of *A Mouthful of Birds*. The older play breaks into and possesses that world, ultimately infusing it with a new power, but throughout the context remains that of the diverse and relatively powerless individuals on the edges of society rather than that of a ruling family divided within itself. Within this context, the action takes a different form as well. This difference becomes evident in the first possession scene of *A Mouthful of Birds*, which uses *The Bacchae*'s most powerful emotional element – Agave's murder of her own son – to show Lena's desperate response to her unhappy marriage. The two movements of the original, which were divided by the non-represented climax of the possession and dismemberment, are re-formed into a before-during-after structure that extends and fully dramatizes the 'during' stage of possession.

Revisioning of the catalytic force that sets the action in motion calls attention to the relationship between structure and nature, or between the will of human subjects and the forces of environment. The way in which Churchill and Lan confront these basic questions indicates a feminist challenge to masculine/feminine polarities structuring nature as feminine and formless, and culture as its opposite – masculine form created through the will of man.[14] Dionysos functions in *A Mouthful of Birds* not as a god, or a representative of any organized belief system, but instead as a model of nature. As such, he/she is neither masculine nor feminine, but both simultaneously – and therefore, essentially non-unitary. From the start, he/she displays qualities and visual emblems of both male and female; later, he/she splits into two androgynous incarnations. Dionysos never speaks, signaling his/her non-participation in the system devised by humans to express thought and will. Without appearing to exert control – only observing, responding, and at times seeming to disappear into the surrounding environment – Dionysos sets in motion the myriad transformations which repeatedly break apart and reconstitute the consciousness of characters in the play.

A Mouthful of Birds repeats and elaborates the image of tearing apart artificially constructed forms and transformation into the condition of disunity modeled by Dionysos throughout all its elements. The scenic environment of the original production suggests the

concept of rebirth through fragmentation in its decaying structure of a derelict house, invaded at the centre by a live sapling.
Role doubling, as in other plays Churchill has written, serves
to theatricalize the concept of non-unitary selfhood through the
reciprocality between player and role. The idea of the 'undefended
day' suggests a dissolution of the structure imposed on time as a
means of defending an artificial unity imposed on life. For the seven
main characters, possession tears apart the structure – be it the profit
motive, the church, or the job – which initially defines their lives.

The triad of Derek, Herculine, and Pentheus most clearly illustrates the interplay between unity and fragmentation. In his introductory segment, Derek lifts weights in an effort to maintain an
image of masculine wholeness which he feels is threatened by the
loss of his job. In his episode of possession, he meets Herculine,
the nineteenth-century hermaphrodite who was forced to deny the
ambiguity of her natural sexuality and live as a man.[15] Through
listening to her story and taking objects from her, then changing
places with her and repeating her words as his own while giving
the objects back to her, Derek experiences non-unitary sexuality and
understands the painfulness of artificially imposed unity. This realization imparts a dual significance to Pentheus' dismemberment: it
is transformation through a fragmentation that merges the self in
the organic disunity of nature. At the end, Derek is a woman, but
still has 'strong shoulders' (71). He/she no longer feels enclosed
and isolated by a unitary structure of identity, as is evident in the
final monologue: 'I come into a room, who has been here? Me. My
skin used to wrap me up, now it lets the world in' (71).

As part of their assertion of natural duality and multiplicity,
rather than division and opposition, Churchill and Lan challenge
the opposition between rational and irrational. In particular, they
offer a view of irrationality that connects it with political resistance.
They mount this challenge to the rational/irrational opposition
at the level of genre, using epic theatre structure, which Brecht
insistently identified with rationality, to overturn the validity of
any view of art or politics that excludes the irrational. The episodic
structure of *A Mouthful of Birds* is clearly Brechtian in origin, but
the content and overall effect are anti-Brechtian. The play explores
the irrational and asserts the value of what cannot be understood
or accomplished through intellect alone. The turning point for
each of the episodes is emotional rather than logical, and results
in each of the characters temporarily abandoning conscious choice

and self-control. The interludes, rather than promoting thought, undermine the attempt to construct a rational narrative of what is being presented. The play, in fact, is premised on the idea that possession, dream, obsession, and other states brought on by an abandonment of reason may provide a means of political change.

In using a Brechtian outer shell to contain a play addressing the political potential of self-abandonment, extreme emotional states, and non-rational forces, Churchill and Lan call attention to the fact that epic theatre, like less explicitly political forms of theatre, is based upon the patriarchal assumption of unified subjectivity. In making its appeal exclusively to the intellect, epic theatre demands a self-possession based upon patriarchal repression of the 'feminine' qualities of relatedness represented by identification, emotion, and non-rational energy. Thus valorizing the binary opposition between intellect and emotion, epic theatre associates effective creativity and political action with the traditionally 'masculine' pole of rationality. This framework denies creative or political expression to the emotional, irrational, marginalized, 'feminine' characters of *A Mouthful of Birds*. The position of these characters evokes patriarchy's invalidation of female creativity by associating it with madness, within the norms of male-dominated culture.[16] Lan and Churchill, by contrast, fuse the concepts of possession, creativity, and political resistance. In this way they suggest an inclusive view of creativity and political action that does not negate the 'feminine discourse', or metaphor, of 'submission'.[17]

Churchill and Lan's questioning of Brechtian epic points the theatre toward forms that may allow emergence of non-patriarchal subjectivity. They question with equal force the more traditional and less explicitly political forms through which myth has been transmitted in theatre. Their attack on the traditional narrative structure of myth opens its generically singular perspective to encompass multiple points of view, subordinates language to image and rhythm, and seeks contact with a level of experience not communicable through simple narrative. Throughout the play, seven stories are told. Moments of 'extreme happiness' or violence present seven images. The 'Excuses' segment that initiates the 'undefended day' shatters the realm of the possible with a chaotically multiplied and increasingly excited chorus of voices that claim: 'I've lost my voice . . . my dog's gone missing . . . there's a power cut . . . my sister's been kidnapped . . . the army's closed off the street . . . there's a bull in the garden' (23). The interruptive episodes

– conceptualized as simultaneous occurrences – show contemporary characters possessed by the spirits of the mythic figures who, as Churchill notes in her preface to the play, were used but not invented by Euripides. These episodes thus fuse the contemporary and the primitive by using the seven main characters to describe and recreate the myth's primary images. When the ancient myth breaks into the play, language ceases: action takes the expressive, rather than representational, form of dance-mime. Over all the wordless sequences Dionysos – in his/her single or double incarnations – presides, linking them with the rhythmic movements of nature. It is rhythm, not language, that brings the Bacchants together in the act of violence against the emblem of a dual loyalty to relatedness and authority.

Only after she has carried out the violent attack that destroys this emblem does Agave, in *A Mouthful of Birds*, speak words of her own. These words radically revise her relationship to the patriarchal power structure. At the conclusion of Euripides' *The Bacchae*, after both the body of Pentheus and the ruling family of Thebes have been torn apart in the ecstatic violence, Cadmus, the grandfather of Pentheus, reassembles his remains for burial. A humbled, as well as grieving, Agave wraps Pentheus' body in a shroud and submits to the dispersal of her family into exile. Thus, Euripides shows restoration of unity through a reassertion of the primacy of physical wholeness, the confirmation of a new divine order (which exhibits its artificiality in the device of Dionysos' above-the-stage suspension on his throne), and the dispersal of the Bacchants. In the original, therefore, the tearing apart of Pentheus serves only as an isolated outburst of women's rage, as they enact upon the body of patriarchy's representative the fragmentation that the patriarchal order continually forces upon them by demanding their conformity to partial, non-subjective roles.

In *A Mouthful of Birds*, Agave communicates a dual sense of her act of violence. In the episode that describes the deed before its enactment, she declares, 'I put my foot against its side and tore out its shoulder. I broke open its ribs' (28). Following the enactment, she says, 'I broke open his ribs. I tore off his head' (70). Her understanding of Pentheus as both a hated figure of authority and a loved son clearly points to the dilemma of women in patriarchal cultures: agonizingly split between triumph and loss by the act of rebellion. Her companions, remembering their abandoned homes, work, and responsibilities to 'look after someone', begin to leave the scene of violence, but Agave refuses to do so, asserting, 'There's nothing for me there. There never was' (70). Having broken the primal tie of relatedness, she will not return to the empty shell of patriarchal society. She decides to remain on the mountain, the site of fragmentation and loss, but also of power and change. The Bacchants, instead of following their first impulse to disperse, turn back and stay with her, forming a community which fuses the power of possession and decision. Satisfying closure is denied, however, in Doreen's final lines, which testify to relentless pain in the constant feeling that her 'mouth is full of birds which I crunch between my teeth' and that 'feathers . . . blood . . . and broken bones' are choking her (71). Neither the terrible act of resistance nor the multiple transformations that culminate in a vision of non-patriarchal subjectivity for some of the characters have dislodged the actual structure of patriarchal power. Trapped in this structure, Doreen continues to 'work as a secretary' (71).

Those pushed to the edges of society by prejudice, fear, or economic imperatives – blacks, women, the poor, the sexually deviant, the unemployed – are shown, in *A Mouthful of Birds*, to be 'open to possession'.[18] This openness to transformation, rather than an assertion of conscious will, allows them to challenge their oppression and resituate themselves in relation to society. They possess and are possessed by the power of myth, in a reciprocal relationship with images that evoke the struggle of human beings from time immemorial to establish themselves in a truthful relation to their natural and created environments. This reciprocity calls attention to the power of relatedness – that capacity defined as the essence of femininity and both repressed and oppressed within patriarchy – to redefine and re-present human consciousness.

ICECREAM

In writing *Icecream*, Churchill again moved away from collaborative work. In an interview with Linda Fitzsimmons, she stated the need to 'draw back and do something of your own and be clear what's yours and not just response to other people'.[19] This latest of Churchill's plays is a personal venture into the arena of contemporary myth. In a short, simply organized interweaving of three narratives, Churchill explores American and English mythologies of national identity. Directed by Max Stafford-Clark, the play opened at the Royal Court on 6 April 1989, and ran for six weeks. After rehearsals of *Icecream* had begun, Churchill wrote a very short companion piece, 'Hot Fudge'. Intended to utilize the same combination of actors, but reverse the pattern of which ones play Americans and which play English, this play extends the exploration of myth to its operation within the relationship of a couple in today's London. 'Hot Fudge' played as a rehearsed reading with *Icecream* during the final two weeks of its run.[20]

Icecream begins with stereotypical American tourists Lance and Vera driving in the country singing snatches of half-remembered songs they associate with the charm of the British Isles. They have come to England to trace Lance's ancestors and cultural heritage, within which he grandly includes his wife, the descendant of European Jews, on the principle of the 'joint bank account' (3). After marvelling at the age of castles and visiting the now-vacant cottage of a great aunt, the two track down Phil, a distant cousin living with his sister Jaq in East London. Phil, a sinister young man who has never had a job and keeps an Alsatian dog to guard the flat, involves Lance and Vera in a crime. He kills his landlord and persuades them to help him hide the body in Epping Forest.

A year later, having long since returned to their home in the suburbs of an American city, Vera and Lance are still trying to purge themselves of this contact with murder. Vera tells her psychiatrist about it, and Lance tries unsuccessfully to discuss it with a colleague. When Phil and Jaq arrive unannounced for a visit, however, Phil immediately gets drunk and relates the whole incident to guests at a party. The guests, far from being horrified, see the story as an exciting adventure in which he 'got away with murder' (35).[21] Phil has little opportunity to further disrupt the lives of his American cousins, because he is hit and killed by a car.

In the wake of Phil's death, Jaq steals a car from Lance and Vera and sets off across the US. She gives a ride to a hillbilly who invites her home for dinner; both he and his mother turn out to be religious eccentrics who attempt to engage Jaq in their on-going dispute over when the end of the world will occur. In the far west, she picnics with a college professor; their conversation, in which he talks about the recent death of his wife and Jaq muses about the differences between Americans and the English, culminates in his attempting to rape her. Back with Lance and Vera, Jaq pleads for 'a thousand dollars' (45) to go home. They refuse to give her any money, but when she tells them about the latest violence in which she has indirectly involved them – the death of the professor, whom she pushed over a cliff in self-defence – they agree to pay her way back to England. At the airport, Jaq meets a woman from South America who is returning home after witnessing the death of her grandfather. The woman tells Jaq to change her destination and come with her; as the play ends, Jaq hesitates, then goes, at the South American woman's urging, to inquire about the possibility of changing her ticket.

Returning to the subject of emigration to America abandoned many years previously, Churchill uses *Icecream* to explore the quest by contemporary people to find connection with a mythological framework of place and time. Lance and Vera seek a bridge across the Atlantic Ocean through a patriarchal mythology of the past – an unbroken genealogy participating in a narrative that goes back 'before 1066' to 'Alfred and the cakes' (2–3). Instead they meet a contemporary reality – the two young East Londoners who disdain connection with anything but their immediate environment and the present moment. Unwilling to accept the denial of their expectations, Lance and Vera insist, with loquacious friendliness, on forging a link of relatedness with Phil and Jaq. Their tide of friendliness propels the four through a conversation which brings an outburst of anger against American hegemony from Phil, an assessment of English people as 'stupid and violent' from Lance, and uneasy agreement that both the United States and England are 'terrible countries' (9–11). Neither pair learns anything from this exchange, going on from it to express appreciation for things about the others' land that best serve to reinforce existing preconceptions. The Americans admire the English countryside, accents, and pubs – aspects of England that contribute to a non-threatening and easily consumed image of quaintness. The English pair, who think of America in terms of superfluous richness and easy consumption, admit to being tantalized by the flavors of American ice cream: 'butter pecan. Rocky road. Mocha. Blueberries and cream. Peppermint stick' (11).

What cements the relationship is not friendliness, or even sex – as Phil discovers when he tries unsuccessfully to seduce Vera – but violence. The Americans, who have asserted their control in forming the relationship, find themselves involved in an act that they did not will and cannot control. Their involuntary connection with the murderous anger of an urban underclass endures even when they return to their protective suburban enclave. Despite their efforts, they can neither purge themselves of this violence-forged link nor make sense of it in a way that allows them to continue believing in their own essential blamelessness. Thus, the contact with their English cousins shatters Lance and Vera's illusion of a reassuring relatedness to the past and substitutes for it an uncertain view of themselves in relation to the future.

While it problematizes Lance and Vera's future, the link with cousins on the opposite side of the Atlantic gives Jaq and Phil their first impulse toward a future. Their lives have previously been devoid of purposeful direction, as evidenced by Phil's never having had a job and Jaq's cheerful recitation of an endless and random series of temporary jobs. It is in pursuit of a future, and in response to the capitalist mythology of making a 'fortune' which (6) Phil associates with emigration, that they break their exclusive orientation toward the present and travel to the United States. Unlike the talkative Americans, the two English visitors do not voice their expectations of America: they merely agree that the 'American cop with a gun' looks 'really American' (30–1). Any expectations they, as a pair, have for the future are, of course, shattered: Phil's fatal accident immediately cuts short any future for him.

The death of her brother sends Jaq off in search of a more personal connection with a larger framework of meaning. She conducts her quest within North America's geographical vastness, driving across the country – heading, perhaps, for Disneyland, the quintessentially American land of technology-aided fantasy she has insisted she wants to visit. Though she seizes control of her own direction and enjoys the 'interesting characters' she meets on her journey, Jaq's 'road movie' (44) sequence of experiences does not establish itself as qualitatively different from the series of disconnected jobs she held in England. Through observing the larger 'scale' by which things in the United States are ordered, Jaq does begin to articulate a difference between the English and Americans: 'Americans are happier than the English . . . they think they have a right, while the English feel more comfortable if it rains every day in August' (43–4). However, before she can situate herself in relation to this perception of 'right', Jaq finds herself the unwilling object of it. Jaq's assertion of her right of personal autonomy ironically throws her back into a dependent relationship with Lance and Vera, because, as the audience later learns, it causes the death of the professor who attempted to rape her.

Icecream emphasizes the futility of seeking to establish a definitive relation to reality through existing systems of myth or symbol. These frameworks do not actually contain the overarching meaning sought in them. The production's segmented pictorial backdrops, designed by Peter Hartwell, emphasized the inadequacy of an image or concept to sum up either England or the United States as separate nations or cultures. Stereotypical views of verdant English hills in the first part and high mountains against a wide American sky for the second were chopped into vertical and horizontal sections, respectively, to call attention to the partial, post-card impressions received by foreign visitors to either country. Subject to arbitrary selection and rearrangement, these partial views indicate that the sum of the parts does not equal a definitive whole.

The play's structure negates reference to external symbol systems other than the clichéd and explicitly invalidated images of nationality. *Icecream* unfolds in a linear series of brief episodes – ten in England and ten in the United States. Each episode begins without referring to the one preceding it, as though initiating a new story or sub-plot, but contains a line or two of exposition at some point in the action that reveals its link to the previous episode. This internal chain of reference, however tightly causal, shows a blackly humorous implausibility that calls attention to the gap between story and reality and prevents the audience from firmly linking the two.

The four disturbingly incomplete and inconsistent main characters resist identity as strongly as they inhibit identification. Lance and Vera are abstractions dressed in the rain gear and clashing plaids sold in tourist shops. Connected only with an unnamed suburb in the United States, they use British-isms in their speech, refer to native Americans as 'aboriginal people', and knowledgeably discuss the inmate population of Broadmoor. Phil and Jaq reveal so little of themselves that the audience never knows why Phil hates his murder victim enough to kill him, what prompts Phil and Jaq to go to the United States, or how Phil happens to be hit by an automobile. The bare plot line and indecipherable characters function, like the disconnected scenic elements, to give an illusion of continuity where none exists.

Areas of commonality that might serve as shared points of reference do not exist even within the play, as the title – pronounced *ice* cream by some characters, ice *cre.:n* by others, emphasizes. Lance's insistence that knowledge of his ancestors situates Vera in a more authentic relation to history than would knowledge of her own points to the absurdity of patriarchal mythology for women. Neither side of the nationalistic divide can accept the other's definition of English or American.

Actual experience gained in the individual's quest for meaning cannot be communicated to others in a way that enables them to share it or participate in determining its larger meaning. Lance's attempt to be honest with his colleague about the murder gets submerged in the stereotypically male ritual of exchanging tales of sexual conquest, and Phil's revelation of the murder at the party is received in the spirit of an exciting film plot. When Vera tries to tell her psychiatrist about her part in concealing the murder victim's body and asks him to call police, the psychiatrist receives this information exactly as if it were a dream and interprets it for Vera without any change in his calm demeanour. His interpretation, far from showing simple insensitivity, is both careful and caring; it is meticulously truthful to his view of Vera. What makes its definitive framework meaningless to Vera herself is its total lack of contact both with her specific experience and with her capacity to experience. Jaq, similarly, encounters the two hillbillies who insist that she take sides in their argument about the end of the world, even though she has no concern about it. Jaq encounters further frustration when she returns to Lance and Vera's home after killing the professor. They conflate her unintentional killing of this man with Phil's premeditated murder of his landlord and turn her experience of threat into a narrative of further threat to them.

With those connections between past, present, and future, and between symbol and reality that are integral to myth frustrated throughout the play, the final scene comes as a surprise. The scene takes place in an airport departure lounge in, but not part of, the United States. The lack of a pictorial backdrop in this scene makes it clear that this space is free from the control of nationality and national culture. Here Jaq meets an old, unnamed woman from South America. Eager to return home – in fact, the only character in the play who seems to value her native culture – this woman remarks that she does not like airports. Jaq acknowledges this antipathy, but says she has found she does like airports because they contain 'everything you need. Food, toilets. Books. Alcohol' (50). Having learned that Jaq enjoys seeing things on the ground diminish in size when she is flying, the South American woman offers her the window seat. The woman thus assumes and acts upon a relationality that does not exist.

As she waits for her airline flight, the South American woman simply but poetically describes the flight of a soul, referring metaphorically to transformation and rebirth through the image of the butterfly. The purpose of her journey has been to witness her grandfather's death so as to be able to tell 'everyone' back at home how his life ended. She describes his final moments thus:

> My grandfather breathed and stopped, breathed and stopped. Then I saw there was a butterfly in the room. When it went out of the window my grandfather breathed and stopped and didn't breathe again. (50)

Rather than assigning an explicit meaning to this narrative centreing on an ancient mythic symbol associated with the soul, the South American woman asks Jaq what meaning she sees in it. Jaq calls what happened a 'coincidence', connecting the grandfather's death with the present moments and mathematical probabilities that have up to now defined her life. Though Jaq acknowledges the old woman's way of seeing, she does not share in that vision. Informing Jaq that she has received an American university education, the South American woman makes it clear that she is also capable of seeing the occurrence in terms of mathematical probabilities, but quietly reasserts the suggestion of an integral connection between the material and the spiritual.

The South American woman, marginalized by her age and third-world origin (and the final transformative presentation of an actor who has played, in turn, a silent waitress, an incoherently drunk party guest, and the hitchhiker's obsessed mother) presents the unforeseen possibility. This unconsidered option or unexpected connection may allow emergence of a new mythology that is not patriarchal or nationalist, or even revisionist, but originally feminist. This unnamed woman, with her vital but enigmatic presence, is the feminist hero Churchill has considered but never represented before: she combines strength and caring. Like Kay in *Moving Clocks Go Slow*, when she makes an assumption based on relationality, she creates the assumed relation. She does not, however, verbalize myth or meaning. Instead, she tells Jaq to come with her and share the experience of the journey: 'Change your destination', she says (50). Jaq, knowing that if she accepts the invitation she will change her destiny, hesitates. She thinks about the cost of changing the ticket and the appeal of drinking tea back in England. In the end, despite her doubts, Jaq goes to do as the old woman has bid her – find out the cost of changing her ticket. The play gives no indication of whether or not the change is completed, and leaves the audience to wonder what might be the outcome of such an unlikely journey. Jaq, in any case, has made a significant change: she has decided to venture into an unknown future rather than retreating into a safe past. She does not, in doing the old woman's bidding, simply accept the symbol system through which she understands the world, though she retains the double vision of being able to see, to some extent, both through her own and the South American woman's symbol systems. What Jaq does accept is relationality – specifically, the impossible, from a genealogical standpoint, relation with the South American woman. Truth, if Jaq finds it, will consist in relation, but within a non-patriarchal and cross-cultural relationship. The myth she might write will be one in which a reciprocality between two symbol systems acts upon shared experience. Jaq has not, of course, deliberately set out to find such a connection, but is open to the accidental contact. The potential of this newly created relationship empowers her to open herself to further change by going to a previously unimagined destination.

In these final two plays, Churchill seeks new relationships with the material of myth, but even more with the practice of myth-making. She 'steals the language', to use Alicia Ostriker's term,[22] and energy of epic theatre to transmit an experience of multiplicity, relationality, and creative self-abandonment that its patriarchal practitioners attempted to deny. She steals the language of linear narrativity to invalidate that form of myth-making. From the deconstructed elements of patriarchal forms, she imagines new forms in which women and men will produce meaning through, rather than in spite of, relationality. The faces and bodies of Churchill's socialist/feminist heroes are now becoming visible; they have begun the polylogue of their impossible stories.

9

Song of the Mute

Theatre, to Caryl Churchill, means 'making things happen'. The aesthetic, personal, and political implications of commitment to such a view are clear: things happen, not through a passive, closed reflection of reality, but through active intervention in it. Treating theatre as a metaphor for society, Churchill's theatre empowers audiences to challenge social definitions from within the structures created by those definitions. Her work to date shows an active progression from the radio plays' examination of individual dilemmas in a societal context, through disrupting the unity of the patriarchal aesthetic vision and developing a socialist-feminist analytic approach in the television and early stage plays, to creating alternative theatre conventions that challenge traditional ways of situating the self in relation to a play's formal and thematic presences. The motive that has sparked this progression has been that of making something new happen – not just new songs, stories, and dramas, but new ways of singing, telling, and dramatizing available to those who have been culturally silenced.

Although the issues and themes dealt with by Churchill may be encountered in the work of other politically oriented playwrights in contemporary Britain, her use of theatrical form to alter the relationship between play and audience sets her work apart. Through eclectic experiment on the margins of the expected, Churchill's mature work consistently attempts to reorient the audience from reception of an artifact to participation in a transformative process. Her plays invite participation by making the creation process visible through breaks in narrative and style, rather than obscuring it beneath the surface of a consistently finished product. Just as the 'voice' of the mute May in *Fen* calls attention to the process by which voices are produced and heard in public or private places, so Churchill's plays, from the visible alternation between past and present focus in *Vinegar Tom* to the exchange of objects by Derek and Herculine Barbin in *A Mouthful of Birds*, call attention to their own

190

processes of creation. In doing so, they empower audiences to look at society, and at their own relationships with patriarchal/capitalist institutions, from the standpoint of process and creation, rather than as a set of immutable givens.

Churchill's theatre of process, rather than seeking to inspire through the classic projection of an ideal, invites participation through a gestic presentation of existing realities that demand questioning and reformulation. Central to this presentation is the before-during-after structure, with an open-ended conclusion, that gives Churchill's plays an on-going life in the present and projects their imaginative time beyond the boundaries of their actual time. Choice of unusual subjects that offer, in Brechtian terms, 'pleasurable learning, cheerful and militant learning',[1] further promotes participation. Workshops have enabled Churchill to research and share others' experience of a diverse range of subjects. The element of surprise with which she so often involves audiences and stimulates them to reorient their perspectives toward the subject reflects Churchill's own enjoyment of surprise during her period of learning about that subject. In writing the play, she condenses the process of learning in which she has engaged, to share it with audiences. As a result, the form of criticism leveled at a particular power structure or set of conditions does not come as a foregone conclusion – even though Churchill has never hidden her overt biases – but rather appears as a fresh discovery.

The socialist-feminist critique that Churchill has developed since she entered the arena of explicitly political theatre in 1972, focuses on the connections between patriarchal-capitalist ideologies and the material conditions of a particular historical situation. The often devastatingly accurate presentations of social realities with which audiences are confronted, once they have entered the process of the play, demand response. Churchill, however, does not programme this response. Her insistence on complexity and contradiction precludes simple, unidimensional solutions. In asking audiences to take up the challenge of the open-ended inquiry she has initiated, Churchill thus makes clear just how difficult processes of personal and social change must be. At the same time, Churchill balances her recognition of the limitations posed by oppressive conditions with a uniquely theatrical expression of her belief in the possibility of change.

While Churchill presents the structures of oppression through the narrative and thematic elements of her plays, she uses the doubleness of player and role and the 'density of signs'[2] that comprise theatre to challenge the inevitability of oppression and empower audiences to seek change. She has an unusual ability to find in the situations she represents comedic and theatrical dimensions that give audiences the opportunity to view issues with the double vision necessary to see both what is and what might be. Her application of comic and highly theatrical techniques to the portrayal of grim situations results in a dialectic between imagination and material conditions. This dialectic confronts audiences with a dual sense of material reality and imaginative possibility that both acknowledges and challenges the power of stasis. It models for audiences a process by which to analyse and challenge historical conditions.

The theatricality for which Churchill's plays are known derives from an understanding of drama as play-acting and use of the anarchic energy of play to overcome the inertia of static theatrical conventions. Clearly, this practice has evolved out of the experience of developing plays through the workshop method, with its improvisations and games in which both rules and roles are never more than provisional. The creative use of role doubling indicates a game-playing approach toward roles that allows participants in a production to set up a combination such as that of Ellen and Mrs. Saunders in *Cloud Nine* for 'sheer fun'[3] or, in *Light Shining in Buckinghamshire*, to hit upon the idea, 'first as a joke, then seriously', of the actors 'keeping their [original] characters for the meeting but swapping them round for the other scenes'.[4] The game-playing approach is evident, in a related sense, in the many plays – for example, *Fen* and *Serious Money* – which portray a character's death, and then, through a jump backward in time or some other rejection of realistic convention, show that same character taking part in the scene immediately following his or her death. By giving Churchill access to the creative potential of play, the workshop method has involved her in a range of stimuli and demands. The interactive energy, the multiple voices, the intensity of focus, and what Churchill refers to as the 'common imagination'[5] of the collaborative process serve as a source of challenge and invigoration that might be termed Churchill's social muse.

The social muse has consistently nudged Churchill in the direction of experiment and greater freedom from conventions that have served to contain the meaning of theatrical production within the ideological boundaries of patriarchy. Churchill, of course, began with an impulse toward experimental overturning of theatre's 'ordi-nary' and 'safe' orthodoxies: 'Easy Death', produced in 1962, shows an early attempt at the multiple viewpoint by presenting a day in the life of one character and the entire life span of the other within the same conceptual space. The social muse, however, has broadened the experiential context from which Churchill draws the multiple perspectives that offer the audience different ways of seeing. Its demand that she produce roughly equal roles for a set group of actors has encouraged her to break open the player/role dyad. Finally, its emphasis on improvisation and play has given her the chance to create new, and even accidental combinations, that may widen the range of available meanings. As Churchill remarked to interviewer Lynne Truss, 'It's always funny how things can happen by chance and then they seem to have a good reason for being there afterwards.'[6]

The wide range of subjects and styles in Churchill's plays con-verge upon a consistent and coherent thematic emphasis on the societal division between the powerful and powerless. A key to this division throughout the plays is the word *frighten* – the most significant single word in Churchill's lexicon and one used to identify the motivation of a major character in nearly every one of her plays, beginning with the first one-act produced during her student years at Oxford, *You've No Need to Be Frightened* (1959). The reference by a character to being frightened, which invariably occurs in a dramatically heightened context, marks the dividing line between the powerful, who are frightening, and the powerless, who are frightened. The line may be laid down by economic inequal-ity, class privilege, race or sex discrimination, behavioural norms, or crippling of one's self. Insistently, Churchill suggests that the answer to powerlessness lies not in merely reversing the power equation but in dissolving it through the type of co-operation exemplified by Lin and Vic's negotiation, in *Cloud Nine*, of the terms of a new kind of relationship, or by Joint Stock's modeling of a small-scale alternative to institutions based upon traditional economic incentives and power relations in their policies of paying the same salary to each company member and of making collective decisions regarding work to be undertaken.

In a society where women are more likely to be frightened than frightening, and in theatre, where women dramatists and directors still constitute a very small minority,[7] Churchill struggles, as do all feminist writers, within a medium of expression that has a history of appropriation to patriarchal ideology. Her work expresses the struggle of coming to terms with biological femaleness and challenging the culturally imposed ideology of femininity within a medium accustomed to excluding and repressing such material. Even before she evolved a conscious feminist/socialist position, Churchill identified the vital capacity to make things happen with the marginality of the feminine within patriarchal culture. Throughout her work, she has presented the situations, actions, and motivations of characters in ways that can be understood through the experience of being a woman. In all of her writing, she uses the socially marginal positions associated with the powerlessness of childhood, old age, poverty, racial oppression, and lack of education or social skill, as areas of special potential from which to subvert the established power structure. At the same time, she has used common female experiences, such as pregnancy and childbearing, as well as the socially structured emphasis on family relationships, as areas of reference central to an overall definition and understanding of human experience. By making visible both 'the private lives of one-half of humanity'[8] and the interplay between these private lives and public structures, Churchill affirms the feminist insight into the inseparability of the personal and the political.

In her application of socialist-feminist analysis to contemporary power relationships and socio-economic institutions, Churchill has revealed herself as not only an original playwright, but also an original thinker. Some of the ideas she suggests, such as the connection between masquerade and the sexual repression of women[9] in the television play *Turkish Delight*, or the concern with a morality of care[10] in *Top Girls*, occurred either before or contemporaneously with their articulation in theory. Many other ideas show a reciprocity with theoretical explorations of the history and functioning of patriarchal and capitalistic institutions, as exemplified in the writing of contemporaries Michele Barrett, Sheila Rowbotham, and Judith Newton, as well as relevant, but not specifically feminist thinkers, such as Michel Foucault. Without seeming to be a programmatic writer, Churchill has identified and explored many of the most salient questions materialist feminists in all fields have been asking over the past two decades. Her inquiries, while always extending their focus wider than those already committed to feminism, frequently include areas of concern not specifically addressed by the feminist movement, such as the authority of the state over the individual and the effect of capitalistic exploitation on the exploiters.

Churchill's determination to make things happen ensures that ideas are not merely voiced, but put into action: she shows women in ways that are, in twentieth-century theatre, still highly unusual. Women characters occupy central positions in most of Churchill's plays, and in this way her plays contrast to the overwhelming majority of produced works in British theatre over the past twenty years, which present women only in secondary and subordinate positions and portray them only in relationship to males. Churchill's plays show women of all ages and classes, in various historical periods, expressing specific desires and grappling with significant choices in their own lives and the society around them, rather than merely serving as an object or sounding board for men. They speak of and enact their choices, history, sexuality, labour, and myth – thus contributing to a reshaping of how those things are known and what is known of them. Merely in presenting non-traditional images of women, Churchill's plays offer an alternative to the stereotyping of women in traditional drama. Though the images of strength and independence, even those connected to moral failure, have an empowering influence that is necessary if women in the audience are to meet the challenge of Churchill's moral vision, Churchill does not present simplistic arguments for equal access to power or models of new, feminist roles for audiences to passively imitate. Instead, she challenges audiences to create, revise, and re-create both their own lives and their surrounding social structures to foster personal strength, an ethic of care, a commitment to community, access to pleasure, and scope for creative adventure.

The empowering potential of Churchill's theatre lies not only in what is said but in 'the conditions of speaking'.[11] By exposing and deconstructing the 'grammar' of patriarchal authority, Churchill de-authorizes narrative, widening its compass to include a varied and non-hierarchical presentation of voices, stories, and viewpoints. Avoiding the familiar pattern of dramatic conflict – a system of dyadic opposition that binds audience identification to a single viewpoint – she expresses difference through juxtaposition or overlap. Juxtaposition, a technique that confounds the audience's impulse to categorize, insures that no character, even those with whom the playwright or audience might be expected to have little sympathy or commonality, can be logically placed in the category of villain, denied any measure of audience identification, and simplistically blamed for the situation. Juxtaposition thus orients the audience toward a view of social structures rather than individuals and encourages new modes of perception, rather than reinforcing old ones. Overlapping speech negates opposition, precludes exclusive identification with one speaker, and thus demands that audience members situate themselves in relation to what is presented. By using these techniques to set up an interchange in which audiences contribute imaginative energy to the dramatic process, rather than merely receiving the imaginative product of the playwright, the Churchill play creates a potential space for what Teresa De Lauretis has, in her study of feminist cinema, termed 'address[ing] its spectator as a woman, regardless of the gender of the viewers'.[12]

Recognition of a reciprocal relationship between the individual and society has emerged as an integral part of Churchill's project of re-creating structures of meaning and power in non-patriarchal forms. This relationship mandates that cultural and social structures must change to allow emergence of non-patriarchal subjectivity, but that individuals must change to be able to effect change in those structures. Revolutionary potential thus resides in the reciprocal relation, rather than in any specific action or redefinition.[13] Churchill gives form to this potential by means of a transformative reciprocity in the player/role relationship, as well as through the open-ended construction that highlights the capacity for on-going change. Each player entering a new role in a series of transformations within a single play, carries within the immediate conceptual presentation the displaced previous role(s). These roles, except for the stable player/role dyads, such as Marlene in *Top Girls*, that inscribe stasis, do not stand on their own; meaning is produced both in the relation among them and in the reciprocality between player and role. For those plays produced in workshop, of course, there is the additional reciprocity of the project's overall focus determining which actors are involved and who the actors are influencing what roles were written. The reciprocal transfer of energy evident in both role doubling and in the workshop creation of roles activates the potential for revising or recreating traditional symbols or symbol systems, as well as for re-situating the self in relation to these symbols or systems. Each new role or character reformulation – for example, the revised sexual identities the second-act characters of *Cloud Nine* define for themselves, or the revised gender identities the seven characters in *A Mouthful of Birds* find through possession – serve only as provisional, temporary, and strategic points of situation in which to 'welcom[e] further change'.[14]

It is in the space of reciprocity that Churchill overcomes the 'double displacement' of woman in 'the discourse of man'[15] and locates the possibility of non-patriarchal subjectivity. Her plays do not define woman, or woman's place. De Lauretis writes of feminist films:

> They do not assign me a role, a self-image, a positionality in language or desire. Instead, they make a place for what I will call me, knowing that I don't know it, and give 'me' space to try to know, to see, to understand.[16]

Churchill, too, understands that specific roles, images, and positionalities are precisely what has constituted women's objectification. Instead of presenting definitions, she models the deconstruction of such definitions as an empowering process. It is in the space of the deconstructive process – the space of metamorphic relationality, which in patriarchal culture has been displaced by the construction of static presence – that the potential of recognizing a selfhood outside the artificial limitations of gender occurs.

Churchill empowers audiences to find and use the space of potential subjectivity through her assertion, in the face of the apparent limitations of the stage and the hidden constraints within the symbol system of drama, that 'in the theatre anything's possible'.[17] Her dramaturgy employs the inherent density of theatre in a transformative process through which the materiality of theatre is continually reconceived.[18] In Worsely's pistol shot at the end of *Owners*, the multi-layered presentation of time in *Traps*, the representation of unrepresentable choice in *Moving Clocks Go Slow*, the time-period fusions of *Vinegar Tom*, the revolution's victorious failure in *Light Shining in Buckinghamshire*, the mismatch of sex and gender in *Cloud Nine*, the Pig whose death is canceled by the embrace of his lover in *A Mouthful of Birds*, the time compression and rhyming transactions of *Serious Money*, or the dinner party fusing past and present, fact and fiction in *Top Girls*, Churchill demonstrates her ability to bring the literally or realistically impossible to the stage. By presenting her critique of contemporary life in a theatrical context that vaults over the realistic constraints of necessity, practicality, and compromise, Churchill produces plays that, instead of imitating life, challenge audiences to reshape reality using their moral vision and their example of daring experiment and creative play.

Impossibility means fusion of opposites, dissolution of power differentials, and, ultimately, the mute songs of those who are not permitted to sing. It may produce a moment when, just for that moment, the impossible synthesis between imagination and material conditions occurs. One of the most moving of such moments is the final image of *Fen*, in which Val's mother May – who always wanted to be a singer, and for that reason would never sing – sings, in a few seconds of mute release. The conditions of her environment that dictate division of her desire from her strength have not changed, and the strong character that enforces the division so rigidly within herself also continues as it is, but the audience hears 'what May would have liked to sing . . . something amazing and beautiful'.[19] That brief moment in which the not possible is realized communicates Churchill's confidence in the potential of oppressed people to transcend the limitations of their material conditions and her challenge to audiences to go beyond what she has been able to imagine in the process of questioning, reformulating, and resituating self and society.

Notes

CHAPTER 1: QUESTIONING AND EMPOWERMENT

1. Caryl Churchill, 'Not Ordinary, Not Safe', *The Twentieth Century*, vol. CLXVIII (1960) 446.
2. Ibid.
3. Ruth Salvaggio, in *Enlightened Absence: Neoclassical Configurations of the Feminine* (Urbana: University of Illinois Press, 1988) suggests a broad engagement of contemporary feminism with theoretical structures, in her statement that 'woman seems to occupy a place at the intersection of history and theory' (5).
4. Caryl Churchill, interview, *Interviews with Contemporary Women Playwrights* by Kathleen Betsko and Rachel Koenig (New York: Beech Tree Books, 1987) 76.
5. Martin Esslin, *Brecht: The Man and His Work* (Garden City, New York: Anchor Books, Doubleday, 1961) 129.
6. In a 1979 interview, Churchill said, 'If pushed to labels, I would be prepared to take on both socialist and feminist . . . ' (Catherine Itzin, *Stages of the Revolution* [Methuen, 1980] 279). Interviewed in 1984, Churchill again emphasized this dual political commitment: 'socialism and feminism aren't synonymous, but I feel strongly about both and wouldn't be interested in a form of one that didn't include the other' (Kathleen Betsko and Rachel Koenig, *Interviews with Contemporary Women Playwrights* [New York: Beech Tree Books, 1987] 78).
7. Sheila Rowbotham, *Woman's Consciousness, Man's World* (Harmondsworth: Penguin Books, 1973) xvi.
8. Simone de Beauvoir, *Force of Circumstances* (London: André Deutsch, 1965) 192, quoted in Juliet Mitchell, *Woman's Estate* (New York: Vintage Books, 1973) 65–6.
9. Michele Barrett, 'Ideology and the Cultural Production of Gender', *Feminist Criticism and Social Change*, ed. Judith Newton and Deborah Rosenfelt (New York: Methuen, 1985) 74.
10. Ibid.
11. Michele Barrett, *Women's Oppression Today: Problems in Marxist Feminist Analysis* (London: Verso Editions, 1980) 69–70.
12. Rowbotham, *Woman's Consciousness*, 27–8.
13. Helene Keyssar, *Feminist Theatre: An Introduction to Plays of Contemporary British and American Women* (Houndmills: Macmillan, 1984) xiv.
14. Simone de Beauvoir, *The Second Sex*, trans. H. M. Parshley (1953; rpt. New York: Vintage Books, 1974) 174.
15. Rowbotham, *Woman's Consciousness*, xi.
16. Michele Barrett, ed., *Ideology and the Cultural Production of Gender* (London: Croom Helm, 1979) 83.

17. Teresa de Lauretis, *Technologies of Gender: Essays on Theory, Film, and Fiction* (Bloomington: Indiana University Press, 1987) 131.

18. Catherine Belsey, 'Constructing the Subject: Deconstructing the Text', *Feminist Criticism and Social Change*, ed. Judith Newton and Deborah Rosenfelt (New York: Methuen, 1985) 58.

19. Hélène Cixous, in the ground-breaking essay *La Jeune Née* (1975), asserts that the binary, hierachized opposition between the masculine and the feminine structures all discourse in patriarchal culture.

20. Nancy Chodorow, *The Reproduction of Mothering: Psychoanalysis and the Sociology of Gender* (Berkeley: University of California Press, 1978) 169.

21. Barrett, 'Ideology', 69.

22. Rachel Blau du Plessis, *Writing Beyond the Ending: Narrative Strategies of 20th Century Women Writers* (Bloomington: Indiana University Press, 1985).

23. Roland Barthes, 'Baudelaire's Theater', *Critical Essays* (Evanston: Northwestern University Press, 1972) 26.

24. De Lauretis, in *Technologies of Gender*, defines a film which 'addresses its spectator as a woman' as one which 'defines all points of identification . . . as female, feminine, or feminist' (133).

25. This theorization of the stage, clearly, diverges from the view of reception-oriented theorists (see, e.g., Jill Dolan, *The Feminist Spectator as Critic*, 1988) that theatrical representation is structured by the audience's gaze. The film-derived notion of the gaze as the determinant of meaning has been deemed inappropriate for this analysis because it fails to account either for theatre's complexity or for audience multiplicity.

26. Barthes, 'Baudelaire's Theatre', 27–8.

27. Gayatri Chakravorty Spivak, 'Displacement and the Discourse of Woman', in *Displacement: Derrida and After*, ed. Mark Krupnick (Bloomington: Indiana University Press, 1983) 169.

28. This concept is so useful, in fact, that its operation has frequently been observed in actual social life. See, for example Erving Goffman, *The Presentation of Self in Everyday Life* (New York: Doubleday, 1959).

29. Rousseau, Prynne, and other anti-theatricalists, attack theatre on the basis of its 'feminizing' influence. An anti-feminine bias is implicit in other anti-theatrical writings (e.g., St Augustine) as well. See Jonas Barish, *The Anti-Theatrical Prejudice* (Berkeley: University of California Press, 1981).

30. Susan Bassnet, 'Struggling with the Past: Women's Theatre in Search of a History', *New Theatre Quarterly*, vol. 18 (May 1989) 107. Bassnet's essay makes an important distinction between text-based theatre, which excluded women, and the less seriously regarded improvisational companies (such as Commedia troupes), which did not.

31. Henrik Ibsen, initiator of modern realism, did expose the conflict and contradiction inherent in women's societal roles through such characters as Mrs. Alving in *Ghosts*, Nora in *A Doll's House*, Hedda in *Hedda Gabler*, and Rebecca West in *Rosmersholm*. Though Ibsen never

went further than the suggestion that with the proper husband, advisor, or environment, women should be able to reconcile these contradictions, his emphasis on them shocked audiences of his time and earned Ibsen his undeserved reputation as a feminist.

32. Hélène Cixous, 'The Laugh of the Medusa', *Signs* I (Summer 1976) 880.
33. Sandra Gilbert and Susan Gubar, *The Madwoman in the Attic: The Woman Writer and the Nineteenth-Century Literary Imagination* (New Haven: Yale University Press, 1979) 45–6.
34. Spivak, 'Displacement and the Discourse of Woman', 169.
35. Belsey, 'Constructing the Subject', 53.
36. Belsey, quoting Roland Barthes, 53.
37. John Willett, ed., *Brecht on Theatre* (New York: Hill and Wang, 1964) 92.
38. Carl Weber, 'Is Brecht in Eclipse?' *The Drama Review*, vol. 24, no. 1 (1980) 114–24.
39. Janelle Reinelt, 'Feminist Theory and Performance', *Modern Drama* vol. XXXII, no. 1 (March 1989) 55.
40. Blau du Plessis, xx.

CHAPTER 2:   QUESTIONS OF POWER: THE RADIO PLAYS

1. Caryl Churchill, personal interview, 8 July 1987.
2. Ibid.
3. Caryl Churchill, *Plays: One* (London: Methuen, 1985) xi.
4. Caryl Churchill, *Easy Death*, ts. (1962) 65, 72.
5. E. Martin Browne and Tom Maschler, *New English Dramatists*, vol. 12 (New York: Penguin, 1969) 7–8.
6. Churchill, *Plays: One*, xi.
7. Judith Thurman, 'The Playwright Who Makes You Laugh about Orgasm, Racism, Class Struggle, Homophobia, Woman-Hating, and the Irrepressible Strangeness of the Human Heart', *Ms* (May 1982) 54.
8. John F. O'Malley, 'Caryl Churchill, David Mercer, and Tom Stoppard: A Study of Contemporary British Dramatists Who Have Written for Radio, Television, and the Stage', unpublished dissertation, Florida State University, 1974: 54.
9. The unproduced plays, described briefly in Linda Fitzsimmons's *File on Churchill* (Methuen, 1989), seem quite similar to the produced radio plays in subject and theme.
10. Gresdna A. Doty and Billy J. Harbin, eds., *Playwrights at the Royal Court Theatre 1956–81: A Discussion by Representative 'Court' Writers* (Baton Rouge: Louisiana State University, 1981) 5.
11. Caryl Churchill, *The Ants, New English Dramatists*, vol. 12, (Harmondsworth: Penguin Plays, 1969) 90–103. All quotations are from the script as published in this volume.
12. The tape of the original BBC production, directed by Michael Bakewell and broadcast 27 November 1962, is held at the National

Sound Archive, Division of the British Library, Exhibition Road, London.

13. Caryl Churchill, *Lovesick*. All quotations from the original script held by the BBC Play Library, Broadcasting House, London. The play, for which no tape is available, was directed by John Tydeman and aired by BBC radio on 2 May 1967.

14. Caryl Churchill, *Identical Twins*. All quotations are from a tape of the original production directed by John Tydeman and first broadcast by BBC Radio on 21 November 1968. The tape is held in the BBC Sound Archives, Broadcasting House, London.

15. Caryl Churchill, *Abortive*. All quotations are from a tape of the original production directed by John Tydeman and first broadcast by BBC Radio 3 on 4 February 1971. The tape is held at the BBC Radio Sound Archives, Broadcasting House, London.

16. Caryl Churchill, *Not . . . not . . . not . . . not . . . not enough oxygen*. All quotations are from the original script held in the BBC Radio Play Library, Broadcasting House, London. The play, for which no tape is available, was directed by John Tydeman and broadcast by BBC Radio 3 on 31 March 1971.

17. Churchill, personal interview, 13 August 1987. In the same interview, Churchill noted that she was not aware of the case history of Schreber written by Freud, using Schreber's memoirs, until after she wrote the play.

18. Showalter, in an observation which parallels the major theme of *Schreber's Nervous Illness*, states that 'madness, even when experienced by men, is metaphorically and symbolically represented as feminine: a female malady'. Elaine Showalter, *The Female Malady: Women, Madness and English Culture, 1830–1980* (New York: Penguin Books, 1987).

19. Caryl Churchill, *Schreber's Nervous Illness*. All quotations are from the tape of the original production directed by John Tydeman and first broadcast by BBC Radio 3 on 25 July 1972. The tape is held at the BBC Sound Archives, Broadcasting House, London.

20. Showalter, *The Female Malady*.

21. Churchill, in a 1987 interview with Geraldine Cousin in *New Theatre Quarterly*, vol. IV, no. 13 (1987) 4, points out that *Henry's Past* was written to be a stage play, then cut and adapted for radio.

22. Caryl Churchill, *Henry's Past*. All quotations are taken from a tape of the original production directed by John Tydeman and first broadcast by BBC Radio 3 on 5 December 1972. The tape is held at The British Library National Sound Archive, Exhibition Road, London.

23. O'Malley, 47.

24. Churchill, *Plays: One*, 246.

25. Caryl Churchill, *Perfect Happiness*. All quotations are taken from a tape of the original production directed by John Tydeman and first broadcast by BBC Radio 3 on 30 September 1973. The tape is held in the BBC Radio Sound Archives, Broadcasting House, London.

26. Churchill, personal interview, 13 August 1987.

27. Illustrative discussions can be found in reviews of *Schreber's Nervous Illness* by Nicholas de Jongh in the *Guardian*, 7 December 1972, and by Frank Marcus in the *Telegraph*, 17 December 1972; and in reviews of *Perfect Happiness* by John Barber in the *Telegraph*, 11 March 1975, and by Charles Lewsen in the *Guardian*, 18 March 1975.

28. Catherine Itzin, *Stages of the Revolution: Political Theatre in Britain since 1968* (London: Methuen, 1980) 279.

29. Toril Moi, *Sexual/Textual Politics: Feminist Literary Theory* (London: Methuen, 1985) 167.

CHAPTER 3:   QUESTIONS OF FREEDOM: THE TELEVISION PLAYS

1. Caryl Churchill, 'Not Ordinary, Not Safe', *The Twentieth Century*, vol. CLXVII (1960) 451.

2. John F. O'Malley, 'Caryl Churchill, David Mercer, and Tom Stoppard: A Study of Contemporary British Dramatists Who Have written for Radio, Television, and Stage', unpublished dissertation, Florida State University, 1974: 56.

3. Caryl Churchill, personal interview, 8 July 1987.

4. Caryl Churchill, The *Judge's Wife*, ts., 1972. This and following quotations, with page numbers given in parentheses, are taken from the original script held in the British Broadcasting Corporation Reference Library, Drama Section Script Unit, Western Avenue, London. The play, broadcast on 2 October 1972, was produced by Anne Head, edited by Richard Broke, directed by James Ferman, and designed by Rosamund Inglis.

5. O'Malley, 49.

6. Caryl Churchill, *Turkish Delight*, ts., 1974. This and all following quotations, indicated in parentheses, taken from the original script held at the British Broadcasting Corporation Reference Library, Drama Section Script Unit, Western Avenue, London. The play was produced and directed by Herbert Wise and broadcast on 22 April 1974.

7. Luce Irigaray, *New French Feminisms*, ed. Elaine Marks and Isabelle de Courtivron (New York: Schocken Books, 1981) 100.

8. Ibid., 102.

9. Mary Russo, 'Female Grotesques; Carnival and Theory', *Feminist Studies, Critical Studies*, ed. by Teresa de Lauretis (Bloomington: Indiana University Press, 1986) 223–4.

10. All quotations taken from the original script of *Save It for the Minister*, by Caryl Churchill, Mary O'Malley, and Cherry Potter, held at the British Broadcasting Corporation Reference Library, Drama Section Script Unit, Western Avenue, London. The program was produced by Graeme McDonald and directed by Piers Haggard.

11. Caryl Churchill, *The After-Dinner Joke*, ts., 1978. This and all following quotations, with page numbers given in parentheses, are taken from the original script held in the British Broadcasting Corporation Reference Library, Drama Section Script Unit, Western Avenue, London.

The play was produced by Margaret Matheson and directed by Colin Bucksey.

12. Linda Fitzsimmons, *File on Churchill* (London: Methuen, 1989) 38.

13. Caryl Churchill, interview, *Interviews with Contemporary Women Playwrights*, ed. by Kathleen Betsko and Rachel Koenig (New York: Beech Tree Books, 1987) 81.

14. For full texts of the original voice-overs, see Catherin Itzin, *Stages of the Revolution: Political Theatre in Britain since 1968* (London: Methuen, 1980) 280–1.

15. Caryl Churchill, *The Legion Hall Bombing*, 1979. All quotations taken from the videotape of the original production, held at the National Film Archive, Dean Street, London.

16. Churchill, interview, Betsko and Koenig, 81.

17. Caryl Churchill, *Crimes*, ts., 1981. All quotations, with page numbers given in parentheses, are taken from the script of the original production, held at the British Broadcasting Corporation Research Library, Drama Section Script Unit, Western Avenue, London. The play was produced by Neil Zeiger and directed by Stuart Burge.

18. Itzin, *Stages of the Revolution*, 279.

19. Victoria Radin, 'Churchill's Adventures', London *Observer*, 15 August 1982: 29.

CHAPTER 4: THE POWER OF CHOICE

1. John F. O'Malley, 'Caryl Churchill, David Mercer, and Tom Stoppard: A Study of Contemporary British Dramatists Who have Written for Radio, Television, and the Stage', unpublished dissertation, Florida State University, 1974: 50.

2 Richard Findlater, ed., *At the Royal Court: 25 Years of the English Stage Company* (New York: Grove Press, 1981) 155.

3. Ibid., 193.

4. Caryl Churchill, note to *Owners*, *Plays: One* (Methuen, 1985) 4.

5. Catherine Itzin, *Stages of the Revolution: Political Theatre in Britain since 1968* (London: Methuen, 1980) 282.

6. Churchill, *Owners*, *Plays: One* (London: Methuen, 1985). All quotations, with page number indicated in parentheses, are from this edition.

7. The 'male gaze' as a determinant in the composition of art works was first analysed by John Berger in *Ways of Seeing* (London: Pelican, 1972).

8. Caryl Churchill, interview, *Plays and Players* (January 1973) 41.

9. Ibid.

10. Churchill, note to *Owners*, 4.

11. Virginia Woolf, 'Professions for Women', *The Death of the Moth and Other Essays* (New York: Harcourt, Brace, 1942) 236–8.

12. Caryl Churchill, 'Afterword' to *Objections to Sex and Violence*, *Plays by Women*, vol. 4, ed. Michelene Wandor (London: Methuen, 1985) 52.

13. *The Stage*'s reviewer stated that 'one hour would have done, for me

at any rate, quite nicely', as reported in Linda Fitzsimmons, *File on Churchill* (London: Methuen, 1989) 27.

14. Findlater, *At the Royal Court*, 155, Appendix I, Appendix II.
15. Ibid., Appendix II.
16. Max Stafford-Clark, '"A Programme for the Progressive Conscience" the Royal Court in the Eighties' (interview), *New Theatre Quarterly*, vol. 1, no. 2 (May 1985) 143.
17. Caryl Churchill, *Objections to Sex and Violence, Plays by Women*, vol. 4, ed. Michelene Wandor (London: Methuen, 1985). All page numbers, indicated in parentheses, are to this edition of the play.
18. Churchill, 'Afterword', *Objections to Sex and Violence*, 52.
19. Caryl Churchill, preface, *Traps* (London: Pluto Press, 1978).
20. Churchill, *Plays: One*, xii.
21. Caryl Churchill, *Traps, Plays: One* (London: Methuen, 1985). All page numbers, indicated in parentheses, refer to this edition of the play.
22. This dynamic is, of course, similar in structure and function to the 'continuous present' in the works of Gertrude Stein. For a discussion of Stein's continuous present, see 'Composition as Explanation', in *Selected Writings of Gertrude Stein* (New York: Random House, 1962).
23. Jacques Derrida, 'The Theater of Cruelty and the Closure of Representation', *Writing and Difference*, trans. Alan Bass (Chicago: University of Chicago Press, 1978) 248.
24. Caryl Churchill, interview with Janet Watts, *Guardian*, 5 February 1977.
25. Derrida, 'The Theatre of cruelty', 239.
26. Paula A. Treichler, 'Escaping the Sentence: Diagnosis and Discourse in "The Yellow Wallpaper"', *Feminist Issues in Literary Scholarship*, ed. Shari Benstock (Bloomington, Indiana University Press, 1987) 63. Also see Rachel Blau du Plessis, *Writing Beyond the Ending: Narrative Strategies of 20th Century Women Writers* (Bloomington: Indiana University Press, 1985).

CHAPTER 5: RECLAIMING HISTORY

1. Sheila Rowbotham, *Hidden from History: 300 Years of Women's Oppression and the Fight Against It*. (London: Pluto Press, 1973) x.
2. Toril Moi, *Sexual/Textual Politics* (London: Methuen, 1985) 8.
3. Judith Newton and Deborah Rosenfelt, eds., *Feminist Criticism and Social Change: Sex, Class and Race in Literature and Culture* (London: Methuen, 1985) xxiii.
4. Rosalind Coward and John Ellis, *Language and Materialism* (London: Routledge and Kegan Paul, 1977) 61.
5. Catherine Itzin, *Stages of the Revolution: Political Theatre in Britain Since 1968* (London: Methuen, 1980) 279, 285.
6. Caryl Churchill, note, *The Joint Stock Book: The Making of a Theatre Collective* (London: Methuen, 1987) 119.

7. Churchill, *The Joint Stock Book*, 119.
8. Ibid., 119, 120.
9. Ibid., 119.
10. Caryl Churchill, 'Author's Note', *Softcops, Softcops and Fen* (London: Methuen, 1986) 3.
11. Caryl Churchill, *Plays: One* (London: Methuen, 1985) xii.
12. Caryl Churchill, preface to *Vinegar Tom, Plays: One*, 129–30.
13. Caryl Churchill, *Vinegar Tom, Plays: One* (London: Methuen, 1985). All quotations, with page numbers indicated in parentheses, refer to this edition of the play.
14. Caryl Churchill, Afterword, *Vinegar Tom, Plays by Women*, vol. 1., ed. Michelene Wandor (London: Methuen, 1982) 39.
15. Churchill, Afterword, 39.
16. Rowbotham *Hidden from History*, 5.
17. Ibid.
18. Ibid., 6.
19. Bertolt Brecht, 'A Short Organum for the Theatre', *Brecht on Theatre*, trans. John Willett (New York: Hill and Wang, 1964) 190.
20. Bertolt Brecht, 'The Modern Theatre Is the Epic Theatre', *Brecht on Theatre*, 37.
21. Newton and Rosenfelt, xxiii.
22. Janelle Reinelt, 'Beyond Brecht: Britain's New Feminist Drama', *Theatre Journal*, vol. XXXVIII, no. 2 (May 1986) 162.
23. Michele Barrett, 'Ideology and the Cultural Production of Gender', *Feminist Criticism and Social Change*, ed. Judith Newton and Deborah Rosenfelt (London: Methuen, 1985) 65.
24. Churchill, preface to *Vinegar Tom*, 130.
25. Ibid.
26. Monstrous Regiment, 'Afterword', *Vinegar Tom, Plays by Women*, 41.
27. David Zane Marowitz, 'God and the Devil', *Plays and Players*, February 1977: 25; Christian Thomsen, 'Three Socialist Playwrights: John McGrath, Caryl Churchill, Trevor Griffiths', in *Contemporary English Drama*, ed. C. W. E. Bigsby (London: Edward Arnold, 1981) 168; Sid Smith, review, *Chicago Tribune*, February 4, 1988, II:12.
28. Monstrous Regiment, Afterword, *Vinegar Tom, Plays by Women*, 41-2.
29. Brecht, quoted in Esslin, 129.
30. Newton and Rosenfelt, xvii.
31. Brecht, quoted in Esslin, 129.
32. Churchill, *The Joint Stock Book*, 119.
33. Caryl Churchill, *Light Shining in Buckinghamshire, Plays: One* (London: Methuen, 1985). All quotations, with page numbers indicated in parentheses, refer to this edition of the play.
34. Caryl Churchill, preface to *Light Shining in Buckinghamshire, Plays: One*, 183.
35. Churchill, preface, *Light Shining in Buckinghamshire*, 183.
36. John Willett, ed. *Brecht on Theatre* (New York: Hill and Wang, 1964) 205.
37. *Brecht on Theatre*, 204.

38. Sheila Rowbotham, *Women's Consciousness, Man's World* (Harmondsworth: Penguin Books, 1973) 27.
39. Rowbotham, *Hidden from History*, 11.
40. Churchill, interview with Geraldine Cousin, 'The Common Imagination and the Individual Voice', *New Theatre Quarterly*, vol. 4, no. 13 (February 1988) 16.
41. Churchill, preface, *Light Shining in Buckinghamshire*, 183.
42. Ibid.
43. Ibid. For a somewhat more comprehensive view, see 'Puritans and Prophetesses', in Rowbotham's *Hidden from History*.
44. *Brecht on Theatre*, 96.
45. *Ibid.*
46. Newton and Rosenfelt, xvii.
47. Caryl Churchill, 'Author's Note', *Softcops* (London: Methuen, 1984) 3.
48. Caryl Churchill, *Softcops, Softcops & Fen* (London: Methuen, 1986). All quotations, indicated in parentheses, refer to this edition of the play.
49. The 'theatre of situation' is a term used by Dario Fo in 'Some Aspects of Popular Theatre', *New Theatre Quarterly*, vol. 1, no. 2 (May 1985) 132.
50. Michel Foucault, *Discipline and Punish: The Birth of the Prison*, trans. Alan Sheridan (Harmondsworth: Penguin, 1979) 14.
51. Ibid., 30.
52. Caryl Churchill, 'The Common Imagination and the Individual Voice', 5.
53. Alison Ritchie, note, *The Joint Stock Book*, 133.
54. Churchill, note, *The Joint Stock Book*, 121.

CHAPTER 6:   SEX AND GENDER

1.   Caryl Churchill, personal interview, 13 August 1987.
2.   Linda Fitzsimmons, *File On Churchill* (London: Methuen, 1989) 8–9.
3.   Caryl Churchill, 'Sex, politics, and other play things', interview with John Simon, *Vogue* (August, 1983) 126, 130.
4.   Caryl Churchill, preface, *Cloud Nine, Plays: One* (London: Methuen, 1985) 246.
5.   Caryl Churchill, *Cloud Nine, Plays: One* (Methuen, 1985). All quotations, with page numbers indicated in parentheses, taken from this version of the play.
6.   Caryl Churchill, preface, *Cloud Nine*, rev. American edn. (New York: Methuen, 1984) ix; Caryl Churchill, interview, *Interviews with Contemporary Women Playwrights*, ed. Kathleen Betsko and Rachel Koenig (New York: Beech Tree Books, 1987) 83.
7.   Churchill, interview, Betsko and Koenig, 83.
8.   Churchill, preface, *Cloud Nine*, rev. American edn., ix.
9.   Churchill, preface, *Cloud Nine, Plays: One*, 247.
10. This tradition, and the association of farce with the 'saturnalian',

is discussed in Richard W. Bevis, *The Laughing Tradition* (London: George Prior, 1981) 100–3.

11. See Hélène Cixous, 'The Laugh of the Medusa', *New French Feminisms: An Anthology*, ed. Elaine Marks and Isabelle de Courtivron (New York: Schocken Books, 1981) 247–8.

12. Alice Rayner, *Comic Persuasion: Moral Structure in British Comedy from Shakespeare to Stoppard* (Berkeley: University of California Press, 1987) 105.

13. Churchill, preface, *Cloud Nine*, 246.

14. Susan Rubin Sulieman, '(Re)Writing the Body', *The Female Body in Western Culture: Contemporary Perspectives* (Cambridge: Harvard University Press, 1985) 24.

15. Claude Levi-Strauss, *The Elementary Structures of Kinship*, trans. James Harie Bell (Boston: Beacon Press, 1969).

16. Churchill, preface, *Cloud Nine*, 246.

17. In a discussion of *Cloud Nine* based on the New York production, Elin Diamond asserts for the embrace the function of 'comic closure and narrative teleology'. See 'Refusing the Romanticism of Identity: Narrative Interventions in Churchill, Benmussa, Duras', *Theatre Journal*, vol. XXXVII, no. 3 (October 1985) 273–86.

18. Luce Irigaray, 'Ce sexe qui n'en pas un' [This sex which is not one], trans. in *New French Feminisms: An Anthology*, ed. Elaine Marks and Isabelle de Courtivron (New York: Schocken, 1981) 100.

19. Erich Speidel, 'The Individual and Society', *Brecht in Perspective*, ed. Graham Bartram and Anthony Wayne (London: Longman, 1982) 45.

20. Judith Thurman, 'Caryl Churchill: The Playwright Who Makes You Laugh about Orgasm, Racism, Class Struggle, Homophobia, Woman-Hating, the British Empire, and the Irrepressible Strangeness of the Human Heart', *Ms.* (May 1982) 57.

21. Attention to the question of authority in literary texts was suggested to me by a lecture on the poet Marianne Moore, titled 'No Moore of the Same', given by Rachel Blau DuPlessis at the University of Wisconsin-Madison, 28 March 1988.

22. Thurman, 54.

23. Caryl Churchill, *Three More Sleepless Nights*, ts., 1979. All page numbers, given in parentheses, refer to the typescript. The play has recently been made available in *Anthology of British Women Writers*, ed. Dale Spender and Janet Todd (London: Pandora, 1989).

CHAPTER 7:   LABOUR AND CAPITAL

1. Victoria Radin, 'Churchill's Adventures', *Sunday Observer* (Review/Arts), 15 August 1982: 29.

2. Caryl Churchill, 'A Fair Cop', interview with Lynne Truss, *Plays and Players*, January 1984: 8.

3. Radin, 29.

4. The concept of a morality of care, based on an individual's recognition of competing responsibilities, has been advanced by Carol

Gilligan in *In a Different Voice: Psychological Theory and Women's Development* (Cambridge, Mass.: Harvard University Press, 1982).
5. Caryl Churchill, *Top Cirls, The Plays of the Seventies* (London: Methuen, 1986). All quotations, given in parentheses, refer to this edition.
6. Caryl Churchill, 'Making Room at the Top', interview with Laurie Stone, *The Village Voice*, vol. XXVIII, no. 9 (1 March 1983): 81.
7. For a discussion of neurasthenia among Victorian women, see Elaine Showalter, *The Female Malady: Women, Madness, and English Culture, 1830–1980* (New York: Penguin, 1987) 135–7.
8. Churchill acknowledges use of *The Confessions of Lady Nijo* and an account of the life of Isabella Bird, by Pat Barr, titled *A Curious Life for a Lady*, in the preface to the play. Both women made major literary contributions. Nijo's memoir, which she wrote in an effort to reclaim her family's literary reputation, has recently been rediscovered and recognized as a major work of mediaeval Japanese court poetry. Bird published more than a dozen books about places she visited, including a cultural geography of Korea which was accepted as authoritative until the 1950s.
9. Frank Rich, review, *Fen* by Caryl Churchill, *The New York Times*, 31 May 1983, reprinted in *New York Theatre Reviews*, Off-Broadway Supplement (Spring/Summer 1983): 208.
10. Mary Chamberlain, *Fenwomen: A Portrait of Women in an English Village* (2nd edn.) (London: Routledge and Kegan Paul, 1983) 11.
11. Jennie Stoller, note, *The Joint Stock Book*, ed. Rob Ritchie (London: Methuen, 1987) 151–2.
12. Ibid., 152.
13. Rob Ritchie, *The Joint Stock Book*, 28.
14. Caryl Churchill, *Fen, Softcops & Fen* (London: Methuen, 1986). All page numbers, indicated in parentheses, refer to this edition of the play.
15. Churchill, production note, *Fen*, 54.
16. Chamberlain, 10.
17. Nancy Hartsock, *Money, Sex, and Power: Toward a Feminist Historical Materialism* (New York: Longman, 1983) 122–3.
18. Linda Fitzsimmons, '"I Won't Turn Back for You or Anyone": Caryl Churchill's Socialist-Feminist Theatre', *Essays in Theatre*, vol. VI, no. 1 (November 1987) 19–29.
19. Churchill, production note, *Fen*, 54.
20. Sheila Rowbotham, *Hidden from History: 300 Years of Women's Oppression and the Fight Against It* (London: Pluto Press, 1973) 24.
21. Caryl Churchill, 'The Common Imagination and the Individual Voice', interview with Geraldine Cousin, *New Theatre Quarterly*, vol. IV, no. 13 (February, 1988) 12.
22. Caryl Churchill, 'Driven by Greed and Fear', *New Statesman*, vol. 114, no. 2938 (17 July 1987) 10.
23. Caryl Churchill, 'Fear and Loathing in the City', *City Limits*, 16–23 July 1987: 13.
24. Churchill, interview with Geraldine Cousin, 12.

25.   Churchill, 'Driven by Greed and Fear', 10.
26.   Caryl Churchill, *Serious Money* (London: Methuen, 1987). All page numbers, indicated in parentheses, refer to this edition of the play.
27.   Neil Collins, review of *Serious Money, Daily Telegraph* 30 March 1987, reprinted in *London Theatre Record*, vol. VII, no. 8: 369.
28.   Maureen Duffy, 'Introduction', *Rites, Plays by and about Women* (New York: Vintage Books, 1974) 350.

CHAPTER 8:   REVISING MYTH

1.   Alicia Ostriker, *Writing Like a Woman* (Ann Arbor: University of Michigan Press, 1983) 134.
2.   Ibid., 132, 134–5.
3.   Caryl Churchill, 'The Common Imagination and the Individual Voice,' interview with Geraldine Cousin, *New Theatre Quarterly*, vol. IV, no. 13 (February 1988) 10.
4.   Churchill contributed text to this performance piece that attempted to communicate the anticipation, actuality, and memory of a resort vacation. 'Midday Sun' was coordinated by John Ashford and performed at the Institute for Contemporary Arts (ICA) in London.
5.   Victoria Radin, review, *The New Statesman*, 12 May 1986; reprinted in *London Theatre Record* 24: 1334.
6.   Churchill, interview with Cousin, 10.
7.   Ibid.
8.   David Lan, 'The Politics of Ecstasy', preface, *A Mouthful of Birds* (London: Methuen, 1986) 6.
9.   Caryl Churchill, 'The Workshop and the Play', preface, *A Mouthful of Birds* (London: Methuen, 1986) 5.
10.   Churchill, 'The Workshop and the Play', 5.
11.   Other contemporary playwrights – notably Maureen Duffy, with *Rites* (1969) have also discovered points of contact within *The Bacchae*.
12.   Lan, 'The Politics of Ecstasy', 6.
13.   Ostriker, *Writing Like a Woman*, 136.
14.   "For a discussion of 'patriarchal binary thought', as put forward by Hélène Cixous, see Toril Moi, *Sexual/Textual Politics* (London: Methuen, 1985) 104–5.
15.   The life story of Herculine Barbin is contained in her memoirs, *Herculine Barbin: Being the Recently Discovered Memoirs of a Nineteenth-Century French Hermaphrodite*, introduction by Michel Foucault, trans. Richard McDougall (NY: Pantheon, 1980).
16.   Sandra M. Gilbert and Susan Gubar, *The Madwoman in the Attic: The Woman Writer and the Nineteenth-Century Literary Imagination* (New Haven: Yale University Press, 1979) 5–7.
17.   Catherine Belsey, 'Constructing the Subject: Deconstructing the Text', *Feminist Criticism and Social Change*, ed. Judith Newton and Deborah Rosenfelt (London: Methuen, 1985) 50.
18.   Churchill, 'The Workshop and the Play', 5.

19. Linda Fitzsimmons, *File On Churchill* (London: Methuen, 1989) 78.
20. Text of 'Hot Fudge' was not yet available when this manuscript went to the publisher.
21. Caryl Churchill, *Icecream* (London: Nick Hern Books, 1989). All references, indicated by page numbers in parentheses, are to this edition.
22. Alicia Ostriker, *Stealing the Language: The Emergence of Women's Poetry in America* (London: The Women's Press, 1987).

CHAPTER 9:   SONG OF THE MUTE

1. Bertolt Brecht, 'Theatre for Pleasure or Theatre for Instruction', *Brecht on Theatre*, ed. John Willett (New York: Hill and Wang, 1964) 73.
2. Roland Barthes, 'Baudelaire's Theater', *Critical Essays* (Evanston: Northwestern University Press, 1972) 28.
3. Caryl Churchill, preface, *Cloud Nine, Plays: One* (Methuen, 1985) 248.
4. Caryl Churchill, note, *The Joint Stock Book*, ed. Rob Ritchie (London: Methuen, 1987) 120.
5. Caryl Churchill, 'The Common Imagination and the Individual Voice', interview with Geraldine Cousin, *New Theatre Quarterly*, vol. IV, no. 13 (February 1988) 3.
6. Caryl Churchill, 'A Fair Cop', interview with Lynne Truss, *Plays and Players* (January 1984) 9.
7. Caroline Gardiner, in 'What Share of the Cake?', a report on the status of women in British theatre commissioned by the Womens Playhouse Trust, found that women comprised only 15 per cent of artistic directors in building-based companies, controlling 11 per cent of money allocated to theatre (and noted that were it not for the relatively recent appointment of one woman to the team of artistic directors at the heavily subsidised National Theatre, the figures would be 5 per cent and 8 per cent, respectively). Michelene Wandor, in her introduction to the first volume of *Plays by Women* (London: Methuen, 1982), reported that of 250 plays produced at the Royal Court Theatre – known for its championship of new plays and playwrights – between 1956 and 1975, only 17 were written and/or directed by women.
8. Carolyn Kizer, 'Pro Femina' (Three), *No More Masks: An Anthology of Poems by Women*, ed. Florence Howe and Ellen Bass (Garden City, NY: Anchor/Doubleday, 1973) 175.
9. See, e.g., Mary Russo, 'Female Grotesques: Carnival and Theory', *Feminist Studies, Critical Studies*, ed. Teresa de Lauretis (Bloomington: Indiana University Press, 1986) 213–29.
10. See Carol Gilligan, *In a Different Voice: Psychological Theory and Women's Development* (Cambridge: Harvard University Press, 1982).
11. Paula A. Treichler, 'Escaping the Sentence: Diagnosis and Discourse in "The Yellow Wallpaper"', *Feminist Issues in Literary Scholarship*, ed. Shari Benstock (Bloomington: Indiana University Press, 1987) 76.

12. Teresa de Lauretis, *Technologies of Gender: Essays on Theory, Film, and Fiction* (Bloomington: Indiana University Press, 1987) 133.

13. This recognition is implicit in the discussion of 'Science and Knowledge' in *The Archeology of Knowledge by Michel Foucault* (New York: Pantheon, 1972).

14. Caryl Churchill, 'The Workshop and the Play', preface, *A Mouthful of Birds* (London: Methuen, 1986) 5.

15. Gayatri Chakravorty Spivak, 'Displacement and the Discourse of Woman', *Displacement: Derrida and After* (Bloomington: Indiana University Press, 1983).

16. De Lauretis, 142.

17. Caryl Churchill, '"Anything's Possible in the Theatre": Portrait of Author Caryl Churchill', interview with Renate Klett, *Theater Heute* (January 1984) 19.

18. Roland Barthes, in *Critical Essays* (Chicago: Northwestern University Press, 1972) 69–70, makes this demand of political theatre: 'it is the very materiality of the theater and not just its ideology which must be reconceived.'

19. Caryl Churchill, production note, *Fen, Softcops and Fen* (London: Methuen, 1986) 54.

Index

Woolf, Virginia   66, 112, 204
Wright, Nicholas   62
Wyndham's Theatre (London)   161

Zeiger, Neil   204
Zen Buddhism   62